THE NON-PROFIT INTERNET HANDBOOK

Gary M. Grobman

and

Gary B. Grant

White Hat Communications
Harrisburg, Pennsylvania

Published by White Hat Communications.

Copies may be ordered from:
White Hat Communications
PO Box 5390
Harrisburg, PA 17110-0390
(717) 238-3787

Contact the authors in care of White Hat Communications, or by e-mail at:
gary.grobman@paonline.com or g-grant@uchicago.edu

Printed in the United States of America.

Typesetting and Layout: Gary M. Grobman

Design: Gary M. Grobman

Editing: Barbara Trainin Blank, Linda Grobman, John Hope

ISBN 0-9653653-6-0
Library of Congress No. 97-061-931

Table of Contents

"Thank you for calling. Please leave a message. In case I forget to check my messages, please send your message as an audio file to my e-mail, then send me a fax to remind me to check my e-mail, then call back to remind me to check my fax."

Foreword

by
Sara E. Meléndez, President
Independent Sector

In asking me to supply a foreword to their book, Messrs. Grobman and Grant have chosen to tap the experience of one who has had to enter the computerized non-profit era from the ground floor. When I began working in the non-profit sector many years ago, the Internet with all its resources was an unimaginable luxury, a science fiction fairy tale that many of us could not even envision thoroughly enough to wish for.

We were still doing so much "manually" that today can be done in seconds in cyberspace. Small, local organizations were difficult enough to run, with their relatively minor communications and resource challenges; but regional and national organizations were strenuous exercises for the philanthropy-minded, and institutions with an international focus faced almost insurmountable obstacles in communication, resources, information and logistics. Days and even weeks could be spent searching for answers among references and research sources. Arranging conferences and meetings could be a nightmare of miscommunication and delay. It was a struggle to seek out and contact like-minded individuals and organizations, to learn about them, or to get in touch.

Considering that these difficulties arose even in the era of telephones, faxes, radio, and television, it is daunting to imagine what the pre-technology non-profit must have faced. If Clara Barton and her Red Cross had had access to modern information technology at the Johnstown flood, think of the lives that might have been saved!

Through Independent Sector's initiation into the wonders of the Internet, I have come to understand just how effective a tool and how priceless a resource it can be to the non-profit of the '90s. Not only can an organization learn and do research through its innumerable sources, but it can establish communications and interact with distant non-profits—so much that was previously difficult or impossible can now be accomplished with the flick of a button.

Many non-profits—including Independent Sector—now have their own Web sites, and we have found that our interaction with the rest of the non-profit world (and the world in general) has increased dramatically since we went "on-line." We get helpful feedback that points out the directions our constituents want us to go, orders for publications, stories from fellow workers and chance-met "surfers"—and we can disseminate information effectively, cheaply, and quickly. A non-profit's Web site can tell you what the organization does, how it operates, what it believes, what it can do for you—and what you can do for non-profits! There seems to be no end to its scope and possibilities—or to the fascinating changes taking place on the Internet every day.

The Internet is, by its very nature and structure, the ideal interactive community for non-profits—it has no barriers of distance, race, gender, age, or any other societally-fostered obstacles to communication. It is available 24 hours a day, fresh and new and vital in its energy! What a world to open up to children—to adults—to everyone imbued with the natural human thirst for knowledge and interaction. And what a tool for the modern non-profit, in our constant quest for relevance, timeliness and effectiveness today and in the new millenium!

I might have said, a few years ago, that such technology was far too complex for the most computer-savvy non-profit staffer, let alone for the novice. But the computer gurus have developed the technology with the aim of making the product itself simple to use and, with a little practice, anyone today can learn to navigate the "information superhighway," and do it quickly and effectively. I have.

Which brings me to this book. If you want to understand the Internet, with all that it has to offer—if you want to know exactly how the Internet can be useful to your non-profit, how it can increase your interaction with your constituency and serve to spread the word about your organization—if you need to learn to search the Web for reliable, up-to-date information on what is happening in the non-profit world, and the world in general—*The Non-Profit Internet Handbook* is the perfect gateway to the Internet galaxy. The authors have produced a volume chock-full of explanations that make sense, instructions on how to begin and where to go, tools for navigating the Web—and, most important, all of this invaluable information is presented with the perspective of its usefulness and relevance to the non-profit world.

Everything is covered here, from e-mail to copyrights, from viruses to HTML. Reviews of various existing Web sites are provided to give you some tips on which sites will be most helpful for your particular needs—and to give you some ideas on what you might want your own site to look like. *The Non-Profit Internet Handbook* is comprehensive, readable, and just about the only manual you'll ever need to guide you through cyberspace.

If you are rather daunted by the Internet, take courage, take a deep breath, and plunge in. With *The Non-Profit Internet Handbook* as a roadmap, I can promise that you won't get lost!

Part 1

Using the Internet

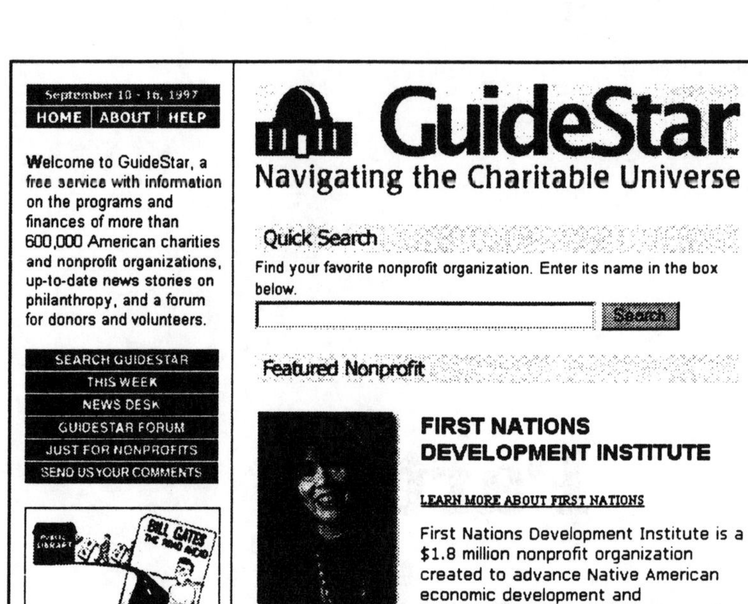

The Guidestar home page (see page 137). GuideStar is a registered trademark of Philanthropic Research, Inc. reprinted with permission.

INTRODUCTION

Silicon Crispies, a cereal for the 90's.

Tens of thousands of non-profit organizations are using the Internet, and thousands of these have their own World Wide Web pages. Some non-profit executives will quickly see the Internet for what it really is—a powerful new communications medium that will help them accomplish their vital missions better. The Internet is being used today by non-profit organizations to hire staff, raise funds, find volunteers, communicate with the public, accomplish advocacy objectives, more efficiently provide information to clients and other agency stakeholders, and bring about collaborations that would not otherwise have been achievable because of time and distance constraints.

But even the most farsighted non-profit executive must learn the technology and the culture of the Internet to take advantage of what it can offer. Many haven't. We hope this book will provide the motivation for non-profit executives who haven't begun using the Internet to do so. We also want to encourage those who are already using the Internet to use it to its full potential to improve their organizations.

The United States and Canada are in the midst of an obsession with the Internet. One can hardly pick up a newspaper without seeing a prominent story about some Web site or another. Whether it is the spectacular pictures being transmitted from the surface of Mars, the untimely death of a princess, the mass suicide of a group of Webmasters in California, the loss of a civilian airliner over the ocean off New York, or the arrival of a brilliant comet called Hale-Bopp, the World Wide Web is front page news, not only telling the news story, but becoming the story itself. More and more Americans are turning up their noses at the 30-second sound bite coverage of network television news and are making the World Wide Web their primary source for news and information. Not only is the Internet replete with "original" documents, interactive opportunities to respond to the news, photographs, video, and sounds, it has the advantage of being "demand-responsive"—it is available when you want it, not just when a broadcast is scheduled. And instead of a handful of networks competing among themselves to be the lowest common denominator and providing a remarkably similar "vanilla" spin on information, the Internet is a Babel, providing simultaneously a cacophony of news, views, and opinion that run the gamut ideologically.

Unlike some other developments in technology, the Internet truly has the potential to transform our lives, perhaps even more than the development of television and the telephone. If the plow was the symbol of the agricultural age and the smokestack was the symbol of the industrial age, then the personal computer is the symbol of the information age. And the Internet is to information what seeds were to the farm and iron and coal were to the industrial plant.

Just as there was resistance to mechanization by our grandparents, and automation by our parents, there are pockets of resistance to computerization by our generation. But just as there had to be groups of pioneers crossing the Continental Divide to blaze a path for their progeny, our generation has become the pioneers for this exciting information technology. The potential of this new technology is so remarkable and revolutionary that we have about as much chance of regressing to our non-Internet past as our children have of giving up their VCR movies and demanding black and white television, after growing up on color.

Technology is, for many of us, a scary new "frontier." The new terms, acronyms, and jargon, are overwhelming. The culture is new. Moreover, the very concepts and ways of thinking that arise are unfamiliar at first, and may generate a certain fear of the unknown. Perhaps some people find this exciting, and leap in with no discomfort, but for most, we doubt that this is the case.

Despite its potential for dangers (see Chapter 12), we believe that in time, the Internet will be as indispensable to non-profit organizations as the telephone. With some background and practice, accessing it effectively can be almost as easy. While we hope this handbook will make the transition from unfamiliarity with cyberspace to a solid understanding of the Internet as easy as possible, the readers must also trust their own abilities to grasp (eventually) all of the intricacies and facets of this new technology. For now, we can at least say that if we were able to learn it, so will you.

After you have an understanding of the Internet, and presuming you have access to the Internet, the next logical questions to ask are: "What does this mean to me? How can I use these resources—these tools—these communication methods—this connectivity to others?"

One way to find the answer to this question is to explore on your own and to experiment. The Internet has become a haven for communities, not in the sense of a geographical community, but communities of people who share the same interests. They may live next door to each other or live on different continents. Imagine that you have an interest in some esoteric field (let's say providing start-up grants for the financing of home businesses for welfare recipients) and you want to find people all over the world who are interested in the same issue. A conventional method of communication might be attending international conferences, which obviously involves great commitments of time and expense. Or you could place advertisements in publications seen by this group—again at great time and expense.

What the Internet provides is a clearinghouse type of infrastructure where people from all over the world have a nexus for communication and interface/interaction that transcends temporal, financial, and geographical obstacles. It is as if you sent a magical invitation to everyone in the entire world interested in your issue to meet at a coffee house down the street and have a discussion and share information, with the exception that it is much more convenient for you than to have to travel down the street to that coffee house—the discussion takes place in front of your computer, and you can have that discussion in "real time" or played out at your convenience.

Our goal is simply this—to give you a jump start into exploring the Internet's practical applications for non-profit organizations—such as fund-raising, volunteer identification, and accessing government information, in order to save you hours, months, and years exploring how to integrate the Internet into your work. You will still have to investigate and think about the Internet's applications to your work, but you will know some of the benefits to be gained from it before you start. Thus, this book represents our efforts to record our journey on the Internet and document the useful places for non-profit managers along the way.

How To Use This Handbook

This handbook is designed for all non-profit executives and staff—those who are using the Internet for the first time and those who have already seriously begun to tap the richness of information and the variety of Internet tools in their work or personal lives.

The first section of this book provides an understanding of the Internet and the landscape described metaphorically as "cyberspace." The majority of the handbook, however, is intended as a "user's guide." We detail the ways the Internet can be used to help those who run non-profit organizations do their jobs, and describe some of the most useful Internet sites for this sector.

The breadth of the non-profit sector is staggering—providing health care, library services, access to the arts and humanities, and education, to name just a few. It would be a monumental task to define all non-profit activities and to detail all the Internet resources applicable to those activities. Instead, we have organized this handbook to provide a base of information that will be useful regardless of your organization's specialized niche. Our intent is to provide information about resources available on the Internet—free, for the most part—that will help you accomplish your tasks easier, better, or faster. If you find that your daily work is not adequately described in any of the sections, then you will find valuable leads for thinking about how the Internet fits into your work.

There are several ways to use this handbook. First, it can be reviewed as a whole. We expect that those who manage non-profit organizations will read this handbook as a way to gain a practical understanding of what is and is not available on the Internet—of what can be done, as well as what cannot—and why. In this regard, use this handbook to:

1. *Determine if you would benefit from having access to the Internet and to what degree.* Our view is that virtually all non-profit organizations that use the Internet can improve their effectiveness; increase donations and grants; enhance the opportunity for collaborative efforts; find a new source of volunteers; expand the number of persons who will know about job openings; and improve communication among the organization, its funders, its board, its clients, government policy-makers, and other direct stakeholders and the public.

2. *Make more informed choices about the cost effectiveness of newer computer purchases for yourself or your staff.* If all you want is to spend a few hours here and there, you can get Internet access at many public libraries and not pay a penny. But for most non-profit organizations, it makes sense to have on-site Internet access. The number of choices consumers have for Internet-related hardware and software is staggering. While this is not intended to take the place of *Consumer Reports* and other evaluative publications, we share some of the issues involved in choosing appropriate Internet hardware and software.

3. *Determine specific ways to integrate the Internet into your existing work.* You will be able to find examples of the work non-profits do, and will find ways to utilize the Internet to reshape your own organization's work to improve efficiency, become more effective, or have a broader impact on those with an interest in your organization. We give examples of how your counterparts in non-profit organizations are using the Internet to their advantage, ways that you, too, can use.

4. *Determine if there are new activities to explore.* It is wise to distinguish between using the Internet for improving upon your existing responsibilities and creating new responsibilities. You will almost certainly find exciting new opportunities through the Internet, but be sure that these are undertaken only if they are truly a higher priority.

A second way to use this handbook is as a desktop resource. Even with the most careful planning of your work, there will likely be times when you must consider whether the best solution is to be found either in the old way, whatever that may be, or on-line. To avoid a fruitless search, this handbook should be a great help in determining quickly and easily which route to take. In this regard, use this handbook to:

1. *Have a ready reference handbook at your fingertips for information about issues relating to the Internet.* Among these issues discussed in this book are Netiquette, trademark and copyright law, encryption, and virus transmission.

2. *Find information about how non-profit organizations are using the Internet.* Learn what is working for them and what is not. We've interviewed non-profit organization professionals who are using the Internet every day, and we share their experiences with you.

3. *Locate specific sites with the information you need.* Start with the handbook's index to see if the information you seek is listed here. Opening this book will be far less time-consuming than aimlessly surfing through the Internet.

A third use of this handbook is as a tutorial on building your own Web site and planning its content and value to the rest of the Internet community. Once the Internet is demystified for you (and you may be surprised at how quickly this comes), you may find yourself assessing the value of contributing to the Internet's content. This book will not only offer a few tips on how to get started with this, but will help to ensure that what you do does not duplicate already existing Internet content. We provide a thumbnail guide on how to use HTML to prepare your files for your World Wide Web site, and provide design tips and related advice on letting others know of the information you have to offer.

A first word of warning: Do not be too put off by the terminology. Words that are unfamiliar in one place will become more familiar as you go on. It is not possible to define all the terms right up front, and much of it must be learned in context and through experience and practice. Do not get stuck wrestling with understanding any particular section, but rather forge forward and trust that your familiarity and understanding will come about soon enough. We've provided a glossary of common Internet terms to help you, but we haven't defined every term now in use, and new words and phrases are coined almost every day.

And a second word of warning: Internet technology is still in its infancy. The World Wide Web was virtually unknown just a few years ago, and no one knows what technological advances will be popular even before the end of the decade. Already, Internet animations, virtual reality (VR), and video conferencing are adding new dimensions to your computer monitor, and each advance requires learning additional software and hardware. Most of the books written about the Internet a couple of years ago appear to be anachronistic, and we would be disingenuous to tell you that this handbook will not suffer the same fate if we don't update it periodically.

If you find that this handbook contains any errors (e.g., Web site addresses that have moved or changed) or omits valuable sites or substantive areas that you would like to see included in future editions, please contact us at:

gary.grobman@paonline.com
or
g-grant@uchicago.edu

with your suggestions or comments. Or write to us c/o the publisher, White Hat Communications, PO Box 5390, Harrisburg, PA 17110-0390.

Acknowledgments

The authors gratefully acknowledge the assistance and support that their families provided to them during the time they wrote and prepared this book. Our wives, Kerry Baronnette Grant and Linda Grobman, encouraged us to complete this project and made it possible to devote the time and effort necessary to achieve the vision we had for it. We also thank "our" children, daughter Alyann Grant and son Adam Grobman, for their patience with their daddies.

For contributions, and other forms of assistance and guidance, we want to thank Arlene Alpert and the University of Chicago School of Social Service Administration's (SSA) Continuing Education Committee, which sponsored the first programs that helped Gary Grant develop some of the original material. In particular, we thank Anna Senkevitch, Robert Tell, Steve Roller, John Aravosis and Mary Carolyn Gleason. Each gave us permission to incorporate articles they authored into this book. We also wish to thank Jennifer Yang and Mika Nagamine for their assistance.

A special thanks goes to Jeanne Marsh, Dean of SSA, for encouraging us to pursue the project and for supporting the work at SSA toward preparing people in the human services for using Internet technology in their work. Thank you also to the scores of people we talked to, and those we formally interviewed for this book. Their time is valuable, and we appreciated it. During the preparation of the technical material in this book, we consulted other books to see how complicated concepts were simplified, and we adopted many of the innovative explanations. Some of these books are listed in the bibliography that appears on page 207, and we would be remiss in not telling you that some of these books not only influenced how we explained topics that appear in this book, but also initially taught us these concepts. Similarly, the Internet itself has been a primary source of information and background material for us. We are especially appreciative of the hundreds of Webmasters who, with no expectation of financial gain, have posted information of high quality and value for the public to learn from, their only reward being the satisfaction of knowing that they have improved society by their efforts.

We thank all of those who gave us permission to use descriptions and screen shots of their Web sites, and to reproduce material we believe will be useful to our readers. Some of the details about these permissions appear in the disclaimer page at the beginning of this book. Almost everyone we contacted for these permissions was enthusiastic in accommodating our needs, and we are grateful.

Our thanks also go to those who read various drafts of the book and provided comments to us, including Joe Geiger and Fred Richmond. Finally, we thank the principal editor of this book, John Hope, for his insights in organizing the material so that it made sense to our readers. John was one of the Webmasters we interviewed, and we shared with him the first draft for some comments. We were so impressed with his comments that we found his talents to be indispensable to the project. He did a great job. We also thank Barbara Trainin Blank for her editing talents. She added clarity and sparkle to the *Up Close* sections of the book.

We are delighted to be able to share the creative talents of internationally-acclaimed cartoonist Randy Glasbergen. Randy draws *The Better Half*, distributed world-wide by King Features Syndicate. You can find a new cartoon by Randy posted each morning at—

http://www.borg.com/~rjgtoons/bio.html

Finally, we wish to thank Linda Grobman for her many contributions to this book. She served not only as the publisher and as an editor and proofreader, but wrote some of the reviews and researched the information on hiring via the Internet and other topics. Without her vision and substantive contributions, this book would not have been possible.

Chapter 1

Introduction To The Internet

"I had to print my new business cards a little bigger to make room for my name, address, phone number, fax number, modem number, Internet address, CompuServe address, America Online address, World Wide Web address..."

It seems as if everyone and every group and every cause is on the Internet now. And that's what makes it so valuable. Imagine you just invented the telephone and decided to place your first call—and then realized that you had no one to call, because you owned the only telephone. It wouldn't be a very useful invention. The Internet is similar, in that it would not be very valuable if only a few elite were connected (which was actually the case only a few short years ago). But that was then, this is now: More than 50 million people are connected to the Internet, and millions more are connecting for the first time each year. Hundreds of thousands of organizations, businesses, and governments are furiously installing the infrastructure to connect to cyberspace. Thousands of schools and libraries are making the connection to the Internet a priority.

If you are looking for information, you can probably find it on the Internet. When you connect, you join one of the fastest growing fraternities/sororities in history. And while this fraternity/sorority does not have an organized system of hazing, there are a few secret hand-shakes involved.

There are no race, disability, age, gender, nationality, class, or other artificial barriers that divide Internet users. The Internet has created a level playing field—the Nobel prize winner and the homeless high school dropout are each judged on the content of their character and what they have to say in the marketplace of ideas, not on their social or economic status. There is a camaraderie among those on-line, and this marketplace is open 24 hours a day and is virtually free. On the Internet, you can meet new friends, "travel" the world, save money (for one example, see the section on Internet telephone starting on page 27), and increase the opportunities for collaboration.

The Internet is like having your own private library, entertainment center, news and clipping service, professional conference, private club, and nightly gala soirée, with several important differences. The library is the largest ever created in the world by a factor of perhaps 100,000, and you have a private genie to conjure up at will who can find and bring you almost any piece of information you want virtually instantaneously.

People who otherwise might not have two words to say to each other if they met at a cocktail reception find common ground on the Internet. Complete strangers see a question posted and spend hours giving advice and discussing the answer among themselves. It has been said that being on the Internet is like having 50 million free consultants. If television is, as it's been often described, an intellectual wasteland, cyberspace is an intellectual Mecca (at least if you are browsing the sites we frequent).

Business transactions that used to take months—through exchanges of faxes, telephone calls, and letters—now take hours or even minutes. There is a welcome and refreshing informality in cyberspace. At least until video cameras become more common, people do not generally wear ties and jackets (or wear pumps) literally or metaphorically. First names are used for the most part, regardless of whether one has a Ph.D. or is entering kindergarten.

There are dangers with this informality, of course. In communicating with someone over the Internet, you cannot verify that the person you are having a conversation with is a Ph.D. as he or she claims, or is someone entering kindergarten. And it is not unusual for people to create identities in cyberspace for a multitude of reasons, some with nefarious intent and some benign. In fact, communicating with people you don't know over the Internet has some of the same drawbacks as communicating by letter or telephone with people you don't know. It is healthy to maintain a bit of skepticism over cybercommunications because, just as in the non-virtual world, there are good folks and bad folks out there. Fortunately, the good far outnumber the bad.

What is the Internet?

The Internet is a term describing the linkage of hundreds of thousands, if not millions, of computers all over the world, that communicate with each other using a standardized connection protocol called TCP/IP (Transmission Control Protocol/Internet Protocol). For the typical Internet user, all of the technical details are totally transparent; communicating from an Atari computer or a mainframe on the Internet makes no difference, provided each computer is running the same protocol. Cyberspace is not a geographical place. There is no mega-computer that holds all of the Internet's information. Instead, the term "cyberspace" defines many thousands of computers around the world all connected to one another by telephone lines.

In one sense, computers have always been connected. It has always been possible to copy any file to a disk, whether it was a software program, a letter or document, a poster or picture. The disk could be given to others who could presumably use it on their computers (providing the computers were compatible, or could read the same software program).

The ability to transfer information by disks was a great convenience. Documents did not have to be retyped or recreated. Instead, they could be printed, revised, or copied to another computer. Other than saving this time, however, transferring the disk was as much a physical act as transferring a document or letter.

The goal of the Internet, and its great achievement, has been to facilitate the transfer of information directly from one computer to another through telephone lines, rather than by disk. The Internet is the means of information transfer, not any specific content or information.

History of the Internet

The Internet evolved from a Department of Defense initiative designed to provide for communication among the armed services that could survive a nuclear attack. It traces its origins back to 1969, with the establishment of ARPANet (after the Advanced Research Projects Agency that administered the first program), a highly restricted bulletin board that linked four mainframe computers. The theory was that in the event of an attack, a centralized system might be destroyed. By creating a decentralized system that could automatically reroute messages around servers that were damaged or destroyed, the government could still get messages through to their destinations. During the next decade, this network was joined by the scientific and academic community's National Science Foundation Network (NSFNET), but public access remained restricted. One application developed was to permit supercomputer centers of NSF to be utilized without actually having to be at a center. The bulk of communications on this network were related to government and academic research. Commercial applications were strictly taboo.

The vast majority of computers connected to this network ran on UNIX, a clumsy, arcane operating system that didn't encourage user-friendliness, and the vestiges of which we are still stuck with for some Internet applications.

It has only been since the beginning of the 1990s that the Internet has become a part of the popular culture and has been available to the masses. New communications software, commercial providers that market to the general public, the emergence of the World Wide Web, advances in technology such as high speed modems, and competition in the industry have made Internet access popular. Even millions without their own personal computers have access to the Internet through libraries, educational institutions, and the workplace. It was not until the 1990s that 1 million host computer servers were connected to the Internet. As of this writing, the number is perhaps five million and growing rapidly.

How the Internet Works

The Internet makes communication possible and information available at any time of day or night to any part of the world, without using long distance phone charges in most localities. To do this, the Internet relies on thousands of specially designed and programmed computers, called servers. A server is, on one hand, just a computer. But it functions in such a way that it overcomes problems of compatibility between computers. Connecting to the Internet means connecting to a server, the term that refers to the computer directly networked with the computers that comprise the Internet, and that responds to the commands of your computer's Internet software (often called the "client") .

Through the server, which knows how to route you to all other existing servers, your computer can reach similarly connected computers on people's desks anywhere in the world for no more cost than the local telephone connection to your Internet Service Provider.

Each resource on the Internet has its own unique address to enable users to find it and connect to it. A unique address is necessary so that information sent from one computer to another is sure to go to the right place. That Internet address is called a URL (uniform resource locator). The URL has a standardized format that is useful in identifying its source.

Think of a server as analogous to a post office. When your friend John addresses a letter to you, from any part of the world, his local post office has one responsibility—to get the letter to your local post office. And it is your post office that is charged with the duty to get the letter into your mailbox.

This is how the Internet provides for electronic mail (e-mail) communication. Each server has its own name, and each e-mail address includes the name of the recipient's server. Let's say you want to send a message to Gary Grant, co-author of this book. His e-mail address is: g-grant@uchicago.edu. Your server sees that the name of his server is "uchicago.edu." Your server sends your message to that server and it is the duty of this server to put it in a file (mailbox) established for him, called "g-grant," to which only he has access.

Gary's computer does not have to be turned on when you send the message for him to receive it. When he turns on his computer and connects to his server using an appropriate e-mail program, he will be alerted to and sent your message, which he can read and respond to at his convenience.

How about the World Wide Web? What is happening when you look at a Web site? Servers are quite versatile. In addition to acting as a post office for e-mail, they can also be the repository for information that is made available to the Internet world at-large. In these cases, readers must connect to a server but, having done so, they can then connect through it to other servers to see documents or other files that have been made available.

For example, if you visit the University of Chicago School of Social Service Administration's Web page (http://www.chas.uchicago.edu/ssa/index.html), you will see a textual and graphical gateway to other pages that together comprise SSA's "Web site."

All Web page URLs have the "http://" at the beginning, which tells the server to use this universal language so that you can (with the appropriate software, called a browser), view that site's home page. Everything between this and the ".edu/" represents the name of the server you are visiting—the server containing the file you are reading on your computer. And if that computer is on the other side of the globe, your connection still is made via local calls with no long distance charges. Everything after ".edu/" represents the name of the file on the server and the path where it can be found.

Another great accomplishment of the Internet, and the language used to make Web sites, is the ability to create "hypertext links." This merely means that the address of another site can be "clicked to" right on the page you are reading, sending you to any other place, either on that server, or some other server anywhere else in the world. The ability to move from file to file, from Web page to Web page, from server to server, as easily as turning the pages in a book, though admittedly not as fast, is what makes it seem very much like a web.

Who runs the Internet?

No one officially runs the Internet. But the policies that relate to it are established by a volunteer board called the Internet Society (ISOC). Committees and ad hoc working groups report to this Society. One influential committee is the Internet Architecture Board, which sets standards for many of the protocols and technical standards that make universal interconnection possible. There is no court to put those who abuse the Internet on trial, although some proposals have been made to create one. Generally, enforcement is through peer pressure—those who violate the written or unwritten rules are either shunned or "flamed" (publicly or privately harshly criticized).

Internet Demographics

In using the Internet to find volunteers, employees, and potential contributors, it is useful to have some idea about the demographics of those who are likely to be on-line. These demographics have changed dramatically since studies were first undertaken. For example, early this decade, men comprised as much as 90% of Internet users. As cultural barriers fell and the World Wide Web became popular, the gender imbalance changed. It is generally believed that women now comprise a third of Internet users. A study by O'Reilly & Associates, a computer publishing house in California, found that Internet users have higher incomes than the general population, but that 41% of users reported combined household incomes of $50,000 or less. In a sampling of 1,500 Internet users found through random telephone surveying, 80% were between the ages of 18 and 44. Almost two-thirds of Internet users said they had a college degree (64%, compared to 28% of the general population).

As the Internet develops, the demographics change and more surveys are being performed. Among the Web sites that have demographic information about Internet users are:

YAHOO!'s Internet Statistics Section
http://www.Yahoo.com/Computers_and_Internet/Internet/Statistics_and_Demographics/

O'Reilly & Associates
http://www.ora.com/research/users/index.html

Euregio.Net
http://stars.euregio.net/joe/zodiac/surveyresults.html

The Internet Index
http://www.openmarket.com/intindex/

Chapter 2
CONNECTING TO THE INTERNET

"I don't worry about what our kids see on the Internet. We've been online for three months and never gotten past the busy signal."

The first step to taking advantage of all the Internet has to offer is getting connected to it. In order to do this, you will need five things:

1. A sufficiently advanced computer and monitor
2. A modem (or an ISDN terminal adapter)
3. A telephone line (or an ISDN line)
4. Access to an Internet Service Provider (ISP)
5. Appropriate software

Computer and Monitor

The computer holds the communications software, provides the mechanism to download and store data from the Internet, provides a convenient way to dial into the Internet, and takes advantage of many new technological wonders, such as using the Internet to have real time audio conversations. Although a printer is optional, you will find it useful to print out much of what you find on the Internet. Almost any new computer you purchase will be advanced enough to access the Internet, but older machines might not be. In particular, older computers may not have the graphical capabilities to view Web sites as they are intended to be viewed, or the memory to support the software typically used for Internet communication. Whether you use an IBM-PC or an Apple (or their "clones") is irrelevant, but you will need to have certain minimum memory and storage requirements for the software you will be using.

Almost every computer can be connected to the Internet, assuming you are willing to settle for text-only characters on your monitor. For personal computers, four megabytes of Random Access Memory (RAM) is a minimum standard for access to the Internet. RAM refers to the computer memory that temporarily holds programs and data, and that can be erased and replaced with new content (unlike ROM, read-only memory). Most browsers that support graphics require a minimum of eight megabytes of RAM and even that amount is taking a chance. Typical computers being sold today come with 32 MB (megabytes, or million bytes) of RAM.

The storage space available for data and programs on the hard drive is also measured in megabytes. Typical computers being sold today come with 1-6 GB (gigabytes, where 1 GB is a thousand megabytes) of memory. It is useful to have sufficient capacity to upgrade your computer's hard disk space; just a few years ago, a 40MB hard drive was sufficient for most personal computer applications. Now, many individual computer programs require more than that.

With a browser, communications software, newsgroup readers, e-mail program, space to store e-mail and the files your browser captures in its caché file (a file that stores data received via the modem), and related Internet programs, consider keeping 100 megabytes of hard disk space available for this purpose. Yes, you can do with less than that, but it can become very inconvenient.

Be sure to ask if and how your computer is capable of accessing the Internet when you purchase it. The computer is clearly the most significant investment you will need for Internet access (starting at about $1,000). In most cases, the computer you purchase will already have a high-speed modem, communications software, an Internet browser, and several "free trial" membership offers from commercial services or Internet Service Providers (ISPs). In setting up your computer, make sure it is near a working telephone jack.

Monitors also make a difference in how you view the Internet. Among the main parameters of interest are screen size (14" is standard, but 15" and 17" are common, but more expensive), viewing area (which is directly proportional to screen size), dot pitch (.28mm is common, and smaller dot pitches, which increase screen resolution, are more expensive), and the frequency, in Megahertz, of the refresh rate (the higher the frequency, the less screen "flicker").

Modem/ISDN Line

Unless your employer uses an ethernet substitute (a technology which uses a Local Area Network to transmit data between computers at 10-100 million bits per section), you will need a modem. The purpose of the modem is to take the digital output from your computer, and change it to analog output (and vice-versa) so that information can be exchanged from your computer to another through telephone lines.

Virtually all new personal computers sold today (1997) have a built-in (internal) modem, typically 28,800 or 33,600 baud. The higher the baud rate, the faster data can be transferred over the telephone line. A 2,400 baud modem is sufficient for the transfer of text, although large files take proportionately longer than smaller files. With the advent of the World Wide Web, which takes advantage of graphics, sounds, animations, videos, and other byte-intensive files, the modem speed becomes critical. The World Wide Web is almost inaccessible using a 2,400 baud modem. Modems are relatively inexpensive, ranging from about $30 to several hundred dollars. A baud rate of 33.6k (33.6 kilobytes) should make using the Internet particularly enjoyable.

Many Internet users find that even a 33.6k baud modem is not fast enough, and there are technological breakthroughs that use special digital cable modems to provide data transfers several times faster than the conventional analog modems of most personal computers.

ISDN (Integrated Services Digital Network) lines are an increasingly popular choice for those who spend a lot of time downloading files from the Internet or "surfing" the Web. As more and more Web sites become sophisticated with flashy graphics, video-multi-media presentations, animations, and even virtual reality, it takes longer and longer to download data through a modem. While technology is improving and 56k modems are now available, there is no reason to believe that the modem speed technology will improve forever. There are limitations with telephone line technology resulting from a transformation of tones back and forth between analog signals and digital signals; after a certain point, data transmission through a modem would likely become unreliable, unless there are unanticipated technological breakthroughs. With ISDN lines, there is no conversion between digital and analog. A typical ISDN line is equivalent to five times the speed of the fastest modem available.

Installation of an ISDN line can run several hundred dollars, and a typical monthly service fee is about $65. Lines are ordered through the local telephone company and most apply a modest charge for each minute the line is in use. The ISDN service must also be compatible with the Internet Service Provider. As you might expect, specialized hardware and software is required to connect using an ISDN line.

Telephone Line

The Internet transfers information from a host computer to your computer by sending packets of data over a telephone line. A non-profit organization may purchase a dedicated telephone line to use only for computer communication. More typically, a non-profit will use an existing line if on-line time is minimal. Many non-profits now use a separate line dedicated to the fax machine, which can be diverted to on-line use. Obviously, when on-line communication is occurring on the dedicated fax line, no faxes may be received or sent on that line.

Internet Service Provider

While it is possible to make a direct connection to the Internet and become, in effect, your own service provider, doing so is expensive, time-consuming, and technically difficult. The choice for almost all non-profits has become to purchase an account with an Internet Service Provider (ISP). Among the commercial service providers are Delphi/MCI (1-800-695-4005), America Online (1-800-827-6364), Prodigy (1-800-776-3449), and The Microsoft® Network (1-800-386-5550). Hundreds of national and local Internet Service Providers have sprung up to compete, and many charge less than the commercial companies. The commercial on-line services provide their own content, in addition to Internet access. The local companies typically offer Internet access only. Typical costs for a service are $10- $20/month. Most offer access for a limited number of hours each month with an additional charge for each hour on-line above that threshold. Unlimited access accounts are also widely available.

The table on the following page compares the advantages of commercial service providers, national Internet service providers, and local Internet service providers. As this table demonstrates, local or national ISPs are generally better choices if you want to be assured that the costs will be minimal and you want the freedom to use any kind of software. If you think you will use the Internet only very infrequently, want to practice in a more easy-to-learn environment, at least to start with, or want to take advantage of being part of a "community" of other Internet users, then a commercial service provider might be preferable.

Note that the choice need not be a permanent one. Nothing prevents you from changing your mind later, or even from trying out more than one provider at the same time and canceling the one you don't like as much. However, changing providers has its inconveniences. You may have printed your e-mail address on your organization's stationery and business cards. Hundreds of people may have your old address. Forwarding your e-mail to a new address can be, at best, a significant inconvenience, and, at worst, can not always be done. In most cases, when a person sends e-mail to an address that no longer exists, the mail is returned with an automated message saying that it is undeliverable.

Communications and Other Software

Basic communications software is included in virtually every personal computer sold, in the form of the Terminal program included in Microsoft® Windows® or HyperTerminal included with Windows® 95. There is an equivalent for MAC-based systems as well. Many personal computers also include demonstration or full versions of communications software designed to connect to the Internet, an e-mail manager, a Web browser, File Transfer Protocol (FTP) software, and a newsgroup reader. Some examples are: Internet Office!, The Instant Internet Kit, Quarterdeck InternetSuite, and Internet In a Box. Many of the programs included in these packages may be

Internet Service Providers

Comparison Chart

	Commercial Service provider	National Internet Service Provider	Local Internet Service Provider
Examples	America Online, Microsoft Network	Netcom, Pipeline, AT&T	Pennsylvania Online, Epix, Ezonline
On-Line Content	Proprietary content (access to publications, services, and forums) provided in quantity.	Limited or none.	Generally none.
Relative Costs	May be most costly; charged by hourly or monthly usage time. May offer flat rate monthly fee.	Charged by usage by the hour or month. May offer flat rate monthly fee.	May be least costly; charged by hourly or monthly usage fee. May offer flat rate monthly fee.
Local Access Numbers	Yes; may offer toll-free number when local service is not available, but may impose an hourly charge for use of that number.	Yes; may offer toll-free number when local service is not available, but may impose an hourly charge for use of that number.	No; local access numbers are restricted to the limited geographical area served by the company.
Community	Members are part of an on-line community.	Members are generally not part of an on-line community.	Members are generally not part of an on-line community.
Special Events	Yes; such as celebrities available in a chat room.	No special events.	No special events.
Connection and Browser Software	Easy-to-load software is provided by the company, and usually cannot be modified.	Basic software is provided by the company, but consumer can usually upgrade or modify it.	Basic software is provided by the company, but consumer can usually use own software.

obtained in some version for free from various sources. In order to use these packages, you will need to pay a fee to an Internet Service Provider.

Over time, you may find yourself needing a variety of different software applications to do various things, such as sending files to your server or viewing video clips on-line. You may obtain many of these software programs for free over the Internet. But for our current purposes, we are only concerned about four kinds of applications:

(1) one that connects you to your server;
(2) one that allows you to view Web pages on the Internet;
(3) one that allows you to send and receive e-mail; and
(4) one that allows you to use the Internet to conduct telephone conversations.

Each of these, other than Internet telephone software, should be available from your Internet provider, who can also help you configure them properly.

Internet Telephone

With the right equipment and software, it is relatively easy and not very expensive to use the Internet for voice communication. The equipment includes a computer sound card that supports duplex transmission (or else only one person can speak at a time, as with a walkie-talkie), a microphone, external speakers (although they are not required), and a high quality Internet connection. Your modem should be at least 14,400 baud. Much of the software required can be downloaded free from the Internet, or is included with Web browsers. For most applications, the person you are talking to must have a similar software configuration.

Internet telephone is one strategy non-profit managers may consider using to cut long distance telephone costs, particularly when many calls are made to the same number. The thought of saving thousands of dollars makes it a tempting option. For more information about using Internet telephone, visit the Internet Telephone Consortium at http://rpcp.mit.edu/~itel/.

Chapter 3

INTRODUCTION TO E-MAIL

"My husband passed away eight months ago, but we still keep in touch. His e-mail address is WalterZ@Heaven.com"

E-mail (short for "electronic mail") is a "store and forward" system that permits someone to send a message to someone else for later retrieval. Each Internet user has an e-mail address for sending and receiving these messages. E-mail is relatively simple to use and offers a number of features worth discussing. E-mail does not replace the many other ways we have to communicate (phones, letters, faxes). Instead, it adds a new way to communicate—one that is sometimes appropriate and better, and sometimes not.

Benefits of E-Mail

E-mail features the following benefits:

(1) *Low cost.* The total cost is the local call to your Internet Service Provider, even if the message is sent internationally.
(2) *Speed.* Messages arrive at their destinations almost instantly, although they are not read until the recipient checks his or her e-mail.
(3) *No busy signal.* Unless a computer or server is down, the message gets there regardless of whether the recipient is on-line or off-line. There is no "telephone tag."
(4) *Broadcast capability.* A single message can be sent to multiple recipients simultaneously.
(5) *Attachments.* Documents and files from your computer can be attached and sent to the recipient's computer.
(6) *Indexed content.* Most e-mail programs allow the recipient to prioritize reading of messages based on the subject line.
(7) *Saving/Printing.* The text of a message can be saved for documenting a conversation or to be used in other documents, can be filed electronically, and can be printed out immediately or later.
(8) *Forwarding capability.* E-mail messages can be immediately forwarded to a third person via the Internet.

Some of these benefits are also drawbacks. You might not, for example, want the recipient to have your written word on his or her computer. There are also confidentiality issues involved, since e-mail can potentially be intercepted and read by others in transit. This is not likely to happen given the increasingly large quantity of e-mail traffic and automation of the process, but it is technically possible.

E-mail's convenience can also result in your becoming overwhelmed with communication. E-mail communication becomes much less effective when you receive 100 or more e-mail messages per day. The president has an e-mail address at president@whitehouse.gov, but one wonders how effective it can be, given the volume of mail sent to this address. On the other hand, this medium does provide a way for more people to respond to issues and for opinions to be tallied, even if messages are not carefully read.

Overall, you will likely find that e-mail enhances your communication in a variety of ways. E-mail has made it possible for us to communicate with more people more frequently than before. The idea for the authors' collaboration on this book evolved from a series of e-mail exchanges. The bulk of this book was written collaboratively even before we physically met for the first time. Various drafts were exchanged over the Internet as e-mail and attached files.

To be sure, all essential communications happened before e-mail came along, but now we can communicate with a number of people we did not have the time to communicate with in the past. We are in touch with distant friends with whom we had previously lost contact. We correspond more broadly and regularly with colleagues. When we receive a message that we find useful to share, this does not require making a photocopy, writing a cover letter or note, finding an envelope, addressing the envelope, finding a stamp and affixing it, and taking the envelope to the post office or depositing it in a mailbox. Merely clicking a mouse button a few times, (depending on the e-mail program and its configuration) automatically makes an electronic copy take a flight in cyberspace, of a city block or a half-world circumference.

Yet, from time to time, we all have changed our minds about sending a letter to someone. Often, the time it takes to prepare a letter for mailing has given us the time to reflect on whether it really is to our advantage to send it now or ponder some more. Perhaps we did not have the right nuance to our language; we may, in the heat of the moment, have been a bit too strident or confrontational. We may have forgotten to include an essential piece of explanatory information or an attachment. We may, at times, realize that we are acting like jerks by what we said or how we said it. We remedy this situation by simply tearing up the letter and writing a new one. Perhaps the most obvious disadvantage of "snail mail" is it takes so long to finish the communication and accomplish the logistical effort of communication. And, in some cases, this is a powerful advantage. Most of us who rely on e-mail and take it for granted have, at one time or another, dashed off a message and hit the "send" button too hastily, in response to something that got our blood pressure up, and then immediately regretted it. And once it is in the "pipeline," you just can't get it back.

But if this disadvantage was so compelling, people would be clamoring for a system that automatically held on to the message for 72 hours before delivering it into cyberspace. Now wouldn't that be a ridiculous feature of e-mail!

And the stories are legion of those who clicked on the wrong Internet address from an "address book" and inadvertently sent the right communication to the wrong person. The consequences of doing so have ranged from simple embarrassment to family breakup or job loss. One friend of ours sent a message to the executive director of a Harrisburg charity chewing out one of that person's subordinates, not realizing that the subordinate in question shared the e-mail account of the executive director and got to read the message first.

Every system has its advantages and disadvantages. Become familiar with the limitations of each system and use them to your best advantage. Sometimes, it is to your advantage to send a letter, sometimes faxing is appropriate, sometimes a telephone call makes sense, and at other times, e-mail is the communication method of choice. Those who master each of the options have a pronounced advantage compared to those who don't. As you become more experienced, you will recognize when you are writing an e-mail message that is better put together after an hour or day of mulling it over and waiting for the effects of anger, fatigue, or mind-altering substances (such as coffee) to wear off.

How E-mail Works

It is possible to send information from all kinds of computers with all kinds of communication software. In transmission, all e-mail assumes a standard form called "simple mail transfer protocol" (SMTP). In writing and sending mail, though, you do not have any direct exposure to SMTP, but instead use software such as NuPop, Eudora, or Z-Term.

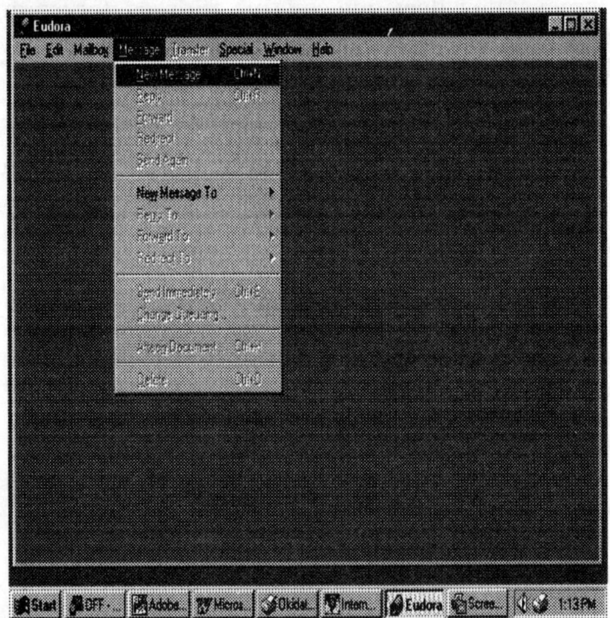

The Eudora screen. Courtesy of QUALCOMM, Inc. Reprinted with permission.

A message sent from the other side of the world will use computers along the way like stepping stones along a path. The message eventually (in seconds or minutes) arrives at the computer in your local area network (LAN) that acts as a repository for mail. Messages "addressed" to you are "dropped off" in your "mailbox" at regular intervals and await you to collect them. Mail can not only be "read," but it can also be "saved" to your hard drive, or you can "forward" it to another person, or "reply" to the sender. You can also get rid of it by "deleting" it.

The notable distinction between e-mail and snail mail, other than speed of conveyance, is one of cost. With the U.S. Postal System, picking mail up is free to us, but sending it has variable costs depending upon the amount mailed and country of destination or, for larger letters and packages, the distance from the mailer. With e-mail, you often pay a monthly fee for your "mailbox" (to your Internet Service Provider) and another, nominal, fee for getting yourself to that mailbox (a local phone call). But you pay nothing additional for sending mail to Michigan, Monterey, or Malaysia.

One of the most convenient uses of e-mail is to get a single message out to a lot of people who have e-mail addresses. You can type a message once, put several e-mail addresses on it (or create a special "mailing list" that serves as a proxy for all those e-mail addresses), and the message will be sent to everyone on the list.

Deciphering an E-Mail Address

If you want to use electronic mail, you will need an e-mail address. All e-mail addresses follow the same format: the person's userid (read "user I.D."), the "at" sign or "@," and the "domain name," or name of the organization whose computer is being used or is providing Internet access. Here is an example:

> tljones@uchicago.edu
> [userid@domain]

A first order of business: how does one say this address, for example, to someone over the phone? Typically, one would follow this convention: "T-L Jones at U-chicago dot e-d-u" where the "tl," the "U," and the "edu" are spoken as letters, and the last name, "at" sign and domain name are spoken as words.

We know several pieces of information immediately from inspecting this address. The address holder is university affiliated (".edu"), and more specifically connected to the University of Chicago ("uchicago"). Further, we might guess that his or her last name is Jones (from "tljones"), though this is not necessarily certain.

By looking at the end of an e-mail address, we can tell what sort of entity an individual has e-mail access through (if in the United States), or what country he or she hails from, if not. In the U.S., the endings can be:

.edu educational institution
.com commercial
.gov federal or state government
.mil military
.net a connection provider
.org a non-profit organization

A public process has been initiated to add to this list of "top level" domain names, motivated in part by the fact that the catch-all suffix .com is considered to be too limited considering the millions of business organizations that have or will seek their own domain names. Jon Postel of the Internet Assigned Numbers Authority, an influential participant in these matters, has proposed as many as 150 new additions. Among those suffixes that are receiving wide support are .firm, .store, .web, and .info. It would not be surprising to have a final agreement in 1998 on those names that are being added.

Outside of the U.S., these codes are replaced by a country code, regardless of the type of institution providing the access. Examples of these are:

.au Australia
.ca Canada
.fr France
.ke Kenya
.uk United Kingdom
.de Germany
.mx Mexico

Finding an E-mail Address

A number of Web sites exist that can help you find addresses, phone numbers, and e-mail addresses or locate businesses and other organizations. BigBook (http://www.bigbook.com/) is an example of a comprehensive and well-designed business listing site, allowing you to locate businesses by name, type, or location/address. In the future, this company hopes to develop a three-dimensional view of cities that will allow you to see a virtual representation of the city. For now, you can view two-dimensional mapping that enhances the amount of information you can obtain in looking for needed services, resources, and products.

In searching for people, there are numerous "white pages" options. One example of these is Switchboard (http://www.switchboard.com/). Switchboard finds people by name and, if desired, by city and state. National in scope, sites like Switchboard expand your ability to find people in regions beyond your local printed white pages, and using it is free, unlike using the telephone company's directory assistance. While Switchboard typically provides information such as that found in telephone directories, it may provide the person's e-mail address, in some cases. You can update your own listing to either give more detail, correct errors, or make yourself unlisted. In creating these white pages, companies have used publicly accessible resources.

Even with the on-line directories, it is often still necessary to use old technology to find someone's e-mail address. Call on the telephone and ask for it, and add it to your e-mail program's address book.

Netiquette and Emoticons

The culture of the Internet has developed over a short period of time and has changed as millions of new users have joined. Most Internet service providers have written rules about proper use of their services. There are general written and unwritten rules regarding the Internet. Among the more useful e-mail rules are:

- Don't type entirely in capital letters. This is considered the computer keyboard equivalent of "shouting," and can result in being flamed (being sent a threatening or denigrating unsolicited message).

- Don't put a message on a newsgroup (see page 36), mailing list (see page 35), or even personal e-mail that you would be embarrassed to have circulated to thousands of people. It just might happen. And don't say anything you would not be willing to defend in court.

- Don't send copyrighted material to a newsgroup, mailing list, or even an individual without permission from the copyright holder.

- Spend time "lurking" (the equivalent of listening quietly) on a newsgroup or mailing list before diving in by posting messages. Many groups and lists have a file called an FAQ (Frequently Asked Questions). Read it before posting your first message.

- Don't post clearly commercial messages on a newsgroup or mailing list. Announcements about new products are fine; sales pitches are strictly verboten and usually result in flame messages.

One of the disadvantages of e-mail is that it is totally text-based. It does not communicate body language, irony, or sarcasm, and this can completely change how the recipient responds to a communication. One system for conveying emotion is known as "emoticons," pictures made from keyboard characters. Among the most popular are:

:-} smiling
:-{ frowning
:'-) crying
;-) winking

There are many more of these symbols. They have their place, but try not to get too carried away.

There is also a short-hand that has evolved for cliché phrases. Among them are:

RTM (read the manual)
IMHO (In my humble opinion)
LOL (laughing out loud)
OTOH (On the other hand)
BTW (By the way)

Signatures

It is common for those who use e-mail to attach a signature file to the end of every e-mail message. The signature provides information about the sender (such as his or her real name, address, telephone and fax number), and may contain an inspirational message, famous quotation, ASCII art (sketches made from standard computer keyboard-generated characters), or witticisms. Remember that if you do include your address and/or telephone number, you are more vulnerable to uninvited communications. Here is a fictitious example:

```
 ____________________________________________________________
|Katie L. Harris              |ph: 900-555-1212              |
|Executive Director           |e-mail: k-harris@BFS.org      |
|Bosmanian Family Service     |fax: 900-555-1000             |
|Weekton, Ohio                |http://www.bfs.org/home.html  |
|____________________________________________________________|
```

Chapter 4

OTHER USEFUL INTERNET APPLICATIONS

"Dad, I met someone in a chat room and it's serious. Did you know a webmaster has the authority to marry people in cyberspace?"

Mailing Lists

One of the most useful features of e-mail is the ability to subscribe to a mailing list, sometimes called a Listserv®, after the software that manages many of these lists. A mailing list allows subscribers to send messages to, and receive messages from, a whole group of people at one time. The mailing list's address is maintained by a server and set up by an individual or organization wishing to generate discussion on a particular topic. To subscribe to one of these lists, you simply send a message to the appropriate address. Once you do, you are added to the list. When you send messages to the mailing list, they are automatically forwarded to all subscribers, who can then respond or send a new message.

This is a very helpful and convenient way to participate in a discussion on a topic of interest and to keep up on what is happening around that topic. It only works well, however, if the amount of communication is not overwhelming. If the messages from a mailing list fill your mailbox, then you will likely be forced to unsubscribe.

You might find a similar topic on a newsgroup (see page 36) to be an alternative.

To subscribe to a mailing list, the subscriber generally sends an e-mail message to a central address in a standard format that automatically processes the request. The command (the text of the e-mail message) to subscribe is usually: subscribe listname <your name>, where <yourname> is replaced by your actual name, not your e-mail address or screen name. The command is e-mailed, without any other message, to the mailing list address, such as: Listserv@listserv.net. The mailing list address is different from the address to which messages are sent that are intended for the entire distribution list.

For example, if you want to subscribe to GIFT-PL, a list for non-profit gift planners, you send a message:

Subscribe gift-pl Your Name

where "your name" is your real name, not your e-mail address or screen name, to listserv@iupui.edu (this is the administrative address for the list) without any topic, heading, or signature.

Within a few minutes, you will receive an e-mail response with a message that you have successfully subscribed to the list. This message often includes useful information, including information for unsubscribing, that you should save for future use. You will immediately begin to receive e-mail messages sent by others to the mailing list. Once subscribed, if you want to send a message to every subscriber on the list, you will send your e-mail message to an address different from the mailing list administration address (which in this case, happens to be: gift-pl@iupui.edu).

Some popular non-profit mailing lists are:

CYB-ACC (Nonprofit Coordinating Committee's Cyber-Accountability Group)
non-profit-net (Non-profit Organizations and the Internet)
NACC (Non-profit Academic Centers Council discussion list)
GIFT-PL (Non-profit Gift Planners)

To unsubscribe to the GIFT-PL mailing list, you would send a message (signoff gift-pl) to the list administration address.

To find a list of current mailing lists, point your browser to:
http://tile.net/listserv

or use the Liszt search engine (http://www.liszt.com, see pages 40 and 196).

There are procedures for starting your own mailing list. For information, contact:
listserv@bitnic.educom.edu and listserv@uottawa.bitnet

Newsgroups

A newsgroup is a form of Internet communication that provides for group discussion of a narrow topic. But, unlike mailing lists, it doesn't come to you in your e-mail box. It is like a bulletin board in the supermarket, where you have to take action to see it and read messages posted there, with an opportunity to post a reply for others to see. Sending a message to a newsgroup results in each subscriber of the newsgroup having the capability of seeing the message without receiving it as e-mail. Typically, someone makes a comment on a newsgroup, another person responds to the comment, and so on until there is a string of related messages on a topic. Simultaneously, others on-line will start another string of messages. All of the messages are stored, often chronologically, and given a title. Viewers can pick and choose using a newsgroup reader to decide which messages to look at.

Newsgroups have a prefix that gives an indication of their content. Those with "alt." prefixes (for "alternative") tend to be more free-wheeling and less politically correct. Other prefixes are:

biz business
comp computers
misc miscellaneous
rec recreation and hobbies
sci science
soc sociology

Historically, the most popular newsgroup of interest to non-profit organizations has been: soc.org.nonprofit (although it was rather quiet during the development of this book). Contact your Internet service provider for information on how to view newsgroups. Most newsgroups have a posting called the FAQ (for "frequently asked questions"). It is good policy to read this file before posting to a newsgroup. If you don't, and you ask a question that is covered in the FAQ (and has been raised a million times already), you risk getting flame messages.

How New Newsgroups are Started

It's not as difficult as you might think to establish your own newsgroup, if you think that the existing 20,000 or so are insufficient to be a forum for one of your favorite topics. Rather than provide all of the details here, we suggest you visit one or all of the following Web sites for more information:

http://www.cis.ohio-state.edu/~barr/alt-creation-guide.html
http://www4.ncsu.edu/~asdamick/www/news/create.html
http://www.cs.ubc.ca/spider/edmonds/usenet/good-newgroup.html

Also, check out the news.announce.newsgroups newsgroup for lots of files and postings related to this issue.

Internet Relay Chat (IRC)

Also known as "chat," IRC is the Internet equivalent of ham radio and was first used in Finland in 1988. Using IRC, you can have a "conversation" with someone by using the computer keyboard, all in real time. What you type and the response of the other participant(s) appear on your screen. It is possible to have a non-profit board meeting entirely by IRC, although we can't say this is the best way to conduct such a meeting. Most commercial providers have a method to provide for privacy among those who participate. More popular, however, are informal chats among those who just happen to frequent an IRC channel. More and more, these channels are becoming specialized, so that participants have something in common.

When you enter an IRC channel, your screen name appears to everyone on the channel. While there are more than 100 IRC commands, you can reasonably participate by knowing a few of the important ones, such as:

/HELP (gives you a list of available commands)
/BYE (exits the IRC)
/JOIN (insert channel# here) (joins an IRC channel)
/LEAVE (leaves the IRC channel you are on)
/WHO (lists those who are on the IRC channel)

Consult your Internet service provider for details on how to log on to an IRC channel. We offer one word of caution, however. This is one of the most potentially addicting parts of the Internet.

Gopher

Gopher is a menu-based tool that allows access to network resources of a variety of types, including Telnet (see page 38) and Web sites. It was originally developed at the University of Minnesota (the name is a multiple pun as the mascot of the campus is the "golden gopher," a gopher is a burrowing animal, which is what the gopher does, and it is also a "go fer"). Before the World Wide Web was developed, the gopher tool was the most popular for logging on to remote computer sites. There are still thousands of useful gopher-compatible sites around the world, but the gopher is fast becoming an extinct virtual animal on the Internet because of the explosion of the Web, which offers graphical abilities gophers cannot.

Up Close: Can We Chat?

Susan Mankita, a social work director at a Coral Gables, Florida, hospital, has developed a national on-line constituency as moderator of America OnLine's Social Work Forum, a part of College Online sponsored by book publishers Allyn and Bacon. She has been running the weekly chat for social workers and social work "wannabees" since the spring of 1995.

Mankita's responsibilities are three-fold: First and foremost, she maintains the bulletin boards—keeping them free from spam (unwanted commercial or other inappropriate messages), facilitating conversations, and developing new topics for the weekly chats. Mankita uses her social work training to encourage newcomers to the site to connect with others who share their interests. She secures content and Web links to keep the site up to date and informative.

Second, Mankita maintains a 300-subscriber mailing list of forum members who wish to be notified of weekly chat topics and other information. "People are constantly sending e-mail messages that they want to be added to, or removed from, the list," she says. "Often these requests include questions about social work. I feel it's important to answer them. Although my affiliation with the Social Work Forum leads some to consider me an expert in all social work matters, my real expertise is the ability to connect these social workers to relevant material, colleagues with similar interests, and informed experts."

Third, Mankita leads the chats. "This is by far the most interesting aspect of my responsibilities for the Social Work Forum," she admits. "Being a chat host is something of an art form. In addition to focusing a room 'full' of participants on a particular topic, I have to greet newcomers and clue them in. If someone enters the room by mistake, I have to steer him or her in the right direction. Often we get students looking for homework help, and they can really disrupt the flow of conversation. I try to answer their questions through internal messaging, but that can take my attention from the room, where it's most needed."

Leading a chat means balancing structure with flexibility. "If you envision the chat room as something of a town square, or local pub, a place where community develops, it's easier to understand the role of the host," explains Mankita. "It's his or her job to make the members feel they're part of something comfortable and welcoming. Without the smiles, hugs, and handshakes offered in real time, the host has to convey warmth creatively through the text."

Why is that so important? "The Internet is a huge, scary place," suggests Mankita. "There are many social workers who use the Social Work Forum as a vehicle to safely explore the larger, less-friendly on-line world. If they feel secure, as if they're among friends, they'll take more risks in their exploration."

What is a typical chat session like? Susan's chat group meets every Thursday from 9-10:30 p.m., EST. Participants are about equally divided between social workers and social work students, and represent all age groups from high school through retirement. They are disproportionately from the East Coast (because of the schedule) and predominantly women. That isn't surprising, since more than 78% of social workers who are employed and members of their professional association, the National Association of Social Workers (NASW), are women, according to a recent NASW study.

An average chat draws 15 participants. Mankita chooses topics from current events—such as welfare reform, health care, and managed care—and from chatter requests. Some chat sessions are devoted entirely to case presentations.

Telnet

Telnet is the protocol to connect with a computer in a remote location and interact with it in real time, as if you are directly operating that computer on-site. Using Telnet, you can use software that is locally unavailable or play games or engage in simulations with others who are also logged in. Telnet is a software program that is text-based rather than graphical. It allows you to find much of the same information as you can on Web pages and some things that are only available through Telnet.

How is chatting like, and unlike, other communication? According to Mankita, chatting has several features unique to synchronous communications, such as telephone or speaking face-to-face. "There are few widely shared norms," she says. "The Internet community actively makes these up, and they show up on the net as 'Netiquette.' One advantage of chatting is that people may feel freer to share intimate details that would be difficult to say face-to-face. But there are also negative outcomes, such as 'flaming.' That occurs when all social norms are flung aside and one communicator assaults another."

Text-based communications such as chatting may be preferable for some individuals, but not others. "They're marvelous for those folks who enjoy talking through their fingertips, or feel they can be clearer by writing," Mankita explains. "On the other hand, they pose difficulties for people who aren't crackerjack typists, or who are more comfortable verbally."

For herself personally, the absence of "physical distractions" in chatting is appealing. "It enables you to consider ideas, devoid of environmental or personal features," she says. "But again, the absence of social cues can be problematic at times. In ordinary conversation, we can usually tell if others want to continue—they look at us with interested expressions, and their mouths might drop open a bit when you share something a bit shocking. We oftentimes hear small gasps and other auditory cues. With chatting, we don't know who's waiting in the background to make a point, or who is being sarcastic. Some people find this freeing. I find myself doing everything I can to add cues as to my mood, such as using emoticons." She reports that she also types "uhm," "er" and "hmmm" alot, because it adds a human rhythm to her on-line communication.

Chatting has at least one unequivocal advantage: it's accessible to people who otherwise might be isolated by geography or illness. Several social workers who participate in the forum are unable to work because of chronic illness, but they can participate fully on-line. Internet communication also offers equality, at least for the computer-literate. "It doesn't matter if you're a student or a professor in the Social Work Forum," explains Mankita. "Everyone gets equal time, and all opinions are considered important."

What advice does she offer to non-profit managers about using the Internet?

"The Internet has a lot to offer, but there is also reason for caution," Mankita suggests. "Perhaps not every non-profit should dive in. Using the Internet—especially if you start signing up for things, developing a Web page, or making your presence known—is creating a permanent body of data that can be used, copied, or misused. In particular, all agencies should ensure that client information not be included in an accessible way, or confidentiality would be at risk."

Mankita recommends that non-profits who consider use of the Internet do everything possible to connect clients as well. "Non-profits tend to have clients who are disadvantaged, and these are the people who will really be left behind, as more and more people access the Internet," she emphasizes. "I feel really strongly that it may be more important in some ways to ensure connectivity for the disadvantaged than for the non-profits themselves."

FTP

FTP, or file transfer protocol, is the tool used to connect to a computer and transfer files from one computer to another. Using FTP, you can upload the file of your non-profit's newsletter to the Foundation Center, and upload files to your Web site. Or you can download a list of the top 40 charities or a document called "Ethics of Fund-raising." FTP connects your computer with the computer that has the file, so that you can transfer it to your own hard drive or floppy disk and then print it out.

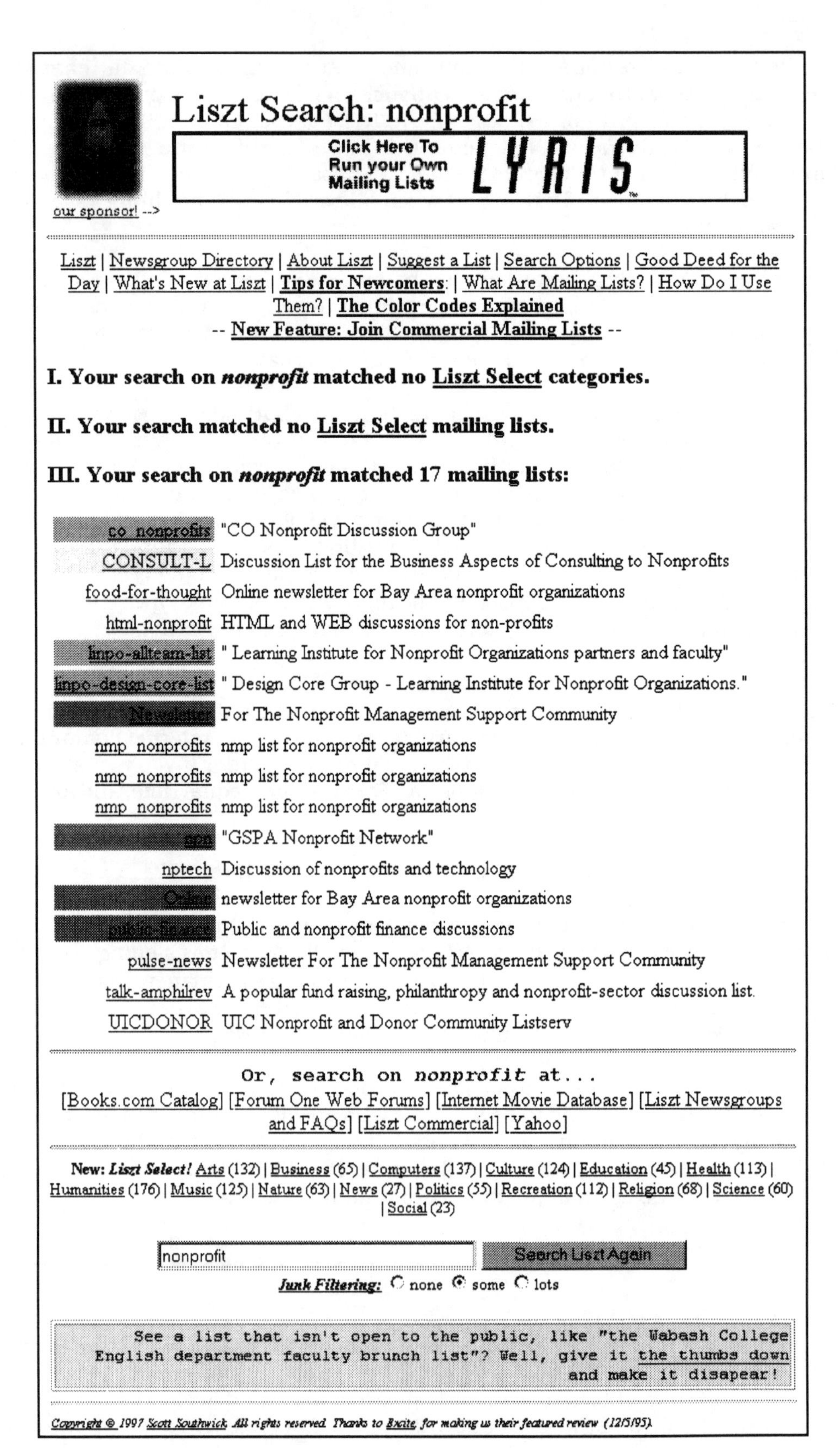

Liszt search screen showing the results of a search on the term "nonprofit." Reprinted with permission.

Chapter 5

THE WORLD WIDE WEB

"This new browser is impressive. I'm downloading an aroma from the Grandma's Bakery Home Page!"

Introduction

The World Wide Web (WWW) is an exciting, relatively new development on the Internet that permits users to link to resources from other computers that are similar to the information they provide, even if those resources physically reside on a computer on the other side of the world. World Wide Web resources are reportedly expanding at the rate of 20% each month. The Web supports not only text, but graphics, photographs, full motion videos, and sounds. Web pages are often formatted to give the appearance of an on-screen magazine, but there is one major difference. World Wide Web pages are formatted using computerized codes, called HTML (hypertext markup language), that permit the user to use a mouse or other pointer device to click on one part of the screen and be connected to a totally different World Wide Web page, which may be generated from a server on the other side of the world. For example, a World Wide Web page relating to libraries can be coded with links to libraries in hundreds of places. By clicking on one of these links, the computer's browser transports the user to the World Wide Web page of that library. To see World Wide Web pages and navigate through these links, "browser" software is required (see Chapter 2).

The Web, that collection of pages you navigate, contains information made available by people and organizations. No one is in charge of maintaining or organizing the Web, so what you see is only what someone else saw fit to make available. Using the Web is free, and it is not directly a money maker in most cases (although that is likely to change in the next few years), so information made available on the Web is usually there because someone wants you to see or know something. It is not necessarily there just because you want it.

Thus, one way to consider navigating the Web's information is to consider if the information that you want is likely to be there. Ask yourself whether anyone has anything to gain by making the information you want available. If you are seeking to purchase something, you are likely to find what you need. If you want information from a government agency, then there is a decent chance it will be out there. But if you want to know a business's trade secrets, you are not likely to find that they advertise these on the Web.

"The World Wide Web" is probably the term most commonly thrown around in discussions of the Internet. You might see it abbreviated "WWW" or "W3." The Web was "invented" by physicists at the European Laboratory for Particle Physics (CERN). Their basic problem was that they wanted to find an easy way to cross reference a document with its end notes and bibliography which, at that time, often required leaving the first document and searching for the second. The objective was to code the link to the second document at the same time one was viewing the first document. The Web you see now—with graphics that can be clicked on, flashy colors, and eye-catching

Up Close: Netscape's Web Browser

Netscape is far and away the most popular Web browser, with about 80% of the market using it. Viewing Web pages requires an Internet browser, such as Netscape Navigator or Microsoft® Explorer, the two leading and most fully featured browsers. Updated versions of Navigator are often available on the Internet (at http://www.netscape.com) or from your ISP free of charge or for minimal costs.

As with all of the browsers and on-line services mentioned here, Netscape is "graphical," meaning that a user can "point-and-click" his or her mouse at an image on the screen to execute a function rather than typing in a command word. Netscape comes with a variety of features, some of which include:

Title Bar: At the top of the document, the name of the current home page.
Menu Bar: The pull-down menus at the very top of the screen, including:

File: Functions for printing and saving.
Edit: Provides the Windows® traditional cut, copy and paste functions.
View: Includes the "refresh" and "reload" commands that update a currently selected Web page.
Go: Function for returning to sites recently visited.
Bookmarks: Marks a URL by name for revisiting later.
Options: Offers choices for settings, or configurations, for your Netscape software, such as what your default [starting when you first turn on Netscape] home page will be.
Directory: Lists Netscape "services," also featured in some of the buttons below the Menu Bar, such as compiled lists of "cool" and new sites, a handbook for using Netscape, search engines, and newsgroups.

Tool Bar: Buttons that speed the completion of certain Netscape functions, including these most frequently used:

Back & Forward: Allows for moving one page back or forward.
Home: Returns you to the default home page.
Open: Lets you type in the address of the Internet site you wish to visit (and transports you there when you hit the "return" key).
Print: Prints the page you are viewing.
Stop: Aborts the transmission of the page you are moving to, or another function in process.

Location/Go to Window: Shows the address of the page you are currently viewing or, by typing in another URL address, sends you to that page.

backgrounds—turned the WWW from what was a sterile, 1850s newspaper style to what looks more like a television or movie screen with an attitude.

The World Wide Web is exactly what its name suggests: a Web of interconnecting sites that span the world. Each "Web site" or "home page" belongs to, and is operated by (or abandoned by), some organization or person. Sometimes the terms "Web site" and "home page" are treated as synonymous, but there is a subtle difference. The Web site refers to the collection of pages of the person or organization, while the home page is the main "gateway," "index," or table of contents to the rest of the Web site.

Scroll Bar: As with many other software applications, the scroll bar allows you to move up and down the page with your mouse to view text above or below the area you are viewing.

The Little Hand, and the Status Bar: When you place the pointer (the arrow) either on a "hyperlink"—the bold-faced underlined text in a home page—or in many instances a graphic—an image of a small gloved hand appears. This lets you know (since it is sometimes not obvious) that you have encountered a link to another Web site. By clicking once, the browser transports you to that link. Before this step, you can identify the URL of the new site by examining the status bar at the bottom of the document. The status bar also includes an indicator of the progression for a page transmitted to you, so that you know when it is finished receiving the page.

As a final note, you can utilize Netscape commands by clicking on any part of the screen you are viewing and holding the right mouse button down for a second without releasing it. This will make a menu appear, and the commands listed can be executed by releasing the button while highlighting the desired command. If you do this over a picture on the page you are viewing, your choices will include the ability to copy the image to your computer for use on or off of the Internet.

The Netscape browser supports e-mail and newsgroups.

The Netscape browser screen and home page. Copyright 1996 Netscape Communications Corp. Used with permission. All Rights Reserved. This electronic file or page may not be reprinted or copied without the express written permission of Netscape.

All Web pages contain only that information that the person or organization wants to make available to the larger Internet public. For individuals, it might be a self-description or a list of interests and links to their favorite Web sites. For an organization, it might be a description or advertisement of its services, or it could be information relating to its mission.

So imagine now, a global newsstand or television network in which each and every person has the ability to create his or her own "home page show." Some people use this ability to entertain, sell goods and services, share news, ideas, or stories. Some home page shows are good, and some are pretty awful. Some are self-serving only and some altruistically offer the world some useful information and communication contacts.

Anyone with a Web browser can view these home page shows. Just as any brand of television shows the same program on the same channels, browsers show the same home pages, even if the tint, contrast, and general layout may vary from browser to browser.

A key feature of the Web, with its millions of home pages, is the ability for each page to lead you to other pages. On almost any home page, you will see some text (or pictures) underlined (or outlined) and/or in colorful boldface. These are the "hypertext links" that, when clicked on with the mouse, trigger your browser to move along to another Web page.

Note that sometimes one of the links will lead not to another Web site when clicked, but instead will link to an individual's e-mail address. A message form will appear, allowing you to write a message to the designated person. These are called "mailto" links.

The ability to create links is the magic of which the World Wide Web is formed, and is one way in which the Internet is different from television shows or newspapers. TV show producers generally want you to keep viewing their shows and not move elsewhere, and written publications are intended to be read in sequential order. The Internet is often referred to as "thinking in parallel," since it allows and encourages you to explore more in depth whatever diversionary routes you wish to take. If TV were like the WWW, you could be watching "Murder, She Wrote," then move on at will to a PBS Agatha Christie special or an Alfred Hitchcock film (since these links are related as mystery shows), and then return to continue where you were in the original episode you were watching.

Deciphering a Web Address

A URL ("uniform resource locator") is the address for Web sites. Each page has a unique address. Typically, Webmasters organize the URLs of their pages in a manner similar to how directories and subdirectories are organized on a computer, by using forward slashes (rather than back slashes) to organize these pages. For example, a home page might have the URL:

http://www.organization.org/webpage.html

The home page might have a link to "press releases" with the URL:

http://www.organization.org/webpage/pressrel.html

The September 18, 1997, press release on the organization's *Legislator of the Year* award might have the URL:

http://www.organization.org/webpage/pressrel/091897.html

This is an important point to understand. Perhaps you are given the URL for a document and your browser gives you a "404" message (which indicates that there is nothing available at that URL). Instead of giving up, you can try finding the page you are looking for by using the URL one directory higher, or two or three directories higher, as may be necessary. There are many times when you can find the information you are looking for even when you are given an incorrect URL.

Let's quickly deconstruct a Web address. The Web site address for the Colorado State University Department of Social Work is:

http://www.ColState.edu/Depts/SocWork

The first thing you might notice is that there are no spaces. This is not a coincidence. No spaces are allowed in a URL, and this is why words are often separated by dots ("."), dashes ("-"), tildes ("~"), slashes ("/"), and underlines ("_").

Starting from the end, in the above address, the suffix, ".html," indicates that the document is a Web page using HTML (hypertext markup language) codes. This is the code used to create Web pages, and these files usually end in "html" or "htm."

Next, each single slash mark ("/") lets you know that you are descending into further file directories in the person's server, just as you do in your own computer to find particular files or documents. This is useful to know, because there are times when you might know an address for a site that is likely to be in the ascending files. For example, suppose you wanted to find the main page for Colorado State University. Knowing the social work department's page, you could guess that the university would be at http://www.ColoState.edu/. Entering this or cutting off the remaining portion of the address will, in fact, get you to the main page for the institution.

To "surf," "browse," or "navigate" the Web (these are all equivalent terms), you simply open your browser and type in the URL of a page, and from there explore various links. You can fully access the Internet's resources even if you hardly ever enter a URL by hand. Your browser will start you off at a default home page (usually the browser company's Web site), but you can set it to start at any site you wish— your own, a favorite organization's, or a favorite navigation launching point, such as the Yahoo! directory (http://www.Yahoo.com). One browser feature you will come to rely on is the "back" button. Suppose you start to jump from page to page during your navigation, and realize that you have gone well off-track. The back button will retrace your steps as far back as you wish to retrace before going forward in a new direction. For a quick return to the beginning, you can always click the "home" button and begin anew.

Most browsers have a "bookmark" function that automatically records a favorite link for future use. Thus, in order to return to that page at a future time, you need only to click on the stored reference in the bookmark, rather than having to type in the entire address.

Searching the Web is a process used to find particular information or otherwise explore the Web's content. It is true that the Internet is disorganized. It has been compared to a library that has no librarian, no index or card catalogue system, just piles of books in random stacks throughout. But fortunately, some individuals and companies have undertaken the enormous task of indexing at least a portion of it for the rest of us. Some people have dedicated all or part of their individual sites to creating lists of other Web sites that have some topic in common. If you are looking for resources of interest to non-profits, you might want to start your search at some of the popular lists of sites created for non-profit managers, and other organizations that have spent the time organizing sites related to non-profits. Perhaps the first large scale directory, and likely the most complete topical directory is Yahoo! (http://www.Yahoo.com/). Here you can start with a set of about a dozen general themes (e.g., business, education, entertainment, health, social science, society and culture). From these, you begin to narrow your search to more specific topics within each category, until you find sites relating to what you want. An alternative search method is to use search engines that are created by a variety of companies, and that are accessible through their Web sites. These allow you to receive a list of related Web sites according to keywords you enter on a form (see page 84).

None of these is perfect, complete, or comprehensive, but they give you an excellent start, and usually produce more information than you want. If you have your own Web page and you want to be noticed, then registering with the more popular search engines will help.

Up Close: Microsoft® Internet Explorer

Microsoft® Internet Explorer, available free for download from Microsoft®'s Web site (http://www.microsoft.com/ie), is gaining in use and popularity. Internet Explorer 4.0 was in the process of being released at the time this book went to press. This version requires a minimum of 16 MB of RAM, and 30 MB of hard disk space, and operates using Windows® 95 or Windows® NT 4.0.

Besides a Web browser, the 3.0 version also has components for e-mail, newsgroups, and on-line conferencing. We will look at the Web browser component here.

Title Bar: At the top of the document, the name of the current home page.

Menu Bar: The pull-down menus at the very top of the screen, including:

File: Functions for opening, printing and saving.
Edit: Provides the Windows® traditional cut, copy, and paste functions
View: Controls what is displayed on the screen. Also includes an Options menu, which offers various settings to customize your IE session.
Go: Function for returning to sites recently visited.
Favorites: Marks a URL by name for revisiting later.

Tool Bar: Buttons that speed the completion of certain Internet Explorer functions, including these most frequently used:

Back & Forward: Allows for moving one page back or forward.
Refresh: Reloads the current page in its most up-to-date form.
Home: Returns you to the default home page.
Search: Loads a page that allows you to search the Internet.
Favorites: Lists your favorite sites, allowing you to click on a site's name to go to that site.
Print: Prints the page you are viewing.
Font: Allows you to increase or decrease the print size of text on the pages you are viewing.
Mail: Allows you to check and send e-mail using Internet Mail, or read and send Usenet newsgroup messages using Internet News.
Stop: Aborts the transmission of the page you are moving to, or another function in process.

Address Bar: Shows the address of the page you are currently viewing, or by typing in another URL address, sends you to that page.

Links: Buttons that allow you to jump to other sites. You can customize these buttons.

Scroll Bar: As with many other software applications, the scroll bar allows you to move up and down the page with your mouse to view text above or below the area you are viewing.

Status Bar: Indicates the progression for a page transmitted to you, so that you know when the browser is finished receiving the page.

Frames

A popular Web page development is the use of frames, a device that allows more than one HTML document to be displayed on your monitor at the same time. Usually, one frame will contain a "Table of Contents" consisting of links. When you click on one of the links, the referenced document appears in another frame, while the first frame remains on the screen. In essence, you are then viewing two Web pages in one. The page that is displayed in the second frame may be another page in the same Web site as the first, or it may be a page from another site.

A significant disadvantage of using frames is that not every Web browser is compatible with them. If you are using a browser that is not, and you try to access a page with frames, you will typically get an error message such as, "Your browser does not support frames. You cannot access this site." Some of these messages may have a link to a site that permits you to download, at no charge, a browser that supports frames. Your only recourse at this point is to download (or buy) a browser that supports frames. Some sites have a frames and a non-frames version, and we recommend that you provide both if you plan to build a site using frames, so you will not alienate (or lose as visitors) those who do not have a frames-compatible browser.

Independent Sector home page (frames version). Courtesy Independent Sector. Reprinted with permission.

Chapter 6

FUND-RAISING

by *Gary Grant and Steve Roller*

Introduction

The Internet is an important tool for fund-raisers. While no one would recommend that you base your fund-raising strategy solely on the Internet, it can help you research and make contact with funding sources in ways that can save you time and money.

A good way to begin thinking about the Internet's uses for fund-raising is to consider which individuals or organizations are most likely to use the Internet for reaching you. If you use a Web site for fund-raising, what audience do you expect to reach?

For example, one might expect, and would in fact find, that foundations are among those leading the way in using the Internet. At least one-third of the top foundations have Web sites and others are moving relatively fast to put proposal information and other content onto Web sites. But foundations are unique in this regard. Few individual donors would feel as interested in making it broadly known that they want to contribute to a particular cause.

Overall, it is probably safe to say that there are more Web sites seeking donations than there are Web sites offering funding. Even in the category of fund-raising educational material, there are more Web sites describing books for sale than there are on-line books or articles on the subject. Simply put, there are few who have incentive to freely give you information about how to fund-raise. On the other hand, people are usually collegial by nature, and are often more than happy to share their experiences and expertise to at least some extent. Thus, you can use the Internet for learning more about fund-raising, simply by using it as a networking tool.

For more information about how to use the Internet in fund-raising (and why), see the on-line article *Fundraising and the Internet: Another Arrow in the Quiver* (http://www.fund-raising.com/intfundart.html). According to this article, a 1995 survey found that the average household income of a "wired" family was $66,700, compared to $42,400 for non-wired families. It also found that Internet users were younger, more highly educated, and were using the Internet more for handling financial matters and making purchases. It reasons that charitable organizations ought to consider this group an important one to reach out to now and in the long-run.

Educating Yourself About Fund-raising

Our first step in using the Internet might be to learn a little more about fund-raising—to seek ideas, to find resources relevant to fund-raising and so on. It is not advisable to use the Internet alone to educate yourself about the field of fund-raising. As with other areas, you should be warned that there is no guarantee about the accuracy of information on-line. Books and courses on fund-raising will likely be more reliable than information you find in documents from the Internet. Chances are that if you enter the term "learn about fund-raising" in any search engine, you will be more likely to find advertisements for books on fund-raising (that might be helpful to you), but you are not as likely to find much detailed and comprehensive material on the subject.

If you really want to learn about fund-raising, and want to use the Internet as a starting point, perhaps the best way would be to use it to access other professional fund-raisers who may be willing to share and discuss issues pertaining to the field and to answer questions for newcomers. You may find colleagues on some Usenet newsgroups such as soc.org.nonprofits. Also, there are some mailing lists you could join, including the following:

CFRNET, a list for people involved in Corporate and Foundation Relations. (To subscribe, send e-mail to: cfrnet-request@medicine.wustl.edu and type message: subscribe cfrnet <your name>.)

FUNDLIST, a general mailing list for fund-raising professionals. (To subscribe, send e-mail to: listproc@listproc.hcf.jhu.edu and type message: SUB FUNDLIST <your real name>.)

GIFT-PL, a mailing list on planned giving (To subscribe, send e-mail to: listserve@vm1.spcs.umn.edu and type message: subscribe GIFT-PL <your real name>.)

Fundraising Online, E-mail to majordomo@igc.org with the message: info fundraising online—which should give you basic information about this list.

More fund-raising mailing lists can be found at:
E-mail Discussion Forums—(http://weber.u.washington.edu/~dlamb/apra/lists.htm)

Creative Fund-raising Ideas

Depending on the kind of fund-raising you do for your organization, you might be interested in exploring creative fund-raising ideas: fun things to do, items to sell as a fund-raiser, and the like. Besides getting ideas from others sharing their success stories, you might also search for companies that offer products for sale by charities. An example of one we found was Music Brokers for Charities (http://www.quiknet.com/dimple/used2.html). Your organization can collect used CDs and videos and Music Brokers will purchase them from you.

Of course, you should be wary of anything you find on the Internet, especially when it involves any financial transactions through the Internet.

Prospect Research

Prospect research can take many different forms. Are you looking for information about an individual someone recommended to you as a possible supporter? Are you seeking to broaden your appeal to new individuals and corporations who have not yet been involved in your organization?

Below are some examples of the sites used by prospect researchers.

Internet Prospector
http://PLAINS.UWYO.EDU/~prospect/

David Lamb's Prospect Research Page
http://weber.u.washington.edu/~dlamb/research.html

Hoover's Online
http://hoovweb.hoovers.com/

Prospex Research
http://prospex.com/Welcome.html

CASE List of Prospect Research Sites
http://192.203.212.6/256/frprspct.htm

The Association of Prospect Researchers for Advancement
http://weber.u.washington.edu/~dlamb/apra/APRA.html

Finding Funding Sources

For finding individual supporters, prospect research provides a tool to identify prospects and to collect relevant public information helpful to the fund-raiser. Many funding organizations, however, use the Internet to make information available to those who may want to apply for funding. Finding these sites is a matter of meeting the funder half-way. The approaches you can use for finding funding sources on-line can range from "hunting" to "gathering."

"Hunting" for funding sources involves embarking on a search through the Internet for support from a variety of sources at a single time when funding is needed. A "gathering" approach involves identifying particular funding sources and visiting them periodically or otherwise collecting their information as it is updated, so that you can be first in line to learn of the availability of support. There is no necessarily preferred method of finding funding but, in general, if you can identify the sources that might regularly be appropriate for you, it is probably best to take a "gathering" approach and to accumulate references to sites of value to you.

Many federal agencies have their own Web sites and use them to post the availability of funding opportunities and detailed information on grant programs. A good place to visit is the Library of Congress's Internet Resource Page (http://lcweb.loc.gov/global/executive/fed.html). This list covers virtually the entire federal government, including the White House, all cabinet departments, and independent agencies.

Good places to start for finding funding sources are:

The Foundation Center (http://fdncenter.org/)
The Internet Nonprofit Center (http://www.nonprofits.org/)
Putnam Barber's Page on Nonprofit Resources (http://www.eskimo.com/~pbarber)
Goodwill Industries of America (http://www.goodwill.org/)

Places for Donors

Next we present some sites that focus on attracting donors and providing them with information about charities and about giving. These donor resources are often helpful to fund-raisers, especially those interested in making sure that their organizations are included among those to which donors might be referred.

While there may be success stories from ventures such as this, there is little hard data on just how successful they are. Such ventures may be worthy of attention as they represent the possible future nature of on-line philanthropy. The proliferation of Web sites and the ease for putting out false or misleading information could make it difficult for donors to know who to trust. Also, just as there are organizations dedicated to helping to disperse traditional charitable giving to worthy efforts, so, too, might there be a role for helping donors to navigate the overwhelming number of options available through the Internet.

Another use for this type of site is to encourage and facilitate giving. Some of the sites referenced in this book, for example, are aimed at helping to simplify employer efforts to promote

Up Close: The Harry Singer Foundation (http://www.singerfoundation.org)

Margaret Bohannon-Kaplan and her husband, Melvin Kaplan, co-founded this national, private foundation.

"One of my husband's goals was to make the point that some people will invest time, effort, and money simply because they care—with no financial motives," says Kaplan, who serves as the Singer Foundation's director. "We pay for the opportunity to do some good."

In 1993 they began as a Bulletin Board Service (BBS) using First Class software. Featured on-line were the annual foundation books first published in print form using excerpts from the essays of high school students across the nation, she says. "We also offered information relating to public policy as well as a Social Security Forum. But few people found our bulletin board, and technology allowed us to consider going on the Internet with a Web site."

Among the most frustrating startup problems was finding a host Web server.

"We sent proposals to CompuServe, America OnLine (AOL), and Connect, a private Web hosting service in Cupertino, California, that catered to an exclusive clientele. Connect agreed to host our site but, unfortunately, it charged members fees far in excess of those charged by AOL and CompuServe. This made it hard to attract our regular clients and Connect discouraged us from advertising our programs to their membership," She recalls. "Connect also restricted the site to ASCII and a small choice of icons."

But the beginning site nevertheless provided a good learning experience for the foundation.

"Remember, this was before the arrival of the small Internet service providers that can now be found in every part of the country," Kaplan adds.

The site was maintained for a few years by part-time computer-literate students. Finally, in the spring of 1996, one of the foundation's volunteers started her own Web design and Webmaster business and offered some of her time gratis to develop the site further. In 1996, she wrote programs for submittal forms, and added links to other sites.

"I submitted the material and direction, and the volunteer added HTML codes and made certain the material looked good on all browsers," says Kaplan. "But we took the entire job back to our office in May 1997. I am now serving as Webmaster using Microsoft®'s *FrontPage*, which inserts the HTML codes automatically. We plan to add a powerful search

employee giving. In essence, they serve as on-line consultants for giving opportunities, either allocating funds to a variety of selected organizations or directing them to the donor's choice.

The National Charities Information Bureau (http://www.give.org/) is an example of a site aimed at donors who wish to ensure that they are giving to charitable organizations that fit this organization's guidelines. Interested donors can order a free Wise Giving Guide and by signing on will receive news via e-mail of new information made available at the site. There is also a set of donor tips available at the site. An on-line reference guide can be used by donors to review whether any of 300 organizations evaluated comply with NCIB standards. These standards are detailed at the site and relate to an organization's governance, purpose, and its programs relating to these. They also evaluate information disclosed, methods of fund-raising, reporting, budgeting, and the engine to the site to enable students who entered essay contests in past years to browse the 12 published foundation books found in our Archive Forum and review on-line what they wrote as high school students."

The foundation is planning further improvements.

"Our data show that the 'Emotional Intelligence' Forum is very popular, and we intend to expand it and the Family and Responsibility Forums, which have a lot of interactive programs," Kaplan continues. "We also offer hundreds of books, audio and even a few video tapes to schools and other interested parties on our Resources Forum. But for the next couple of years, 'Another Way' will be our main focus. We'll highlight grass-roots activities in local communities and host those communities on this Forum."

The project can be viewed 'at-a-glance' in 26 charts and in fictional form at http://www.singerfoundation.org/main/way/

Another Way

How do we get less crime and a more responsible and caring society?

Raise taxes and increase regulations! That's the old way.

In the twenty-first century there will be Another Way.

Everyone thinks government at all levels is spending too much money. Many people think government has extended its reach beyond what is desirable in a free society. Most people think in view of our current social problems there is no other way, but they're wrong-there is another way.

Another Way is the culmination of ten years of Foundation experience; It combines and expands the best of two pilot programs which are described in the Foundation archives: White Hats and Alternatives For Local Governments Struggling With Limited Resources

Click On The Titles For More Information:

- Another Way At A Glance - 26 Charts
- Fictionalized Description Of Another Way
- What's In It For You Personally?
- What's In It For The Younger Generation?
- What's In It For The Older Generation?
- What's In It For The Middle Generation?
- What's In It For Non-profits?
- What's In It For The Harry Singer Foundation?
- What's In It For Political Leaders?
- What's In It For Religious Institutions?
- What's In It For The Nation?
- What's In It For The World?
- How Does Another Way Work?
- How Do I Get Involved?

[Home] [Main Menu] [Archives] [Another Way Menu]

The Another Way home page. Courtesy The Harry Singer Foundation. Reprinted with permission.

use of funds, among other criteria. The quick reference guide provides an easily scanned simple alphabetical list of organizations coded as to whether they adhere to the recommended standards, and whether information has not been disclosed by the organization. Every two weeks, a new charity is featured on-line with the results of its report published.

Another way to ensure the legitimacy of a charity you want to support is through the Council for Better Business Bureaus (http://www.bbb.org/). The Philanthropic Advisory Service (PAS) at the site includes many, but not all, reports made by this organization relating to specific charities (inclusion is based on the frequency of requests). For example, a donor can click on the report for Mothers Against Drunk Driving and find that it does meet CBBB standards for charitable giving under its report written in March 1996 and expiring in May 1997. If an organization does not meet one or more standards, the standards they do not meet are described so that donors giving can make the most informed choices possible.

Other information contained in these reports includes descriptions of an organization's programs, expenses, system of governance and fund-raising methods. CBBB forbids the use of its reports for fund-raising or promotional purposes, but encourages donors to use them to become more educated from this objective source about the organizations they support. Reports not available on-line can be ordered.

The site also includes Tips on Charitable Giving (http://www.bbb.org/about/tipsgive.html), Tips on Tax Deductions for Charitable Giving (http://www.bbb.org/about/tipstax.html), and Tips on Handling Unwanted Direct Mail Appeals (http://www.bbb.org/about/tipsmail.html), among other useful information for donors.

CharitiesUSA (http://www.charitiesusa.com/) bills itself as the "home to over 400 charitable choices." This site organizes charities by the type of services they provide. This site is nicely organized, but many of the service areas have not been updated in more than a year. Donors are encouraged to contribute to these pre-screened organizations. Donors can elect to give on-line via a secure server. The organization's mission is to increase workplace giving and to assist employers to cost-effectively expand their workplace fund drive technology. Charities USA also features a news source, a toll-free "Speaker's Bureau," and a toll-free "Contributor's Assistance" hotline.

International Service Agencies (ISA) (http://www.charity.org/) is a similar effort to increase workplace giving by providing a single site to which donors can contribute if they are interested in supporting efforts to alleviate hunger, poverty, and the effects of war, oppression, and natural disasters. Donors can give to ISA or can designate for particular organizations within ISA. ISA members are organized into categories of Children, Education, Hunger Relief, Medical Care, Refugees/Disaster Relief, and Job Creation/Economic Relief. Members do not need to have their own home page to participate, as ISA includes a descriptive page for each member.

A similar, related project, Relief Web (http://www.reliefweb.int/) is organized by the United Nations Department of Humanitarian Affairs. Emergency areas around the world are monitored by the site, allowing individuals to focus on aid where it may be most needed at any particular time. The site also gives data on the amount of humanitarian assistance that has been provided each year from each nation. And it provides data on the humanitarian assistance provided in response to complex emergencies. Another humanitarian relief site is ReliefNet (http://www.reliefnet.org/),which features an innovative "virtual relief concert" in support of humanitarian relief efforts.

Of course, the well-known centralized resource for donors seeking to contribute to a variety of efforts is the United Way (http://www.unitedway.org/).

The Corporate Community Involvement Resource Centre (http://www.charitynet.org/CCInet/noframes/pages.html) provides a place to learn about corporate philanthropy efforts (and provides corporations with a place to be recognized for their contributions to the community). For example, fund-raisers interested in the Ben and Jerry's Foundation (http://www.benjerry.com/foundation/index.html) can find its site here and learn what projects have been funded, its mission and guidelines, and procedures for applying.

This site is a product of the UK's CHARITYnet (http://www.charitynet.org/), which serves as another resource center for non-profits and contributors. Some of the highlighted things to do at this site include:

1) Add your organization or your corporate philanthropy site to its listing.
2) Learn about the tax effects of giving.
3) Use free Internet space from CHARITYNet to build your own Web site that you can use for fund-raising or other purposes.

News, Articles, and Publications On Fund-raising and Philanthropy

Fund-raising is a time-consuming occupation. Time is in short supply for keeping up with news in philanthropy, the latest knowledge in the field, and participating in advocacy efforts related to current legislation and policies affecting fund-raisers. The cost of subscribing to professional journals is not always a part of the fund-raiser's budget and, if so, is often limited. The on-line solution is to visit relevant news sites or to subscribe to e-mail services providing such news in a way that is easier to search, convenient, and cost-effective.

On-line articles and publications on philanthropy can enhance a fund-raiser's ability by allowing for access to the largest number of information sources, usually free of charge. Keep in mind that you can't carry your computer on the bus for reading on the way to work, so we might recommend keeping your most important subscriptions arriving in hard copy through the mail. Using the Internet, however, can be especially helpful for accessing information from sources that are either only available on-line, or that are secondary in importance to you. Even if you don't read your on-line sources for news regularly, it may be helpful on those occasions when you want to look through a variety of perspectives on a hot topic.

The following sites are among the on-line publications relating specifically to fund-raising.

Philanthropy News Digest (http://fdncenter.org/phil/philmain.html)
Philanthropy Journal Online (http://www.philanthropy-journal.org/)
Chronicle of Philanthropy (http://www.philanthropy.com)
NonProfit Times Online (http://www.nptimes.com/)

Using E-mail to Attract and Solicit Support

One question that is often discussed is whether e-mail can be used for direct solicitations. The newsletter *Successful Direct Mail & Telephone Fundraising* cites a recent study that projects that 80 million people will be using e-mail in 1997 and 130 million by 1998. More than twice as many people use e-mail than use the World Wide Web.

The Internet is too new to be sure one way or another but so far, it appears that the culture of the Internet frowns on soliciting people on-line. In general, there is a degree of fear among many e-mail users that they will soon be inundated with e-mail. Already, the presence of e-mail advertisements or "junk e-mail" (also referred to pejoratively as "spam") is raising fears and sending some back to their more traditional ways of communicating. In addition, e-mail is an informal method of communicating, and solicitations should probably still be made in a more formal manner, such as a letter on your agency letterhead with an original authorized signature.

This could change. When the telephone first became popular in the general population, it was quite unclear what etiquette it would demand. In fact, one very early practice was to send a letter to the person you wanted to call, announcing that you planned to call at a particular date and time, rather than surprising him or her with an unexpected call. It was not until much later, well into the 1970s, that phone solicitations began to be commonplace—at least those from institutions with which people were already involved, if not "cold calls" from organizations seeking new supporters. Still, it is common to precede phone solicitations with a letter informing your prospect base that you will be phoning to request their support.

Up Close: Trolling the Internet for Grants

Steve Roller works for the Chicago Housing Authority and is particularly interested in grant programs through the U.S. Department of Housing and Urban Development. Each month, Steve visits the HUD Web site (http://www.hud.gov/) and finds his way to the funding opportunities page (http://www.hud.gov/fundopp.html). Here, he reviews the current HUD Tentative NOFA (Notice of Funding Availability) Schedule (http://www.hud.gov/nofas.html) where he gets the earliest possible news of soon-to-be-announced programs. For example, seeing that the HUD Office of Community Planning and Development has already made available information on the Continuum of Care Homeless Assistance program, he downloads the complete document to his computer and prints it out the day it is released.

Other funding information on the HUD site includes details of programs by categories, including help for the homeless, youth programs, drug prevention programs, counseling services, research support, and more.

Similar information is available at sites for the U.S. Department of Education (http://www.ed.gov/) through its Money Matters page (http://www.ed.gov/money.html), the U.S. Department of Health and Human Services (http://www.os.dhhs.gov/) through both its Funding page (http://www.odphp.osophs.dhhs.gov/nonprofit/funding.htm) and its Partnership page (http://www.hhs.gov/partner/), and other social service-related federal departments and agencies.

There are comparable resources available at the state level. For example, at the State of Illinois Web site (http://www.state.il.us), you can click on "state agencies" to find a long list of links to various state departments, agencies, and offices. You may need to navigate around these sites a bit to determine if they have information posted on grants they award. If you don't see a heading for grants, or Requests for Proposals (RFPs), then look for such headings as "Programs," "Services," "Resources," or "About the Agency."

For a list of the Internet World Wide Web home page addresses for the 50 states and the District of Columbia, see Appendix C.

Up Close: Development At a School of Social Work

Gary Grant is a development officer at a school of social work. His interest in funding opportunities covers the gamut of topic areas, providing that the funding applies to research in areas of social work. Reviewing agency sites on-line periodically is impractical for him; however, several key agencies and organizations provide automated searches or reports as funding announcements are made. Gary receives the weekly National Institute of Health (NIH) guide via e-mail, as well as several other alerts. Skimming these for the ones applicable to social work research, he forwards them by e-mail to the faculty and doctoral students at his school. Most of what he receives could be obtained in printed form, but by using e-mail, he gets it into the hands of those who need it almost immediately, for less cost, and with less time spent in the effort than ever possible before.

Information like that provided at agency sites makes possible a level of searching and information-gathering never before possible. But to be realistic, only if you have a narrowly tailored interest area can you spend the time necessary to search each one. You may, therefore, want to find sites that either do the gathering for you and provide a comprehensive listing of opportunities, or enlist the assistance of a service that searches for you while you are off-line. Once you identify a possible funding opportunity on-line, the site describing the opportunity is likely to contain more helpful information necessary to you as you work through the application process.

E-mail solicitation is tempting on another level—reaching out to find new supporters. It offers an opportunity to solicit gifts from the largest possible audience in a way that is inexpensive and less time-consuming than either direct mail appeals or phone solicitations. As such, it may one day help to minimize the dollars spent finding new funders. But some of the same factors that make this a tempting opportunity also make it a dangerous risk. Step without caution on the wrong toes, and your organization could be the talk of the Internet in all the wrong ways. Angry words about your organization's overzealousness could spread quite quickly and create problems far exceeding the advantages of the dollars you might raise.

One place to be especially cautious is on mailing lists and newsgroups. In both cases, participants defend the topical turf of their particular group with ardor. Even the most well-meaning appeals for action or support of ideological values not inherent in the subject that brings the group together may be attacked by flame messages. The reason for this is that most of these groups suffer from (or at least fear) being overwhelmed with irrelevant dialogue. To prevent this, they stamp out such tangential discussions immediately. Those who persist after a friendly, or not-so-friendly, warning risk the group moving to the next retaliatory step—spamming—in which hundreds of participants e-mail the wrong-doer, effectively flooding his or her mail box with angry messages. And if this still does not work, they may contact the offender's service provider and petition for his or her removal from the system.

So, unless you are participating in a group you know welcomes solicitations, you should refrain from this. As with any group, you should always read the discussions first, until you get a feel for what is proper and not proper in the group.

If you've used your e-mail for some time, you may have already noticed that commercial advertisers have started reaching out to lists of e-mail addresses they acquire. There are companies that compile e-mail address lists and provide others with the service of sending their message to them. Again, the benefits of this are unclear at best and the risk of being labeled for inappropriate behavior too great for anyone to advise non-profits to use these.

But what about your existing constituency? Would they be put off by an e-mail solicitation? Even here, it's hard to tell for sure, but right now it is probably not advisable, except perhaps in the most special and extraordinary cases. A routine of doing this could lead people to request that they be taken off your list.

Perhaps a better use of e-mail is to simply interact with your constituency and to provide them with information and services that make them feel closer to your organization. E-mail can be a most convenient means for increasing the direct communication between you and your organization's actual and potential supporters. Sharing timely and informative news about what you are doing can keep you on donors' minds and make sure your work has visibility.

One way to do this is to organize a regular e-mail newsletter. Providing a consistent and dependable flow of information can allay fears of being overwhelmed by e-mail. As use of the Internet and e-mail grows, this can help ensure that your e-mail lists grow, bringing a larger portion of your audience closer to your organization.

Another way is to develop a mailing list that you use to encourage dialogue among your organization's constituency. Some organizations, such as the Children's Defense Fund, provide an advocacy alert by e-mail and encourage their members to share information with others. This gives the organization the ability to almost instantly get word out to untold numbers of people, and in turn may bring many of these people closer to the organization.

Your constituency will enjoy the opportunity that e-mail gives them to provide input to your organization. Communicating, asking questions, and on-line surveys are some methods you can use to demonstrate how seriously you take such input. E-mail may also be used to inform people of events. This may be more successful than solicitations.

Finally, e-mail is used frequently to inform people of updates to a Web site. This can help to bring people back when, although they find your site useful, they do not remember to return on a regular basis or know when to do so. A good way to increase your organization's constituency is by including a "guestbook" at your site. Visitors "sign in," perhaps sharing what attracted them to your site. Those so inclined to sign an on-line guestbook are probably more likely than the average person to be involved over time. Web site administrators of organizations can collect guestbook signees and add them to the list of those who are kept up-to-date by e-mail.

In short, e-mail today is an outstanding tool for building a new kind of relationship with a broader base of participants in the life of your organization. It can help to develop a stronger bond without having to spend inordinate resources on events that bring people together. Building such relationships can only benefit your institution's short- and long-term fund-raising prospects. Not only does it help to convey that your agency is doing important and exciting work, but it can help to make others feel as if they get something in return for their involvement by way of the close association e-mail communication allows.

Using a Web site to Attract and Solicit Support

Increasingly, non-profit agencies with Web sites are including information or even special areas of their sites dedicated specifically to soliciting visitors for gifts. These range from noting the mailing address for donations to providing secure, on-line forms for making credit card contributions.

Sites asking for donations may:

(1) detail how funds are used by the organization;
(2) elaborate on the need for or impact of support;
(3) detail giving vehicles such as charitable gift annuities;
(4) recognize current supporters or sponsors; and
(5) allow for inquiries about giving.

How effective these sites are is still to be determined. Some organizations, particularly larger ones, have reported substantial success in raising funds through their Web sites. In general, many people today are hesitant to give on-line—either because of the perceived lack of security of the Internet, or because of uncertainty about whether the non-profit organization is legitimate. The larger agencies overcome the latter fears and may even offer secure pages for sharing credit card information.

A few examples of successful on-line Web sites that solicit donations are:

American Civil Liberties Union (http://www.aclu.org)
American Cancer Society (http://www.cancer.org)
American Red Cross (http://www.crossnet.org/)
Second Harvest (http://www.secondharvest.org/)
ALSAC/St. Jude Children's Hospital (http://www.stjude.org/)
Habitat for Humanity International (http://www.habitat.org/)
March of Dimes Birth Defects (http://www.modimes.org/)
Larry Jones International Ministries/Feed the Children (http://www.feedthechildren.org/)

Some common themes can be seen in these examples of fund-raising sites. First, each makes it clear how support relates to, and advances, the mission of the organization. Each one directs visitors to on-line giving opportunities through various "how can I help" links. In the case of the American Cancer Society, support is appropriately solicited around the concept of providing a memorial to friends and loved ones lost to the disease that the organization battles. The ACLU focuses on attracting support to fight for freedoms relating to cyberspace, since so many visitors on-line are interested in this.

Second, many of them focus on attracting members, so that giving is not a one-time activity or a "one-way street," but rather establishes an ongoing relationship between the visitor-turned-donor and the organization. Visitors may be more likely to answer the call to become supporting members than simply to send a gift to an organization without establishing a formal relationship.

Third is the opportunity used to provide donor recognition on-line. In the case of Project HOPE, the mere fact that it has a Web site sponsor is an example of successful fund-raising. Many commercial sites are funded through paid advertisements, so it's somewhat surprising that non-profits are not taking more advantage of the publicity they can offer donors through their sites (especially if they provide something of value to a large audience). It is likely that the future will see more of this kind of funding arrangement and could help to reinvigorate corporate giving.

Fourth is the idea of providing donor education on-line. Providing some detailed explanation of such concepts as endowments, planned giving, and in-kind contributions is easy to do on-line, where the donor can control how much he or she reads. Doing this through printed media is more costly and risks overwhelming the potential supporter with too much information too early.

Issues to Consider

In general, good common sense and an understanding of cyberculture should be applied to any organization intending to build a fund-raising site. Begin by asking some of the following questions:

1. Who is most likely to visit your organization's Web site? Not every organization will find a ready on-line audience receptive to supporting it. Those more likely to have a receptive audience are those dealing with current topics in a rapidly changing environment (like the ACLU) or those addressing global needs (like Project HOPE). Organizations that have a large potential constituency that is not easily identifiable (like the American Cancer Society and the Rivers Network) are among those that can benefit most from being on-line, because many people looking to become involved in personally important issues will seek them out on the World Wide Web.

   Agencies dealing with local or community issues may be less likely to benefit from a fund-raising site, since their appeal is to a narrower audience that is perhaps less likely to use the Internet to communicate with an organization located in the neighborhood.

2. If you are unsure that your agency can find an audience on-line likely to seek it out, can you offer content on-line that is likely to attract individuals who may be prepared to support it? Any organization that produces an on-line product, such as a service, newsletter with current information, or other value-added information, may enjoy a larger flow of traffic, especially if the site is properly marketed to search engines and directories and maintained regularly.

   It is not likely that people will donate on-line merely because they enjoy it more than traditional methods of giving. However, if visitors use your site in their work or other interests, they may feel sufficiently grateful—and perhaps impressed with the quality of your organization—and may want to support it.

Up Close: Rockefeller Brothers Fund (http://www.rbf.org)

According to Karin Skaggs, communications assistant for the New York City-based Rockefeller Brothers Fund, the Web site was developed by Jennifer Hortin, a systems administrator no longer with the fund, about six months after the foundation determined that establishing a World Wide Web site was both technologically and economically feasible, and that it was an appropriate way to reach its intended audience more efficiently and with more timely information.

Formatting and coding were done in-house; graphics were designed by an outside source. Set-up costs were $800 for the Rockefeller Brothers Fund pages—which receive about 400 hits each week—and $2,250 for a related site called Project on World Security. That site went on-line in 1997.

Both sites are updated in-house, and a major graphic redesign of the RBF main site was in the works when we talked to Skaggs. She says that while the Web site has increased the public's exposure to the Fund's mission and programs, the number of inquiries received from prospective grantseekers has increased dramatically. In addition, because communication between grantseeker and foundation is as easy as a click of the mouse, some grantseekers do not focus as carefully on the RBF's specific grant guidelines. When the site was first established, staff members were not sufficiently prepared to deal with the increase of inquiries, but they now feel they have an effective response system in place.

The site's target audiences are grantees, grant seekers and, on the linked site for the Project on World Security (www.rbf.org/rbf/pws), researchers and experts in the security field.

Skaggs uses the Internet for research on products, other foundations, grantees, and grants given. She subscribes to Dow Jones, Lexis Nexis, and CompuServe.

Skaggs credits the Web site with a significant increase in the number of inquiries received from prospective grantseekers.

"Once we develop our new site, it will become much easier for us—it already has, in fact—to send publications and requests for information to people in electronic form, including eventually putting our annual report on-line," she says. "Certain foundations are considering an electronic version of their reports over and above the printed

Depending on a "brilliant" idea for a valuable on-line service to attract visitors carries a serious risk that it is either already being done or will not be as valuable as you expected. Also, the material on your site should be related to your organization's mission. Using a commercial example, a telephone company providing health and fitness information is more likely to generate shrugs than they are links. On the other hand, a diaper company providing child care and child development information for parents may be more likely to succeed (see *Pampers' Parenting Institute*at *http://www.pampers.com/*).

Be cautious about the time commitment you invest in a site seeking potential funders. It is probably best to be certain that you are committed to what you offer on-line and then treat donations that your site attracts as a reward.

3. If you are committed to at least making it possible for donors to give, consider how much of an effort is appropriate. Should you provide information on all forms of giving and address every

version. We would like to encourage even more communication among grantees; we will work toward this goal on our revamped site."

Skaggs believes the Internet has made a positive contribution to improving communication between foundations and grantees, as well as between foundations and the public.

"In general, grant-giving organizations are finding the Internet to be an effective tool for reaching grantseekers and grantees," asserts Skaggs. "It also appears that grantseeking organizations are taking advantage of the Internet to seek funding sources and volunteers. In both cases, the Internet provides an opportunity for organizations to communicate substantive information about their mission and work."

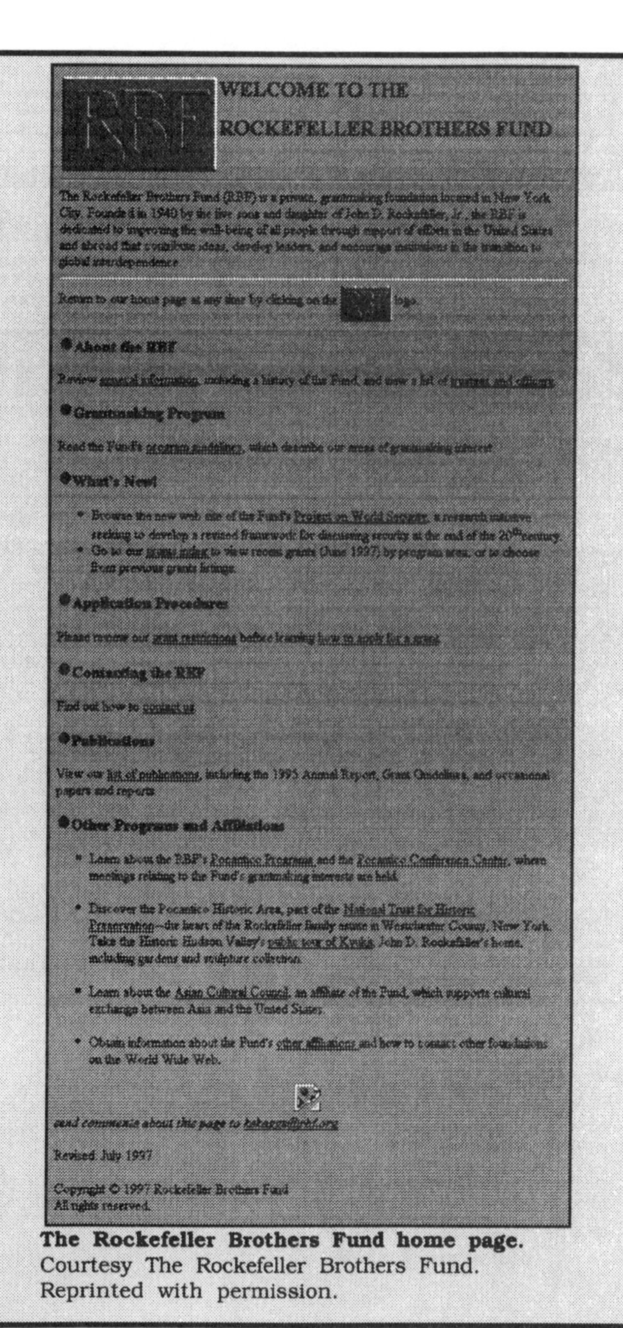

The Rockefeller Brothers Fund home page. Courtesy The Rockefeller Brothers Fund. Reprinted with permission.

possible method of making on-line gifts, or is it best to provide a simple request for donations? The answer here will depend on the extent to which you expect to attract funders. If you are building an organizational Web site for other purposes, then adding the ability to give on-line may be simple enough to be worth doing, even if you expect only a handful of gifts.

4. Can you use your fund-raising site to encourage traditional forms of giving? The idea of donor recognition on-line is becoming increasingly popular, even for organizations that do not otherwise solicit gifts on-line. Pictures of groundbreaking ceremonies, spotlights on donors, and other kinds of on-line donor recognition methods can enhance your stewardship programs while providing a good example to visitors. Should you include an entire honor roll of supporters on-line? This answer may depend on your constituency and whether or not they are likely to see it and appreciate it. The idea is somewhat intriguing, especially if your donors are particularly active on the Internet.

As with e-mail, one of the best uses for a Web site is simply to begin attracting prospective donors. Cultivation, on-line and through traditional means, can then be used to involve people in your organization and to develop their interests in the long-term.

For some more thoughts on using the Internet in fund raising, see http://www.fundraisingonline.com/.

Chapter 7

Non-Profit Organization Advocacy

"It started with *Bring Your Daughter To Work Day*. Now they want to have Bring Your Son To Work Day, Bring Your Parents To Work Day, Bring Your Cat To Work Day, Bring Your Parakeet To Work Day..."

by *Gary Grant and John Aravosis*

Introduction

Can I participate in existing advocacy efforts on-line? How can I build an on-line constituency for advocacy purposes? What are some of the ways to carry out advocacy efforts on-line? Does on-line advocacy really work? What advocacy resources exist?

For the non-profit organization staff member whose work involves advocacy, the Internet seems like (and is) a natural resource and tool. It is a resource for obtaining information necessary in the quickest possible way, and it is a tool for networking and making information available to others. The sites included in this book are considered advocacy sites if they do one or more of the following: (1) make advocacy-related information, alerts, press releases, and reports available in a timely manner; (2) organize people or generate action; (3) collect or report opinion data on current issues; (4) describe advocacy efforts and events on or off-line; (5) urge specific political responses on particular issues; or (6) present political positions on a topic, along with arguments in favor of one side in the debates.

There are many advocacy organizations that have established a Web presence describing the kind of work they do. Our exploration of advocacy Web sites, however, will focus primarily on those that use the Internet for actual advocacy efforts. These may include, for example, sites that organize on-line events, network people and agencies, or provide direct on-line responses for people who want to do something about an issue. These on-line advocacy activities and on-line supports for advocacy efforts are where the Internet really begins to realize its largest potential.

In 1995, for example, Antonia Stolper and Bob Fertik, the publishers *of Political Woman Newsletter*, brought their in-depth coverage of women's issues on-line as *Political Woman Hotline*. They invited their print subscribers to subscribe by e-mail, and offered it free to the Internet community as a benefit of joining *Women Leaders Online*. They announced WLO on the Internet in March 1995, and had 1,000 subscribers within a month. They then held a press conference with U.S. Representative Nita Lowey, Frances Fox Piven, and other feminist leaders to announce it to the world at large. Since then, they've built their list to more than 5,000 subscribers. While the e-mail list initially started as a comprehensive compilation of short interesting news stories and advocacy tips (sometimes as many as 50 per e-mail), the newsletter has since evolved into a more standard issues update/action alert.

Political Woman Newsletter is not just a good example of using an on-line effort in conjunction with other more standard approaches—the newsletter itself was unique (at that time) in its ability to solicit a large number of quality submissions from its growing list, and then re-disseminate those that were relevant to the list at large.

Focusing on actual on-line activities like this, rather than on sites that simply describe advocacy organizations whose work takes place primarily off-line, is not meant to devalue the good work of such organizations. On-line advocacy holds many actual as well as potential benefits but, so far, it is unlikely to replace the off-line work advocates have always pursued, so it should usually be considered "something extra." Nothing in this section should be construed to mean that your traditional, off-line efforts should be abandoned or even reduced. At the same time, we want to focus on the Internet and on the cutting edge work happening on-line.

You will probably not be able to use the Internet to recruit hordes of demonstrators for your rally. But with the simple and cost-effective ability to spread the word about such events, you may boost the numbers and serve to enhance some of your goals while, at the same time, building for a future involving ever-growing use of this kind of technology. Simply put, the advocacy you do on-line is both advocacy for your particular cause and advocacy for the increasing use of the Internet for achieving such goals.

Perhaps the most exciting facet of on-line advocacy is that it is so much more convenient than traditional methods of civic participation. Anyone who has ever felt guilty about remaining silent on important issues merely because they did not have the time to write and send letters, make phone calls, or attend relevant events and demonstrations, may find a rewarding and time-saving solution in the Internet.

For example, e-mail makes it a simple matter to send an editorial letter to your newspaper. The first time one of us took advantage of this, responding to the e-mail address given on the editorial page and commenting on a disappointing editorial about welfare reform, his letter was published two days later. Oftentimes, the newspaper will publish the e-mail address of the person commenting, who may then receive comments from other readers (for good or bad!). If you don't want your e-mail address published along with your comments, make sure to specify this when you send your message. Similarly, e-mail views can be expressed to legislators. Many local newspapers routinely publish the e-mail addresses of elected officials on their editorial page.

An example of the changes such tools are bringing to our society was demonstrated in 1997, when Air Force pilot Kelly Flinn faced a court-martial and possible imprisonment on charges of adultery. Through the ability of people to respond electronically, the Air Force was flooded with e-mail from people across the nation, mostly sympathetic to Flinn and viewing her treatment as overly harsh. What would have likely been a relatively private matter suddenly became a public referendum.

These and other uses of the Internet are examples of why many believe that on-line technology will reinvigorate and broaden democratic participation. Many people today complain about citizen apathy, and the causes cited for this seeming disinterest have ranged from the distractions of entertainment options to the demands on our time of work and family life, particularly in the single-family and two-job households. But whatever the cause, and regardless of whether the apathy is real or imagined, the Internet provides a great potential for people to ask for, give and receive input, and to educate themselves about the issues that affect them locally and globally.

Many believe that the future of the Internet will include formal voting through on-line means. Referenda and regular elections may one day be as easy as logging in to the appropriate Web site. While this is probably some time away, there are many who are using on-line voting to collect their own data useful in both national and local advocacy efforts.

Getting the Word Out About Your Advocacy Effort

So, your organization is on the Internet. You have e-mail and a Web site and you're planning an event—say a rally to prevent the demolition of public housing units. You consider how to use your e-mail and Web site to generate local and national attention and to attract a larger group of people to the rally.

What can you do to make your event known to those on-line who might be interested?

One answer to this kind of practical problem is to do some preliminary work long before the event is to take place. Begin compiling an audience with whom you interact electronically, using both e-mail and the Web site.

You might first start to ask those in your existing membership or on your mailing list for their e-mail addresses, so you can keep them posted on developments relating to your organization. Use your Web site to attract more interested individuals and give them the chance to submit their e-mail addresses to join your mailing list. Develop a regular schedule of communication to this group, urging them to pass your communications on to those individuals or groups they represent or with which they interact.

Asking people to forward your messages to the groups they correspond with electronically can greatly enhance your reach. Most individuals on-line for any length of time will have some group of colleagues or friends with whom they are happy to share appropriate communications. People in organizations are often happy to share such relevant information with their entire staff through e-mail.

The Children's Defense Fund, for example, has done this with great success. CDF sends advocacy alerts and calls to action to a list of interested subscribers. Since these messages contain a good deal of information and are more than just pleas for involvement, they are particularly easy to share with others. While there is no way to tell for sure how many actually get the CDF alerts, the evidence suggests that they get to many more than receive it directly from the organization. As a result, the alerts can have a widespread anticipated benefit and lead to unexpected successes, as well.

Complement your e-mail communications with news on your Web site. You can, for example, use your Web site as a place for supplemental information, briefing people by e-mail, but offering more substantive and complete additional information on the Web site. This will keep people visiting from time to time, which is something they are less likely to do unless they know there is new information there since the last time they visited.

With these strategies you can, over a short time, find that you are spreading your influence and network in ways and to a degree you would never have expected. The quantity of your communications can be increased, and the quality of your relationship with your constituency can be deepened.

Ultimately, when the time for your event comes around, you can provide an e-mail alert and post detailed information on your Web site, if appropriate. You might even get a better read on the event by encouraging responses from those planning to attend.

Whether you organize your on-line network well in advance or not, there are measures you can take to get the word out about your event to targeted individuals and groups on-line.

By investing a few hours of work researching the appropriate places on-line to send news of your event, an alert, or a call for action, you will have available a ready way to respond electronically now and in the future. Below are some examples of the steps you might take in initially compiling such a list.

Up Close: HandsNet (http://www.handsnet.org)

HandsNet is a national non-profit technology intermediary that has built and managed an on-line community for the past 10 years. It has connected some 5,000 human service organizations throughout the United States. Steven Gershik, Webmaster for HandsNet, says the idea for the site came from Sam Karp, HandsNet's founder and executive officer.

The site went on-line early in 1995 after four months of development. There was no resistance within the organization, but HandsNet did experience several problems—notably, finding the time and staff resources to maintain the site and a lack of in-house technical expertise. An outside consultant set up the site. The site is achieving about 1,000 hits each day. Set-up and maintenance costs have exceeded $20,000.

"Our mission is to help non-profit organizations utilize technology more effectively within their organizations," says Gershik. "We currently link our community through an Intranet, having extended our client-server environment to the Web."

One problem the site has experienced is the harvesting of e-mail addresses from its public postings by "spam" e-mailers who want to add these addresses to their own mailing lists.

HandsNet plans to add search capability to its site. That will offer human service organizations and non-profit professionals a fast and simple interface to find the information they need for their day-to-day work.

HandsNet uses the Internet to market its services and preview its membership network, and also to train personnel. Staff members use GPO's Federal Register site and the Library of Congress Thomas database for legislative information. The organization often utilizes its members' Web sites for information gathering as well.

The site has already received the Activism Online's *Best of the Web* Award, Impact Online's *Best of the Web* Award, and Point.com's *Top 5% of the Web* Award.

"We're the oldest network serving human service workers only," Gershik emphasizes. "We happen to think HandsNet is the most useful on-line service for non-profit professionals." (See review, p. 138).

HandsNet home page. Courtesy HandsNet. Reprinted with permission.

Step 1: Collect the e-mail addresses of people from relevant organizations and groups on-line.

By using some of the basic search techniques detailed in this book, you can locate the Web sites of national and local groups whose work is related to your own. These sites typically include the e-mail contact address for the organization. Collecting them into your e-mail program's address book will give you a way to instantly spread your word to people who can then pass it on within their organizations and among their constituencies.

One can think of these contacts as "gatekeepers" for the lists they are likely to have compiled for internal or external communication. Your contact with them can seek to enlist their aid in building a network, starting with the urgency of the current event you are working on.

Over time, such gatekeepers are probably a good group to cultivate a relationship with for mutual advantage. As you create your own networks, you can benefit one another in this way and others. Information and resources can be shared over time, making possible connections and the avoidance of duplicative efforts that may have been the norm in the past.

Through your continued relationship with gatekeeper contacts, you can begin to get a solid feel for how far and wide your message is spreading. Find out what groups they represent and with whom they communicate electronically.

Tips for Finding Possible Gatekeepers

Search the Web for organizations that are on-line. You can locate relevant local, national, and world organizations, as well as groups that may have formed and exist primarily on-line. For organizations that you know have Web sites, you can often find them fastest with a keyword search engine (see page 84). For regional organizations, you can look in the Yahoo! Directory under your region. For organizations dedicated to specific causes, you can look in a search engine, a general directory subject area, or a particular specialized directory.

What other organizations could help? How about schools of public policy or universities in general? Perhaps you can find contacts there willing to serve as gatekeepers.

Once you find all relevant organizations, visit their pages and locate the contact people. Send them a brief message asking them if they are the appropriate contact person for that organization. Cut and paste their e-mail address into your e-mail address book. For example, you can begin a list of related organizations so that you can send a message simultaneously to all of them.

Next, you can look for on-line Web sites dedicated to relevant topic areas. In the above example, for organizing a rally about public housing, you might look for a Web site that organizes people interested in fighting homelessness. Chances are, you will uncover some more people who have gathered a collection of helpful contacts and who can serve as another kind of gatekeeper. Add these individuals' e-mail addresses to your lists.

What other Web sites could help? Are there on-line journals related to your topic that might include your alert in their publications on the Web or via e-mail? Look to the reviews section of this book on on-line publications to begin finding some of these.

HandsNet is one excellent example of an on-line community covering a variety of areas. If you are a member, there are forums in which your alert can be posted and shared weekly with all other members. Even if you are not a member, you might find a contact person at HandsNet willing to post your alert for you.

Up Close: HungerWeb (http://www.brown.edu/Departments/World_Hunger_Program/)

Peter Uvin, associate professor of research at the Watson Institute of International Studies at Brown University, administers the HungerWeb Web site. The site averages 30,000 hits each week from users in the United States and 25 other countries.

HungerWeb was established by a student who couldn't continue it after graduation and looked for a place that would guarantee its survival. "I took it from there, but changed most of the content," says Uvin.

Uvin took over the site in December 1993, after just a few weeks of development. In the beginning, he found the technical aspects slightly overwhelming. "I had no computer training at all," Uvin explains. "But I discovered maintaining a Web site was extremely easy to do and people liked the results.

"Recently, maintaining a Web site has become at once much more difficult and much easier," he says. "It became easier as the result of excellent programs that convert word-processing files into HTML language, a job I once did 'by hand.' It became more difficult, however, as a result of the new programming capabilities offered by Java and the introduction of frames. Professional sites use these new possibilities, including animation, music, frames, and the like in their sites. The HungerWeb has become a technological dinosaur now, and I do not have the time or capabilities to significantly upgrade its technological level," he laments. "Moreover, as I seek to be accessible to people in Third World countries, I keep the site deliberately simple as far as graphics go, to minimize their downloading time."

There was no organizational resistance to putting up the site. "The university was very interested in exposure beyond our usual publications, as well as in public relations," says Uvin. "The only issue at the end of the day is the cost. There really isn't any money for this, so maintaining the site remains quite voluntary on my part. Actually, our general computer person has been given co-responsibility by the director of the Institute, so I guess that does equal an institutional commitment."

Occasionally, Uvin hires a computer consultant for one or two hours a week, at about $25 an hour.

"Price and control were foremost on our minds, so we used a student-run server rather than the

When you have finished spending some time gathering possible gatekeeper addresses, draft an e-mail message describing your event or effort and encouraging others to participate. At the top of your message, provide a statement introducing yourself and courteously asking that they assist you by forwarding your alert within their organizations and among their constituencies, colleagues, and friends as they see appropriate. Encourage them to share with you the groups they are contacting on your behalf. If possible, promise to do the same for them if they need such assistance in the future.

Try to make your message as personalized as you can within the context of a general mailing. Make it short enough that it is easy to understand what is being asked, but try also to make it informative enough so that it is not just a plea for involvement. Make it as exciting as possible and state the importance of their participation. You might want to modify your letter for the specific kind of groups contacted. You should probably also suggest that people print it out and post it in their offices for those not using e-mail.

university," Uvin elaborates. "However, over a year the student-run server broke down repeatedly, once for as long as three weeks. We decided to switch to the university server, which in the meantime had relaxed its policies and decentralized control. Costs are now minimal."

One of Uvin's objectives in taking over the site was to make its pages more professional. "We're an academic institution, so we have to project an intellectual quality and impartiality," he points out.

Uvin uses the Internet for research, advocacy, and communicating with his board of directors and the public. "To distribute information widely and fast, the Internet is vastly superior to paper publications," he says. "The latter costs much more, takes more time, and reaches only a fraction of the people you can reach through the Internet. Now, I get feedback from people I would never have thought of sending information to. Of course, the HungerWeb is quite unique. It isn't so much a site about the World Hunger Program as a public service to the entire hunger community. Our Web site has a worldwide reputation."

HungerWeb home page. Courtesy HungerWeb. Reprinted with permission.

Step 2: Newsgroups and Bulletin Boards

Newsgroups are a good way to get the word out to relevant people. A few minutes of work is sufficient to uncover at least a handful of newsgroups to which you can address messages. It is recommended that you spend a little bit of time getting to know the tenor and type of discussion that takes place so that your message is not inappropriate to the topic of the newsgroup.

Examples of newsgroups that are likely to be appropriate for posting information about a demonstration are regional groups (e.g., chi.general for general discussion relevant to Chicago or whatever city you are in), topical newsgroups (e.g., alt.planning.urban or alt.activism or misc.activism.progressive), or organizational newsgroups (e.g., soc.org.nonprofit).

In all cases, post your message as a courteous request and make the subject line as clear as possible, so those not interested can avoid it. Your posting to larger newsgroups may very possibly generate some negative responses. These may, to some extent, be legitimate if your read on the nature of the group was wrong. Even if it *was* appropriate, an individual participant may feel otherwise. No matter what, you should ignore these. No matter how correct the complaining party is, an apology to the group is usually seen as making matters worse (i.e., the apology is itself another off-topic communication). No matter how rude and inappropriate or wrong the complaining party is, we recommend that you do not respond.

A number of Web sites have their own bulletin boards. These create the same kind of threaded discussion, but they take place directly at the Web site, rather than in the newsgroup format. If you find such bulletin boards related to your effort, treat them like newsgroups and post your message.

Step 3: Post to Mailing Lists

Like newsgroups, the mailing lists you join can become a place to spread the word about actions in which you want to encourage the participation of others. In some cases, you need not join the list to get your message mentioned. By developing a list of mailing list administrators or even people you know who participate, you can spread your message to a larger audience in the same way as through gatekeepers for e-mail lists.

Just make sure that you post only to appropriate mailing lists and newsgroups. It is not uncommon for advocacy efforts in newsgroups and mailing lists to spill over into other forums on unrelated topics. People often carry their interests in one area to another. A person who posts to the gardening mailing list might decide to mention the rally he or she is planning. While you really cannot prevent this, you should not encourage it, since people tend to be very protective of their discussion forums and respond negatively to discussions that distract from it.

Mailing lists and newsgroups relevant to social advocacy efforts are too numerous to name them all here. In fact, Liszt's directory (at http://www.liszt.com, see pages 40 and 198) contains information on more than 71,000 total mailing lists and 18,000 newsgroups! A search of the Liszt mailing list database on the terms "non-profit" and "nonprofit" yielded 30 mailing lists. Among them were:

alnp-list: literary non-profit publishing
boardinfo: National Center for Non-Profit Boards
boardtalk: National Center for Non-Profit Boards
boardtalk-digest: National Center for Non-Profit Boards
CONSULT-L: a list for consultants who have non-profit clients
fscnews: Information relating to a certain non-profit organization named FSC
Gift-pl: Non-Profit Gift Planners
html-nonprofit: Internet and WWW related for non-profits
kappa-alpha-psi: information relating to a specific non-profit community organization
NACC: the list of the Non-profit Academic Centers Council
Ozarknet: a list connecting government, and non-profit individuals
peak-non-profits: Non-profits hosted by the PEAK server
pnpnet: The list hosted by the Kellogg School of Management
public-finance: for those interested in public and non-profit finance issues
talk-amphilrev: a fund-raising, philanthropy, and non-profit-oriented list

Chapter 8

VOLUNTEER RECRUITMENT

"This project is extremely important, but it has no budget, no guidelines, no support staff and it's due tomorrow morning. At last, here's your chance to really impress everyone!"

Introduction

The World Wide Web hasn't replaced conventional methods of volunteer recruitment—such as passing around volunteer sign-up sheets during speaking engagements, developing public service announcements, and sending out press releases. But an increasing number of charities are utilizing their Web sites to share information about volunteer opportunities with their respective organizations.

According to Independent Sector, 48.8% of adults volunteer an average of 4.2 hours each week. In 1995, the value of this volunteer time was more than $200 billion. Non-profit organizations rely on volunteer assistance to perform organization functions from receptionist to board chairperson. Indeed, the term "voluntary sector" is a working synonym for "non-profit charities." The changes in demographics during the 1990s—more single-parent households, more two-parent working families, more women in the workforce, and an increase in the incentives to defer the retirement age to maintain income—have placed increased pressure on non-profits to identify and recruit volunteers.

Yet, despite these factors, there has been increasing attention in recent years on the value of volunteering.

First, educators have identified service learning as an effective teaching strategy. Study after study indicates that students who participate in these programs are less likely to drop out. The lessons learned in environments outside of the classroom, in "real life" situations, are not only remembered but put to use during work years. More and more school districts are adopting service learning in their curricula. In 1992, Maryland became the first state to require all of its students to participate, beginning with the 1993-94 school year, in a program as a prerequisite to graduate from high school. Many of the students have Internet access.

Second, public officials intent upon decreasing government expenditures for human services have challenged their constituents and the private sector to fill the gap left by cuts in government spending. While no credible study suggests that the private sector has the capacity to accomplish this, there are indications that the public is responding by giving at least a second look to volunteering in their communities. Almost 80% of respondents to a recent survey by Independent Sector agreed with the statement, "The need for charitable organizations is greater now than it was five years ago." As the rhetoric is replaced by actual public policy implementation in which the Congress and the Administration both agree that the federal budget must be balanced by the year 2002, government funding for programs administered by charities will be decreasing.

Up Close: Independent Sector (http://www.indepsec.org)

One of the non-profit advocacy organizations on the cutting edge of the new technology is Independent Sector—a coalition of more than 800 organizations representing both mainstream charities and their national associations. The coalition serves as a national leadership forum for the voluntary sector—encouraging philanthropy, volunteerism, and advocacy on behalf of charities.

The Web site was the brainchild of Dr. David R. Stevenson, who was associate director of the National Center for Charitable Statistics when the site was conceived. There was little resistance to the concept on the part of the executive staff or the board of Independent Sector.

Now at the Urban Institute, Stevenson didn't actually develop the site. But he was the individual with the vision at a time when few in the non-profit sector recognized the value of a Web site.

The site went on-line in October 1995, after a four-month development and construction period. Webmaster Elizabeth Rose, who left Independent Sector at the end of April 1997, put the site together in-house, with some minor adjustments provided by an outside consultant.

According to Rose, Independent Sector invested approximately $7,000 in the site, in addition to her salary as assistant director of communications. AT&T updates the site now, but earlier updates were done in-house. The number of hits averages1,000 a day.

Even before establishing a Web site, Independent Sector recognized the possibilities of saving money by using the Internet for communication. "It's cheaper and faster to send out information to a large list of people over the Internet," Rose points out.

Still, using the Internet can be frustrating. There have been technical problems, which made the site unavailable for one reason or another. "When it's down, we have to fix it," Rose laments.

Another major frustration has been visitors who are not part of the target audience but somehow stumble onto the site. "I get a lot of random questions and wonder how some of these people found our Web site," Rose says.

Rose periodically reviews the way the pages might be reconstructed so as to appeal more to members and the public—taking into account both the limitations and advantages of the new medium. "We have to constantly rethink the content and organization of our Web site," she says. "We found, for example, that we had to make our text leaders more bite-sized to get readers' attention. We really listen to feedback from our visitors, both members and the general population."

One of the highlights during Rose's tenure as Webmaster was collaborating with a colleague at OMB Watch to set up the site for "Let America Speak Coalition" (http://www.rtk.net/las). This group was formed to fight the Istook Amendment, legislation designed to place limits on the ability of tax-exempt organizations to engage in advocacy.

As Rose was leaving Independent Sector, the Web site was setting up an area for real-time conferencing for members. The Webmaster was bubbling with enthusiasm over this Internet application. "It's certainly possible that organizational planning, strategy meetings, and brainstorming sessions will take place one day entirely in cyberspace," she speculates. "Independent Sector is ready to offer that feature to our members."

Having a productive meeting in cyberspace can create problems, particularly when there are few standard rules for participants to follow to prevent the meeting from degenerating into babble. But Rose expects such rules will evolve—moderating, if not eliminating, many of the interpersonal difficulties involved in real-time conferencing.

In the meantime, the Internet is likely to strengthen its hold within the non-profit sector. "As non-profit organizations realize the money-saving possibilities offered by electronic communication, we will change the way we communicate," Rose predicts. "But you can't replace one with the other immediately. It will take time."

In any case, she says, non-profits needn't be afraid that what they do on the 'Net is permanent. "If there's one distinguishing characteristic of the Web, it's that you can change it—and quickly."

Independent Sector Home Page (non-frames version). Courtesy Independent Sector. Reprinted with permission.

Can volunteers and charitable giving replace it? It doesn't really matter. Competition among charities for volunteers will be keen, and using the Internet can give a charity an edge over those that don't.

Third, a Gallop Poll indicated that the percentage of adults between the ages of 65 and 74 who volunteered during a one-year period in 1995-96 was 45%, up from 40% in 1988. Whether this is the result of corporate downsizing that resulted in lucrative retirement buyouts, improved healthcare and life span for the elderly, or other factors, we can't say definitively. But the elderly are an active, able resource for charities. Many of these potential volunteers are at home with time on their hands, using their personal computers to surf the Web.

For an increasing number of non-profits, "advertising" on the World Wide Web is one effective strategy to find a source of loyal, devoted volunteers.

In April 1997, General Colin Powell convened a three-day "Presidents' Summit for America's Future," at which President Clinton and two of the remaining three living former Presidents (Nancy Reagan filled in for the ailing Ronald Reagan) met with thousands of business, charitable, and government leaders to encourage an increase in volunteering. Even before the gavel came down concluding this summit, charities across the nation reported a measurable increase in demand for information about volunteer opportunities. The summit followed several years of increased rhetoric in Washington, and within state and local government, concerning the role of government funding to solve social problems.

The "Virtual Volunteer"

Consider allowing volunteers to volunteer at home using their computers. The advantage of this to the volunteer is obvious. Work can be done during non-business hours. Work can be done without having to be supervised directly. The volunteer can choose his/her own work schedule, making it consonant with the demands of having a full-time job and family. There is no need to waste time commuting to the charity, and paying travel and parking costs. There are several advantages to the charity as well. There is no need to provide office space, parking, and equipment for these volunteers.

What can these volunteers do? One task is obvious: They can design, construct, and maintain the organization's World Wide Web site. They can write or lay out the organization's newsletter, design brochures, write fund-raising letters, and perform research on the Internet. They can maintain mailing lists. All of the advantages of telecommuting for conventional workers are available for volunteers.

And you can communicate with your volunteers via e-mail, saving time and money.

World Wide Web sites have sprouted up to allow charities to post information about volunteer opportunities, among them Actions Without Borders (http://www.idealist.org), Impact Online (http://www.impactonline.org), and SERVEnet (http://www.servenet.org). Most of these sites are administered by non-profit organizations that rely on volunteers to maintain their Web sites.

Before requesting volunteers on the Internet, as in any recruiting effort, it is important to have a detailed job description, which includes at least the following information:

1. examples of duties to be performed;
2. specific skills or training needed;
3. the location where the duties will be performed;

4. the hours per week required or expected;
5. the time period (weeks, months) the duties will be performed;
6. the supervision, if any, that will be provided;
7. whether any organizational resources will be available;
8. what training, if any, will be provided; and
9. whether any special equipment is required (for example, if the organization requires the material prepared by the volunteer to be in IBM format).

You also need to have a policy on what your response will be once a prospective volunteer responds to your on-line recruitment announcement.

Among the best Web sites for those interested in issues relating to volunteers are:

Accesspoint (http://www.accesspt.com/civicsys/volunteer/volunteer_m.html)
American Red Cross Volunteer Facts (http://www.redcross.org/volunteer/fact.html)
CASAnet Resources on Volunteer Management (http://www.casanet.org/volman.htm)
Impact Online (http://www.impactonline.org)
Internet Nonprofit Center (http://www.nonprofits.org)
Legal Handbook for Nonprofit Corporation Volunteers (http://www.polarnet.com/users/vlh/)
SERVEnet (http://www.servenet.org)
Volunteer Management Resources (http://www.halcyon.com/penguin/svm/newvpms.htm)

Chapter 9

HIRING

"Our company lost 900 million dollars last quarter. Your job is to make this look like the best thing that ever happened to us."

Introduction

As you become more Internet savvy yourself, you may find it desirable to have staff on board who have the ability to take advantage of all cyberspace has to offer them in their jobs. One way to increase the chances of attracting and finding Internet-literate job candidates is to use the Internet as part of your recruitment strategy.

There are numerous places to advertise job openings on the Internet. As a non-profit manager, you will want to try to find resources that attract job seekers who are looking for non-profit jobs, or who are looking for the specific type of job you are advertising.

One way to announce jobs on the Internet is by sending an informal note to any related mailing lists to which you subscribe, briefly stating what the job is and how to apply, and asking members of the list to pass the information along to their associates and colleagues. Word can spread quickly through this electronic "grapevine."

More commonly, you will use established Web sites to get your job announcement in front of likely candidates.

National Job Search/Recruitment Sites

One such site is Philanthropy Journal Online's Nonprofit Jobnet (http://www.philanthropy-journal.org/jobnet/jobs.htm). *Philanthropy Journal* has been published since 1991 in the Sunday Business Section of the Raleigh, North Carolina, *News and Observer*, and is becoming a national resource on non-profit issues. Touting its on-line classifieds as fast (they can post the announcement the same day they receive it), affordable ($.50 per word, plus $1 per day), and effective, this on-line version of the print publication is seen by thousands of viewers each month. When we looked, there were jobs listed representing a variety of job titles and organizations.

The Community Career Center (http://www.nonprofitjobs.org/) is self-described as "an on-line gathering place where not-for-profit employers and management personnel can meet one another." Employers or organizations can post jobs on this site for $125 for 60 days. Member organizations can access candidate profiles, which are posted by job candidates for a 6-month period for a $25 registration fee. There were 214 jobs listed here when we looked.

JobWeb (http://www.jobweb.org), the Web site of the National Association of Colleges and Employers (NACE), offers job postings for $80 per month.

The American Society of Association Executives (ASAE) has several options for recruiting association staff. These include ASAE Career Starters (http://www.asaenet.org/aboutASAE/

Up Close: Catholic Charities (http://ccsj.org)

Frank Arnold, Webmaster for Catholic Charities in San Jose, California, retired from the organization in 1992. He updates the site from his home office.

The origin of the site was an electronic Bulletin Board that Arnold and Hans Anderson, then MIS Director for Catholic Charities, started running to provide information to the disabled community.

"Hans's skills with Unix/Linux and my experience in providing information and designing menus and screens were complementary," Arnold says. "As it became obvious the Web was the way to go, I shut down the BBS and we started the Web site project."

It took about three months of startup time before the site went on-line in late October 1995. Its creators faced some technical and "political" problems.

"The CEO gave me general support, but some staff members—including a few project directors—thought the whole idea of a Web site was 'frivolous,' " Arnold recalls. "Others thought it was a misuse of MIS time."

Because of their attitude, Anderson did most of his work during off-hours. Arnold volunteered his time.

But the major obstacle was the almost-universal complaint: "How can we find the time in a busy schedule to do the work?" Cost was not a particular problem. The site was set up in-house using a 486 Linux box connected to the Internet with an ISDN line—the most costly piece of equipment. But while startup costs were indeed minimal, hardware and software upgrades and maintenance costs needed to be budgeted.

CCSJ home page. Courtesy Catholic Charities of San Jose. Reprinted with permission.

"The server has been running almost nonstop since startup and needs upgrading," Arnold says. "The software is also in need of an upgrade. Additionally, the Chief Financial Officer has now expressed an interest in connecting the server to the existing Novell network to give staff both internal and Internet e-mail at their desktops. That will require an upgrade to both Novell and the Internet server." Work on this project is now in progress, he says.

As with most non-profits, "money is tight" at Catholic Charities. It wasn't clear whether the necessary funding for these upgrades would be included in the budget when the organization began its 1997-98 fiscal year.

CCSJ's Internet use is typical of that of many small to medium non-profit organizations. E-mail is the most visible component. Staff members use search engines to find information on the Web, particularly about immigration and other legal and public policy issues. They have used the Internet to research foundations and other potential funding sources.

The site is also used to publicize events. It includes a donations form, but Arnold finds people still hesitate to share credit card information over the Internet. The site is used to recruit volunteers and to enroll disabled clients in training and job placement programs.

At the time we spoke, this site was averaging 300 "hits" per month, but Arnold later reported this number increased as a result of the site receiving a good review on a *Resources for the Homeless* Website in South Carolina. The target audience consists of local residents—who may need the types of services provided by Catholic Charities—of staff, and of helping professionals and other interested people anywhere who might find the information helpful. "I get a lot of requests from adoptees searching for their birthparents," Arnold says. "Even our Guestbook contains many such requests."

Arnold aims to keep the design as simple as possible, noting that the site was a recipient of the Speech Friendly Site Award. This award is bestowed on sites that meet six criteria. They make Web-surfing easy for sight-impaired individuals who use specialized software. For example, "links that are embedded in paragraphs are placed one to a line and clearly labeled." For more information about this award, check out http://www.wwwebit.com/magical-mist/ribbon.htm.

"We are an information provider, not an entertainment site," he says. "I want the site to be accessible to a disabled user with a slow modem. The site is also designed to be user-friendly to individuals who use software that reads aloud what appears on their screen."

Copyright law and Internet addiction are two of the issues about which Arnold has strong opinions. "The answer to copyright infringement is just don't do it," he says. "But sometimes it's difficult to determine just what is, and what is not, infringement."

The Web can be addicting, Arnold admits. "I know that from talking to Webmasters at other agencies who have tried putting it on the desktop of their computers. Catholic Charities has two machines with Web access, one in training and one in MIS." This is changing; a few months after our initial interview, he told us that the World Wide Web will be made accessible to those staff who need it, along with internal e-mail and Internet e-mail.

JobServices/index.html), for listing non-profit jobs that pay up to $30,000 annually; ASAE Career Opps (http://www.entremkt.com/ceo/asae.htm), for jobs in the $30,000-50,000 salary range; and CEO Job Opportunities Update (http://www.entremkt.com/ceo/ceopps.htm), reserved for senior staff positions paying more than $50,000.

Regional/State Sites

Opportunity NOCs, a print publication that is available for different regions of the U.S., has several Web sites (try: http://www.tmcenter.org/op-noc/on-ba-jobs.html), which are on-line versions of the printed job listing.

The Minnesota Council of Nonprofits' (http://www.mncn.org) Online Nonprofit Job Board is a good example of what can be done on the state level. When we checked, there were 28 jobs listed, ranging from Executive Director to Secretary/Receptionist to Development Director to Museum Lesson Instructor. The job board was up-to-date, updated weekly, with all jobs having been posted within the previous month. Each included a posting date and a closing date. If your state has a statewide association of non-profits, it may provide a similar on-line job service.

Profession-Focused Sites

Another type of site to consider is one that advertises jobs for a particular profession. If your organization is a family service agency, you can advertise on George Warren Brown School of Social Work's Social Service and Social Work Jobs site (http://www.gwbssw.wustl.edu/~gwbhome/services/career/career.html), or The New Social Worker's on-line career center (http://www.socialworker.com/career.htm). If you're looking for a communications or PR professional, advertise on the Public Relations Society of America's site (http://www.prsa.org). There is an Internet Classifieds, positions available page at that site. Handsnet (see pages 66 and138) is also an excellent site for posting non-profit organization professional job openings.

Your Own Site

If your organization has its own Web site, consider including a page that lists job openings. The people who visit your site are likely to have an interest in the organization's work and mission, and they might have just the qualifications you are seeking in applicants. Don't miss this simple, yet sometimes overlooked, opportunity to recruit staff who are in your own virtual backyard.

Chapter 10

NON-PROFIT ORGANIZATION RESEARCH

"First I searched for Larry in Yahoo, then Lycos, Excite and Infoseek. Eventually, I found him in the bathroom."

Introduction

No longer do you have to hire a commercial service to find a definitive answer to a question, engage the services of an expensive consultant to develop a public policy issues report, spend an entire day at the library trying to find the text of a law or court decision or, more importantly, go to a travel agent to find an attractive, inexpensive spot to take a vacation. The computer is the equipment of choice to find what we want, and the search engine and directory are the tools we can use to obtain this information on our desktops at any time of the day or night.

Search Engines and Directories

A search engine is a computer program that searches the Internet, or a large database of material from the Internet, and finds matches for keywords. A directory is analogous to a library card catalog, which organizes information you can find on the Internet by pre-selected categories (see page 93 for an example). With practice, you will develop a sense for when to use each. Here are a few hints and tips to ask yourself when selecting a search option:

1. Are you looking for a specific organization's site, and are you relatively certain it exists? If so, the directory may be the best option, since it avoids having to look through unrelated sites. Suppose, for example, you wanted to find the University of Chicago's Web site. Searching with the term "University of Chicago" will find any page that references the University of Chicago, and may bog you down with every site containing either "University" or "Chicago" if you are not sure how to avoid that problem. But you can be sure that most directories would lead you easily and smoothly through "education" to various regions, and then to that institution's home page. If, on the other hand, you are researching a topic and want to access discussion and literature on it, then a search engine becomes the obvious choice, since it will automatically stack up sites relating to that topic for you.

2. Based on what you are seeking, do you think the topic categories will be obvious? A directory is only a good idea if you are looking for something that is easy to categorize. For example, "Universities" may be logically connected to education and only education, but "non-profit management" is a little harder to categorize and may be listed in one directory under business, another under health and welfare, and another under some other category. Thus, consider what you are looking for and use your best judgment in determining whether you are likely to find what you are looking for through a directory. If not, a search engine may be a better starting point.

Up Close: Philanthropy Journal (http://www.philanthropy-journal.org)

Sean Bailey, Director of New Media for *Philanthropy Journal*, is a pioneer among non-profit Webmasters. At the site, you can often find a prominent leader in the non-profit world available to answer questions from participants in a chat room. Real-time chat is one of the innovations on home pages that encourage a targeted audience to return to a site regularly.

"Overall, it is not that terribly difficult to set up a chat room if you have some baseline of design knowledge," Bailey explains. "You do need to have an understanding of UNIX. Chat rooms can be successful when you drive traffic to the room to get the people to come back."

Still, Bailey believes setting up a Web site should not be left to amateurs if you want to ensure its success. "I'm saying that getting the Board Chairman's teenage son to design your Web site is not a good idea," he relates. "You might get some good work for free but, in the long run, you're better off making the necessary financial investment to get a site that meets your organization's needs."

When Bailey's chat room first began operating, there were technical problems. They could be traced to the simple fact that, "We had too many people trying to get in." He expects innovations in Java software to vastly improve the quality and number of people capable of participating in real-time Web chats. Seminars, classes, and other participatory events for those in the non-profit sector will become common on-line events, he predicts.

Did he have any trouble selling the idea to his organization?

"Not really," Bailey says. "There was a complete buy-in at the top; others not familiar with the technology were hesitant. Now, there's a comfort level among all of our staff. All of our computers are connected to the 'Net; it's part of our daily activity. We blast out 7,000 free newsletters each week in e-mail, and the recipients love it because they get great, timely information."

Bailey believes that many organizations in the non-profit sector are behind in computer technology, noting that many non-profits still don't have computer hardware adequate to handle Internet applications. But he sees evidence the picture is changing.

"If any non-profit wants to use the Web to seriously communicate with its supporters, they are going to have to have an e-mail component on their Web site where they are giving people an opportunity to subscribe to a newsletter or some other communiqué that will open up a regular channel of communication between the organization and the supporter," Bailey says. "The key is to make it easy to subscribe and unsubscribe."

The number of non-profits with adequate technology may grow, Bailey theorizes, pointing out that an article in *Wired Magazine* calculated that the current turnover rate for

3. How narrow or specific is your targeted information? If your information is very specific or narrow, it may take a long time to dig it out of a directory since you will have to go through many categories and sub-categories first. In such cases, a search term might get you there quicker, especially if using an engine that prioritizes or "scores" sites. If, on the other hand, you just want to do a self "tour" through a general category of information to explore what sorts of things are available, the directory might be a better option since it will keep you more focused on sites that contain related content as opposed to the variety of sites that might contain the same

computers is three years. Many businesses may choose to donate "outdated" 486s to non-profits.

"There are a large number of non-profits that are already on the Web," he says. "Many of these are ready to move to the next level—such as offering a secure transaction environment to make on-line donations. This would give a non-profit the opportunity to have its doors open 24 hours each day, seven days each week."

For donors of a non-profit organization, an on-line visit needs to be informative and, when possible, entertaining. A thank-you letter for the donation (for IRS substantiation) should be kicked back immediately . "There should be something there to encourage them to return—and elevate their sense of confidence in the organization's use of technology," advises Bailey. "If you aren't using your Web site to provide newsletters and secure on-line donations, you're not using the Internet to its fullest potential."

Bailey predicts some major changes within the next 18 months in the ways audio and video communication are pushed over the 'Net.

"We aren't that far from the Jetsons, where we'll be looking at a screen and talking with our colleagues, clients and service providers through the Internet," he says.

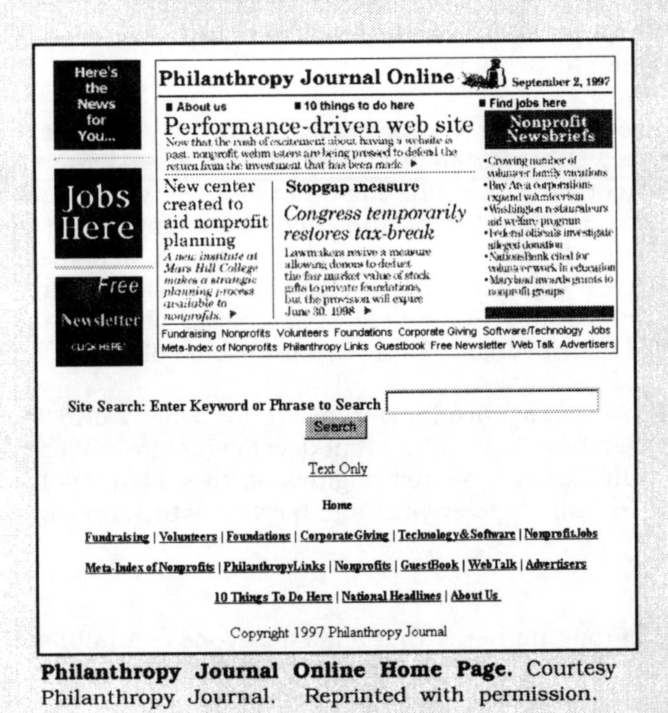

Philanthropy Journal Online Home Page. Courtesy Philanthropy Journal. Reprinted with permission.

search term. For example, if you are looking for information about a city you will be traveling to, the directory will keep you focused on relevant regional information and avoid sites about the region that are unrelated to traveling there, such as articles, histories, or individual home pages of residents.

Using Search Engines

One of the common complaints about the Internet in its early years was that you could find a plethora of fascinating databases, files, and information, but it was almost impossible to find something you were actually looking for. Commercial companies offered services to assist researchers in finding Internet resources, and often charged handsomely. Recently, that has changed dramatically, with the development of powerful search tools, all of which can be accessed free of charge. Among the more popular search engines are Yahoo! (http://www.Yahoo.com), Lycos (http://www.lycos.com), Infoseek (http://www.infoseek.com), and Alta Vista (http://altavista.digital.com). Users access a search engine by connecting to its Web address and then filling out an on-line form with the term or terms to search for.

Many directories, including Yahoo!, offer search engines. Be aware that not all search engines are the same. Each uses a different program (or algorithm) to search the Web for the word or words you enter. They also differ in appearances and how the information is presented to you. So, which search engine is the "best"? There is no right or wrong answer here. One possible response is that any search engine will get you started in your research. Another response is that you can try several in the process of finding what you need. A third response is to try each a few times before settling on the one that you like the most and seems to work for you, but we suggest you keep the others handy as a backup.

What are some of the differences in search engines? In part, this is a hard question to answer, since they are always under development, changing, and improving. One major difference among the search engines is in what is being searched—Web page headers, all Web page text, newsgroups, or gopher, to give some examples.

Some focus on giving you the most sites possible. These may expand your search using variations on the terms you enter. Others attempt to weed out unwanted material, giving you sites that list your terms the most frequently or evaluating them in other ways to eliminate those you are less likely to want. Some include a count of the number of documents found, and others do not. Some give just the links to the sites found, while others include a portion of the text from that site to help give you an idea of what it contains. Some allow case sensitive searching (recognizing capitalization of words) and others do not. Some engines do a better job than others at eliminating sites that no longer exist from their listings. These are just some of the differences.

Search engines usually provide a procedure for registering a new World Wide Web page with them so that it will appear in searches. Non-profits that develop their own World Wide Web pages should register their pages with as many search engines as they identify. There are one-stop service agencies which, for a fee, will register your site for you with scores of search engines.

Credibility of Sources

One major advantage of the Internet is that almost anyone can publish material so that it is accessible to millions of people. That is a disadvantage as well. There is nothing that forbids people to post information that is false, deceptive, or misleading. Obviously, you have a much better chance of finding reliable information when accessing a World Wide Web page of a respected institution than by accessing a personal home page. False rumors flourish on the Internet. There are Internet sites that have files collecting "urban legends" and related misinformation found on the Internet (see: http://www.kumite.com/myths/; http://www.urbanmyths.com/; Yahoo's urban legends site at http://www.yahoo.com/society_and_culture/mythology_and_folklore/urban_legends/; http://www.urbanlegends.com/; and the Urban Legends Reference Page at http://www.snopes.com).

We suggest that you treat information found on the Internet just as you would treat any other information you find when researching a topic. Make a judgment about its reliability based on where you found it and the track record of the information's source. Maintain a healthy skepticism. And don't add to the problem by posting rumors (such as those about new viruses) to everyone in your address book.

Internet News

There are a great many Web sites dedicated to bringing the Internet community daily and sometimes up-to-the-minute news. While you could in theory obtain all of your news via a reputable Internet news source, it is more likely that this will be supplemental to the printed newspapers you read. For example, there may be times when it is easier to go to your computer for information, or when you need more details on an event, or want to compare headlines from different cities or countries.

Free services such as CRAYON (see page 181) make this easy to do. Internet news also gives you the ability to follow older stories that are kept on the Internet, a valuable ability if you've ever regretted missing an old story in a paper you discarded. In addition, printed news is usually regionally focused, but general in scope. On the Internet, you can organize the news you read according to topics such as health or politics. You may also find helpful the ability to follow a story (through the hypertext links) to other related stories and information, giving you more power to control the depth to which you explore a story.

Another feature that Internet news can offer is the ability to interact with the reader. For example, whereas editorial pages offer a few readers the chance to respond to events or articles, many local newspaper sites allow any reader to comment, and others to respond to those comments—an ability that could give you a greater ability to learn how public perceptions are shaping around events. Complementing this is the use of polling, in which the news provider surveys reader response and makes available the ongoing results of public opinion—but be warned that these are informal and not necessarily scientific. For example, you might check to see if there is a mechanism that prevents people from voting more than once.

Of course, Internet news also allows the news provider to add different elements to the articles. Video clips and sound bytes of historic events can be included and, if permitted by copyright, saved onto your computer for use later. The text can be cut and pasted into documents you write, with appropriate citation to the author.

Among our favorite sites for obtaining current general national news are CNN (http://www.cnn.com), Fox (http://www.foxnews.com), and Yahoo! (http://www.yahoo.com/headlines/news).

Up Close: United Jewish Community of Greater Harrisburg (UJC) (http://www.hbgjewishcommunity.com)

Jordan S. Harburger, who has served as executive director of the United Jewish Community for almost five years, is "wired" at both home and the office. At first, he was skeptical about the usefulness of the technology, and had other concerns as well.

"I had questions about the security of communications, and a fear that those who oppose my organization or compete with us for market share would have more access to an insider's view of who we are, what we do and say, and how we operate," Harburger admits. "I was also afraid the Internet might somehow compromise our tax-exempt status."

Now, the Internet is almost like a second staff to him and his organization, which is the central fund-raising and social services/education management arm for the area's Jewish community of almost 6,000.

"We use the Internet for a wealth of purposes, including e-mail, chat, conferencing, news services, professional forums, social service research, investment portfolio updates, and meeting scheduling," says Harburger. "We download documents from professional associations, receive up-to-date news regarding Israel and Jewish communal developments worldwide, research prospects, and access international Jewish association conference calendars and program updates."

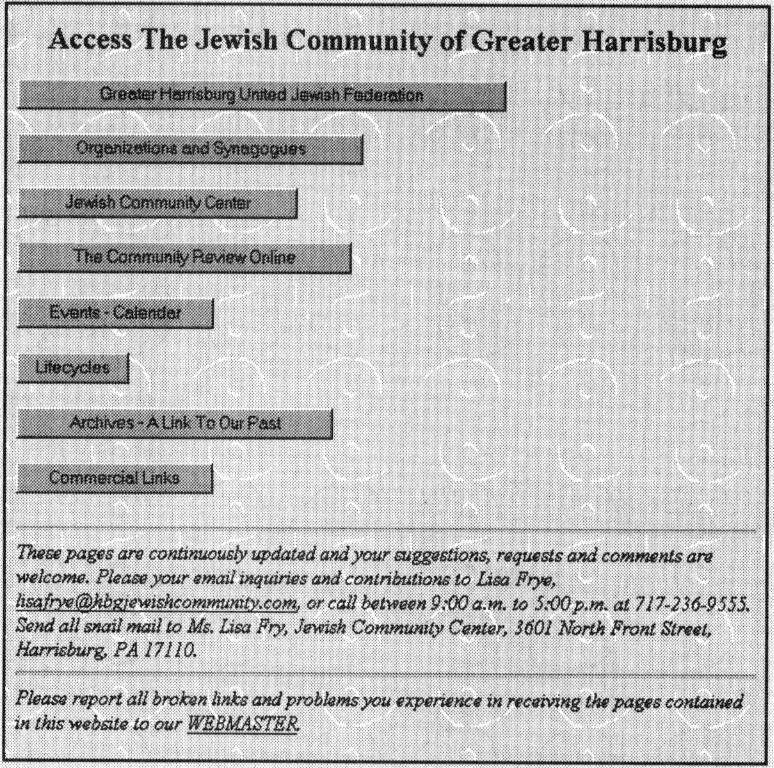

Access The Jewish Community of Greater Harrisburg

Greater Harrisburg United Jewish Federation

Organizations and Synagogues

Jewish Community Center

The Community Review Online

Events - Calender

Lifecycles

Archives - A Link To Our Past

Commercial Links

These pages are continuously updated and your suggestions, requests and comments are welcome. Please your email inquiries and contributions to Lisa Frye, lisafrye@hbgjewishcommunity.com, or call between 9:00 a.m. to 5:00 p.m. at 717-236-9555. Send all snail mail to Ms. Lisa Fry, Jewish Community Center, 3601 North Front Street, Harrisburg, PA 17110.

Please report all broken links and problems you experience in receiving the pages contained in this website to our WEBMASTER.

United Jewish Community of Greater Harrisburg home page. Courtesy UJC of Greater Harrisburg. Reprinted with permission.

The Internet also allows the United Jewish Community to promote community initiatives among professional colleagues worldwide, search for professional openings, do travel planning and flight ticket purchase, hotel and conference registration, and comparative shopping for major purchases. Its uses are as diverse as providing access to consultation services, product searches, genealogical research, program idea research, legal advice, tax advice, staff training, clip art, logos, maps and directions, and mission planning for group travel to Israel.

With all that, Harburger feels his organization has only scratched the surface of how to take advantage of the new communications technology. In the future, the UJC plans to use the 'Net to promote community activism and advocacy to government and private sector leaders, improve attendance at events, obtain current events information on public affairs issues, send meeting notices, and save on printing and mailing and labor costs for community functions.

"I think we can harness the Internet for the circulation of briefing papers and the maintenance of an electronic version of historical archives," Harburger says. "That way we don't have to build a museum or storage facility. I also think we can use our new Web site to attract people to Harrisburg."

The UJC is also in the process of exploring the use of its Web site for fund solicitation, volunteer scheduling, and implementing an emergency communications system, Harburger adds. Homebound services, advertising sales, and sponsorship of Jewish communal information services are among other innovations in service delivery being considered.

"We think telecommuting is one strategy we can use to reduce or cap costs for office space," he says. "We are just beginning to harness the power of the Internet to accomplish on-line conferencing, demographic research, adult education, gift acknowledgment, and polling for decision-making. Other possibilities include doing Internet personnel security background checks, banking, investment management, marketing services, and searching for project and coalition partners for public policy initiatives."

Other possible uses might be tracking for human resource development purposes as people move from community to community, and saving on long-distance phone calls. For Harburger, the applications of the Internet are limited only by the human imagination. "The Internet is a whole big opening to the full world of information. It's very satisfying to the curious mind, reassuring in that you need not risk showing your ignorance."

"The Internet even encourages collaborative behavior," he adds.

Harburger has frank advice for those non-profit managers who are timid about taking advantage of Internet technology. "Join the revolution, become more efficient, allow time to learn, have a ball. Get the fastest modem you can; get a sound card, video card, and scanner to be fully enabled, even if you seldom use these. But use office time to deal with people—real time, live. Limit your on-line time to the hours when you can't be up close and personal with constituents. There is no substitute for the real thing."

TURNING good intentions INTO action

Eager to get involved? Want to volunteer?
You've come to the right place!

VOLUNTEER AMERICA

Find a list of opportunities in your community!

NONPROFIT SERVICES

Click here to register your organization and list volunteer opportunities!

LISTINGS

Directory of nonprofits.

VIRTUAL VOLUNTEERING

Volunteers helping non-profits over the Internet.

ADVICE

Tips on volunteering.

About

Respond

Newsletter

Sponsors

Find

Impact Online home page. Reprinted with permission.

Chapter 11

ETHICAL AND LEGAL ISSUES

"I don't understand #11... *Thou shalt not be obscene on the Internet.*"

Introduction

The Internet is not without its problems. Consumer fraud exists just as it does in the non-virtual world. Although newly developed software has improved the security of communications (particularly important since financial information, including credit card numbers, is routinely sent through e-mail), it is not fool-proof. In general, all World Wide Web page data are transferred through the Internet using ASCII-compatible files, which are virtually (pardon the pun) virus-proof. However, viruses can be transmitted through attached files.

Copyright issues relating to electronic communication are still unresolved. Ethical issues, such as those relating to confidentiality, are unsettled. Finally, the Internet has opened up an entire new world for exploration, and studies indicate that for some people, it is psychologically addicting (see Chapter 12).

Internet Ethics

There are no Web police or Internet police, but some concerned cybercitizens have taken it upon themselves to develop some ethical guidelines for themselves and their fellow travelers in cyberspace.

One such group is the Health on the Net (HON) Foundation (http://www.hon.ch), based in Geneva, Switzerland. It has developed the Health on the Net Code of Conduct (HONCode), which is "an initiative to help unify the quality of medical and health information available on the WWW." The Code provides guidelines for those developing Web sites containing health-related information, as well as for those visiting these sites.

Web sites that display the HONCode logo agree to abide by these principles. If they are in violation, they can be reported to the HON Foundation.

Another group, the Computer Ethics Institute in Washington, DC, has developed the Ten Commandments of Computer Ethics. They are as follows (reprinted with permission):

1. *Thou shalt not use a computer to harm other people.*
2. *Thou shalt not interfere with other people's computer work.*
3. *Thou shalt not snoop around in other people's computer files.*
4. *Thou shalt not use a computer to steal.*
5. *Thou shalt not use a computer to bear false witness.*
6. *Thou shalt not copy or use proprietary software for which you have not paid.*
7. *Thou shalt not use other people's computer resources without authorization or proper compensation.*
8. *Thou shalt not appropriate other people's intellectual output.*
9. *Thou shalt think about the social consequences of the program you are writing or the system you are designing.*
10. *Thou shalt always use a computer in ways that insure consideration and respect for your fellow humans.*

Copyright

Non-profit managers who use the Internet need to be concerned about the copyright laws for lots of reasons. First, non-profit organizations post lots of materials on their Web pages that they don't necessarily want to see reproduced and disseminated without their permission. Second, non-profit managers use a lot of material they find on the World Wide Web, which may or may not be copyrighted. It is important to have an understanding of how these materials may be legally used. Third, non-profit managers send e-mail and post messages to Usenet groups. It may make a difference how you word something if you know that a publisher can include as a direct quote in a book with a 1,000,000 first printing something that you innocently posted on a Usenet group.

Copyright law changes all of the time, based on how individual cases are decided by the courts. Nothing in this section is intended to be legal advice; even if the information here and in Appendix D, *A Short Course in Copyright Law*, is correct at the time of publication, the information can change. And some of this material is an interpretation of statutes and case-law that many legal scholars would feel comfortable refuting. When in doubt, consult a qualified attorney.

Several Web sites keep up with Internet controversies involving what has been labeled "intellectual property"—patents, trademarks and copyrights. Among the better sites are:

U.S. Copyright Office:
http://lcweb.loc.gov/copyright/

RightsBase—ILT
http://www.ilt.columbia.edu/gen/ref/ILTcopy.html

See Appendix D for *A Short Course on Copyright Law*.

Trademarks

Trademarks and service marks are legal protection afforded to words and symbols that identify a product or service in a way that is intended to distinguish them from the goods and services of others. Federal law provides for registration of trademarks used in commerce. Trademarks are acquired as a result of the first use of a valid mark in commerce. No registration is required, although registration, of course, assists those who claim an infringement. Those who register their trademarks are entitled to use a symbol ® after the mark. Registration applications are not automatically approved by the Patent and Trademark Office. Examining attorneys consider whether the word or phrase is already in common use and therefore ineligible, or if the mark is confusingly similar to another already registered. The fee is currently $245 for each application.

The full details can be obtained over the Internet from the Web site of the U.S. Department of Commerce's Patent and Trademark Office:

http://www.uspto.gov

For additional information on this topic, point your browser to:

http://www.eff.org/pub/Intellectual_property/

"Romeo and Juliet met online in a chat room. But their relationship ended tragically when Juliet's hard drive died."

Up Close: Yahoo! (http://www.Yahoo.com)

Yahoo! is, by almost any account, the most popular search engine and directory on the 'Net. The site has grown to include numerous features, in an effort to be one of the most comprehensive available. It is one you will almost certainly want to use with frequency.

Yahoo!'s main directory is enormous, and well organized—an important combination for the Internet— resulting in a valuable, but easy-to-access way to find what you need. Sites are added to the directory both by the staff of Yahoo!, who proactively look for sites, and by people who want their sites placed in the appropriate categories.

The Yahoo! Search Engine accomplishes two goals. First, it allows you to search by words for material that is included in the Yahoo! directory. Second, it gives you results from Alta Vista's search engine, which specializes in broad searches of the larger Internet. A search of just Yahoo!'s directory using the term "non-profit" gives three directory category matches and 3,069 Web site matches. A search on the term "nonprofit" yields 12 category matches, including the one which is most valuable, "Nonprofit resources," and 5,471 site matches. By contrast, the same search on Alta Vista yields 204,377 matches.

Yahoo! has also put together an impressive list of specialized subdirectories including:

Society and Culture: Organizations: Nonprofit Resources
Business and Economy: Companies: Financial Services: Insurance: Commercial: Nonprofit Organizations
Business and Economy: Companies: Consulting: Management Consulting: Nonprofit Management
Yahoo!ligans: A directory of sites created for (or by) children
National Yahoo!s: Directories for several other countries, in other languages (including Canada, France, Germany, Japan and the UK at the time of this writing)
Yahoo! Metros: Directories of sites relevant to large cities, including Boston; Chicago; Washington, DC; Los Angeles; New York; and San Francisco at the time of this writing.
My Yahoo!: A feature which allows you to customize a directory for your own personal news and information, and create a default page.

Yahoo! also serves as a guide to the latest news items, from sports events to stock quotes to world events, and connects you conveniently to other news services and stories. Some of Yahoo!'s other features include tools for finding a map of any address in the U.S., and links to various search engines for finding people, their addresses, phone numbers, and e-mail addresses, as well as businesses and organizations. There is even a magazine called *Yahoo! Internet Life,* which is quite useful for finding new and practical Internet sites.

Princess Diana 1961-1997

non-profit | Search | options

Yellow Pages - People Search - Maps - Classifieds - News - Stock Quotes - Sports Scores

- **Arts and Humanities**
  Architecture, Photography, Literature...
- **Business and Economy** [Xtra!]
  Companies, Investing, Employment...
- **Computers and Internet** [Xtra!]
  Internet, WWW, Software, Multimedia...
- **Education**
  Universities, K-12, College Entrance...
- **Entertainment** [Xtra!]
  Cool Links, Movies, Music, Humor...
- **Government**
  Military, Politics [Xtra!], Law, Taxes...
- **Health** [Xtra!]
  Medicine, Drugs, Diseases, Fitness...
- **News and Media** [Xtra!]
  Current Events, Magazines, TV, Newspapers...
- **Recreation and Sports** [Xtra!]
  Sports, Games, Travel, Autos, Outdoors...
- **Reference**
  Libraries, Dictionaries, Phone Numbers...
- **Regional**
  Countries, Regions, U.S. States...
- **Science**
  CS, Biology, Astronomy, Engineering...
- **Social Science**
  Anthropology, Sociology, Economics...
- **Society and Culture**
  People, Environment, Religion...

My Yahoo! - Yahooligans! for Kids - Beatrice's Web Guide - Yahoo! Internet Life
Weekly Picks - Today's Web Events - Chat - Weather Forecasts
Random Yahoo! Link - Yahoo! Shop

National Yahoos **Australia & N.Z.** - Canada - France - Germany - Japan - **Korea** - U.K. & Ireland
Yahoo! Metros Atlanta - Austin - Boston - Chicago - Dallas / Fort Worth - Los Angeles
Get Local Miami - Minneapolis / St. Paul - New York - S.F. Bay - Seattle - Wash D.C.

How to Include Your Site - Company Information - Contributors - Yahoo! to Go

Yahoo! home page.

Chapter 12

DANGERS OF THE INTERNET

"I just joined a support group for Internet addicts. We meet every night from 7:00 until midnight on CompuServe."

Introduction

Dominating public discourse about the Internet has been a variety of concerns about the risks and dangers involved in Internet use. The non-profit sector has a lot at stake in the outcome of public policy debates relating to this promising new medium of communication. The enactment of the *Communications Decency Act,* on the surface, may not have seemed to be of major importance to the non-profit sector. Yet the erosion of First Amendment rights that this law could have brought about, were it not for being overturned by the U.S. Supreme Court, would almost surely have had repercussions on the ability of charities to communicate freely without fear of government reprisal. There will always be a tension between those who want to use government to protect us from ourselves, and those who believe that government has no role at all in regulating what can be said and done on the Internet. Perhaps neither extreme can work, but finding a consensus, a reasonable and workable middle ground, will take many years to evolve.

Some of the major issues articulated in newspaper editorials, talk shows, public policy forums and legislative arenas we have observed are:

(1) Overuse of the Internet. There is growing concern about whether spending many hours on-line is physically or emotionally harmful.

(2) Internet Content. The *Communications Decency Act* flourished on Capitol Hill as a result of a fear that the Internet was responsible for making pornography freely accessible to children. Other fears are that information dangerous to the functioning of a safe society, such as instructions about making explosives, and material that expresses hatred and bigotry toward particular groups, is available on the Internet.

(3) Privacy issues. Cameras are broadcasting real-time images onto the Internet, and some feel that this violates confidentiality. Also, you can use the Internet to access databases quickly, easily, and inexpensively, and there is the fear, legitimate or not, that you could be stalked by potentially dangerous people, and that personal computer files and other information can be downloaded from your computer without your knowledge or permission when you are on-line.

(4) Social Issues. There are fears that Internet communication will serve to erode traditional social skills. For example, people could lose their ability to interact face-to-face or, taken to the extreme, there may not even be a need to interact face-to-face anymore because people could "live" their entire lives on-line.

(5) Internet Crime. There is a concern that the socially naïve will be preyed upon by disreputable and dishonest people on-line, and that supposedly "secure" financial transactions could be intercepted.

We will not seek to convince you that the Internet poses no danger whatsoever. The fact is that each of these issues has a legitimate component to one extent or another. On the other hand, do not expect an exposition on how the Internet threatens to tear down the fabric of our society. There are reasons why it is easy for fears to become overblown in thinking about the Internet, and to forget that many of its downsides and dangers are balanced or outweighed by its corresponding benefits. Let us not forget that almost every technological advance has fomented fears of one kind or another about its overall impact on society.

Evaluating the Risks of the Internet

An important first step toward objectively evaluating the Internet's costs and benefits is to consider the reasons why objectivity can be difficult. On one hand, it is easy for those who see its vast potential for positive uses to focus only on these and to dismiss the downsides out of hand. At the same time, there are reasons why our fears about the issues can become distorted or overblown.

One reason for this is that the Internet is something that is very new and that can be difficult to understand. While many attempt to understand the Internet by analogy to more familiar forms of communication, sources of information, and resources, none of the analogies is perfect. Is the Internet a library? Is it a television? Is it a video game? Is a chat room analogous to a coffee shop? Am I talking or writing when I am on-line? Often, these analogies raise as many questions as they do explanations.

We do know that the Internet will bring changes—a fact that can be most disturbing in itself. Knowing there will be changes, but being unclear on exactly what they will be, is a source of excitement and anticipation for some and a source of fear and anxiety in others.

In addition, the public holds widely divergent views about that segment of the population that "resides" on-line. For many, there is a strongly negative perception of the "kind of people" on the Internet. These people may be at best different and at worst dangerous and uninviting. Those not on-line may feel that getting on-line means something more than just getting access to new resources. They may in fact feel that they are entering a new, perhaps cultish "society" that is different from what they are used to. And they would be right!

Some people have the perception that Internet users are *not* representative of mainstream society. For example, they may see the Internet as comprised principally of "egg-heads" who enjoy and feel more comfortable with their computers than they do with actual human interaction. Perhaps similarly, there is a perception that the Internet community contains a disproportionate number of anti-social, perhaps even psychopathic people, who use the Internet as an escape and who pose a threat to others.

Other people may believe that the Internet *is* representative of society, but may hold equally strong fears about what this means, worrying about the lack of protections from those who may threaten them. On the Internet, there are no gated communities, neighborhood watches, guard dogs, or burglar bars. There are no "Internet Police" cruising down the Information Superhighway, checking to see that laws are not being violated. How we view mainstream society may influence how we view the Internet community. For some, the Internet provides a haven to interact with others without the threat of physical harm that may result from venturing outside into the "real" world.

Also, being on-line often means judging people by their writing alone and not being able to categorize them or pre-judge them according to their age, gender, or physical attributes, which often are not revealed. For some this is a great advantage as we are left to judge others by the content of their characters, so to speak. But for others, this is more disconcerting since, ironically, it may mean they must distrust what they hear/read.

One's basic slant on humanity itself would have obvious implications to how one views the Internet community. Whether one views the Internet as representing a broad and threatening society or as an unrepresentative "bad element" would cause fear in any parent considering whether to encourage or discourage children from roaming cyberspace. Others are thrilled by the prospects of broad democratic participation in dialogue on-line, and the non-profit community has much to benefit from by the expansion of communication opportunities to those who, as a result of their social and economic status, may have been previously cut off from participating in discussions about social policy issues.

Thus, while many think of the Internet as comparable to a library, and find it an exciting opportunity for children and adults alike, others see it as a red-light district where the unprepared may be stalked and victimized.

Security Issues

Non-profit organizations have lots of reasons to protect the security and privacy of the computer files they generate and the communications they send over the Internet. Human service organizations, for example, routinely use client files that, if disclosed in an unauthorized manner, could cause irreparable harm to their clients and could result in lawsuits. E-mail exchanges may involve sensitive personnel matters or contract negotiations with unions and other entities. Non-profits that sell publications and other products or services over the Internet want their purchasers to know that the credit card information provided will not be intercepted by an unauthorized party. Even if nothing sensitive is discussed in a file or e-mail message, you still do not want any nosy person, within your organization or outside of it, to be able to browse through your business.

For most businesses, privacy is second nature. How many businesses send out communications discussing business matters using postcards or unsealed letters? Our guess is that if they did so, most of these communications would never be read, other than by their intended targets. But we have peace of mind believing that when we put a letter in an envelope and seal it, the letter will reach its destination without being read by someone else.

Software such as PGP Mail encrypts messages, so that the only person who can see the message is the intended user. Encryption scrambles the message when it is sent, and the recipient deciphers it. The message looks like gobbledygook to any third party without the "key" to open it.

Anonymity

Anonymous remailers, also called "anonymous servers," permit people to send anonymous e-mail messages without the recipient knowing the name or e-mail address of the sender. A non-profit organization might make use of this service if an employee wants to post a message on a Usenet bulletin board, and the posting is possibly not "politically correct." The employee might want to send a message to a government agency pointing out organizational misconduct, and not want to be victimized by retaliation by the organization. Or employees may not want responses to a posting tying up their e-mail account. More likely is that the non-profit may receive

New!

- MCN's 11th Annual Conference - "The Responsiblity of Leadership" is the theme for this years conference held at the Radisson Hotel in St. Paul on October 6, 1997 There will be five major speakers, three plenary sessions, nine seminars and a whole lot more.
- Minnesota Futures Fund - The Fund will provide grants to Minnesota nonprofit organizations to encourage thoughtful, systematic planning in response to changes at the federal and state levels. Grants are intended for organizations whose core missions are to assist those most affected by federal and state policy and program changes, especially organizations assisting individuals and families with low incomes.
- **JOB SEEKERS ALERT!** New jobs are added weekly (well, almost) to the Online Nonprofit Job Board
- Public Policy Forum - Now includes Telecommunications and Information Policy sub-forum, the Minnesota Legislative Update, and plenty of good information about welfare reform
- New Federalism Web Site - Minnesota Responds contains analyses of welfare reform and its impact on housing, food stamps, SSI, AFDC, and more.
- About the Minnesota Council of Nonprofits - Get to know us better through our staff, our board and our mission. Updated for 1997.
- Searchable Databases of Minnesota Nonprofits - An important step in locating information on Minnesota's financially active nonprofits NOW WITH MAPS!!!
- Links for Nonprofits - New links to many national and local nonprofits and funders Also, several great papers about nonprofits and the internet.

Resources for Nonprofit Organizations

- Fundraising Information - Get the skinny on giving programs in Minnesota and fundraising in general.
- How to Start a Nonprofit - Ever wondered how to start a nonprofit organization in the state of Minnesota? Here is some great information to get you on your way
- **Job Seeker's Guide** - Looking for a new or different job in the nonprofit sector in Minnesota? These documents will give you resources and a better understanding of what you can expect.
- Links for nonprofits - Including links to government organizations, other state associations and important information for nonprofits.
- Management Resources - Personnel, lobbying and management challenges are available to assist you and your organization's management
- Public Policy - Information about current legislation and issues facing Minnesota and Minnesota's nonprofits. Links to other policy related sites.
- Nonprofit Announcements - A bulletin board for nonprofits including programs and opportunities

Projects

- Civic Engagement - A long term project focusing on new ways nonprofit organizations could increase citizen participation
- Partnership for Minnesota's Future - The Partnership for Minnesota's Future will provide policy makers and the public with a new vision for how public and private resources should be developed and applied to effectively meet the public needs in Minnesota.
- Nonprofit Economy - Released in November, 1995, this report details the contributions that nonprofits make to Minnesota in terms of jobs, revenues and expenses.
- Nonprofit Library - A project to provide valuable information to nonprofit organizations via a variety of electronic media
- Standards Project - The overview of an examination of nonprofit standards in the areas of 1)Nonprofit Board Structure/Governance, 2)Openness/Public Accountability, 3)Fundraising Practices/Financial Management, 4)Evaluation/Outcome Measures, 5)Staff Composition/Selection/Compensation, 6)Collaboration/New Organizations

MCN Information

- **New!** MCN's 1997 Publication List - Complete and up-to-date with descriptions of the publications
- About the Council - Our mission, our staff, our board
- Calendar of Events - We're busy planning our 1997 calendar The link should be reactivated soon.
- The 1996 - 1998 edition of Minnesota Nonprofit Directory is now available Get your copy now!
- Membership Information - Get information on the benefits of membership in the Minnesota

Minnesota Council of Nonprofits home page. Courtesy MCNP. Reprinted with permission.

Up Close: Minnesota Council of Nonprofits (http://www.mncn.org)

Chris Sullivan, MIS Director for the Minnesota Council of Nonprofits, put his site on-line in May 1996 after about half a year of development and construction. Everyone in his organization supported the idea. Everything was done in-house except some of the site content; Sullivan coded all the HTML files by himself.

Did he run into any problems?

Sullivan voices a complaint common to Webmasters. "I lost what little life I had," he says. "Development, upkeep, and maintenance are time-consuming. This could easily be a full-time job, but I have to work it in with the other duties for which I had been hired."

Content creation was also more difficult, time consuming, and expensive than the Minnesota Council had budgeted for. "It included converting content from existing in-house formats to suitable HTML documents, as well as writing and editing new documents of interest," explains Sullivan.

Working with a new server brought challenges of its own. "We had been using our Internet Service Provider for over a year when we were ready to get the Web site going," he says. "The ISP was a project of a local non-profit organization that provides low-cost Internet connections and Web site space to other non-profits. They had approached us earlier about being beta testers of their service. As a result, we didn't have to do any

anonymous messages from clients (e.g., a women who is the victim of domestic violence may be communicating through these services to avoid being traced by her abuser).

There are lots of issues involving remailers, whether you use them yourself, or receive anonymous messages. For more information, browse the Web sites:

http://www.cs.berkeley.edu/~raph/remailer-list.html
or
http://www.well.com/user/abacard

shopping around. Their prices were pretty low and we already had ongoing relationships with their technical support staff."

The approximate cost to set up and manage the site was $15,000. Updates are done in-house. The site averages 550 hits daily and its target audience is Minnesota-based non-profit organizations and anyone interested in them.

"Given the boundless nature of the Web, our secondary audience is much larger," says Sullivan. "But we successfully reach them both, I think. We reach the first audience via state-specific content like the new Minnesota Futures Fund (http://www.mncn.org/mff.htm) and the job listings (http://www.mncn.org/jobs/jobs.htm). The second we reach through our more general content, such as board development and non-profit management issues (http://www.mncn.org/manage.htm).

Sullivan is constantly looking for ways to improve and update the site. "We're trying to be a one-stop-shopping location for non-profits in Minnesota," he says. "While access is not universal by any means, our site provides easy information retrieval for those who are on-line and a carrot for those who aren't. We hope non-profits new to the Internet who find our site find something useful."

The organization publishes a directory of non-profits in the state of Minnesota that Sullivan would like to put on-line in a searchable format. Other more interactive content areas, such as Guestbooks, event registration, and book purchases, are under consideration. The Council's publications and membership information are already on-line. "Whether any of these will happen in the next six months is uncertain," he says.

The Minnesota Council of Non-Profits uses the Internet to promote its advocacy agenda.

"Our staff public policy person does most of her work in person," says Sullivan. "But she uses the Internet to gather information and network with colleagues in the field. The Internet allows us to research organizations, legislation, and other topics easily."

A list of remailers can be found at the newsgroup site:

alt.privacy.anon-server

Virus transmission

A computer virus is an unwelcome and uninvited program that is designed to execute a frivolous or, in some cases, destructive action on your computer. In the worst case, viruses can cause your system to crash and all of your data to be lost.

They may come in the form of worms (programs that replicate themselves and devour your system's memory resources) or Trojan horses (programs that appear on the surface to be benign or useful, but are destructive in some way to your system).

Viruses cannot be transmitted to your computer over the Internet within e-mail messages, because everything is in ASCII format (a format that uses only numbers and letters and is not conducive to making the commands that constitute viruses) rather than binary files. One way viruses can be transmitted in e-mail is through attached binary files (files that contain symbols and other instructions to your computer). But millions of binary files travel through the Internet every day. Just as it is good advice never to put a disk into your computer from a source you do not trust, you should never download a file or open a file attached to your e-mail from a source you do not trust. The major on-line services routinely check their shareware/freeware libraries for viruses, although this is certainly not a fail-safe system, because it is run by humans. Many Internet users routinely get binary files and compressed files attached to e-mail, and this is another potential source of virus transmission.

Even if you have a virus checker, new viruses are created all of the time. Venders of anti-virus software typically update their products several times each year to respond to new strains. Most virus checkers will check to see if there is a virus already on your system, and have a terminate-and-stay-resident (TSR) component that stands as a sentinel on your system whenever it is turned on, alerting you when a new virus is introduced into your system.

It is important that you routinely and frequently employ the use of a virus checker, particularly if you are a frequent Internet user. It's good advice to have a general idea of how much empty disk space you have on your hard drive. And if you notice that your hard drive is inexplicably filling up despite the fact that you are not knowingly adding files, it's time to get some professional help.

We are not alarmists with respect to viruses. We know people who are so terrified of picking up a virus that they refuse to even go on-line. That is their choice, but they are missing out as a result of a myth that viruses are a significant worry. Our view is that picking up a virus is just one of many things that can go wrong as a result of using a computer. There are millions of long-time computer users who have never picked up a virus. In contrast, there are few that haven't had the pleasure of having a floppy or hard disk fail and losing hours of work, having software they depended upon get corrupted, or having their Internet Service Provider go down for a few days.

There are many false alarms about viruses circulating on the Internet. You can access a file on the Internet that uncovers false reports about viruses at this URL: http://www.kumite.com/myths/.

If you follow common sense and act cautiously with respect to binary files, viruses should not be a problem for you.

Addiction and Overuse of the Internet

It is hard not to sympathize with the parents who worry that their child is spending too much time on-line or to agree that adults face a problem when they feel compelled to sit for hours deep into the night wandering Web sites or talking in chat rooms. The fact that these are problems seems so apparent that it does not need to be examined. Or does it? What is a healthy amount of time on-line? Are people getting addicted to the Internet or are they simply spending extra time now learning their way around?

Overuse of television and video games has long been a topic of discussion and research. Many societal problems are attributed to these activities and their overuse. There has been a tendency to think of the Internet as the next wave in this line—the newest attraction on a video screen for people to sit and stare at. The Internet, it is feared, may further reduce the time our children spend in the outdoors playing sports or in the library reading books. It will further encroach on the social interaction necessary for their healthy development.

Once again, some of this may be a legitimate concern. Consider, however, the differences between the Internet and either television or video games. While they appear similar in that the viewer watches a screen or monitor, the assumption that they are similar in every respect is false.

While television encourages people to passively view whatever program may be shown, the Internet requires one to determine his or her own direction. Microsoft® markets its Internet Explorer Web browser with the question "Where do you want to go today?" This speaks to the Internet's unlimited options.

While the television and video games excite viewers with special effects and action, the Internet is much more a medium for text, with pictures and moving images that are unable to compete. Thus, children on the Internet are far more likely to be reading than they would be when watching television or playing video games.

On the other hand, one feature of the Internet that television does not offer is interactivity. Both through computer programs and communication with people, the Internet can serve as a teacher, answering questions. For example, there are popular sites at which children can ask questions relevant to their homework. There are also sites which, by computer program, allow for learning in much the same way as an educational program or CD-ROM.

Many interactive Web sites seek responses from their readers, encouraging them to think, formulate opinions, and articulate them in writing. Discussion forums involve dialogue with real people. In these ways, the Internet is more like a classroom or café than a video. Thus, children on the Internet are more likely to be writing and thinking than they would be when absorbing MTV, or playing Nintendo.

It is true that the Internet offers games and a fair share of frivolous entertainment, unrelated to educational objectives. For perhaps most children, this is the first lure of the Internet. There is a connection to video games as some can be played on-line, or programs can be downloaded to one's computer and played off-line. Nevertheless, the quality of these rarely competes with modern video games and requires a higher level of sophistication to obtain and enjoy. Here again, children's entertainment on-line tends to involve reading. While their choices may be more akin to reading a comic-book, it may still be a positive step back to reading.

Differences such as these demonstrate the problem trying to analogize the Internet to our familiar forms of activities. We may be looking at a screen that resembles a television, but in doing so, we may be reading a book or talking with people. The only clear similarity is that the Internet does not involve much physical activity. However, there has been some research indicating that the time people are spending on-line is coming from the time formerly spent watching television rather than the time spent in physical activities. If so, then the Internet may pose less of a threat to children's time spent outdoors than feared. Instead of cumulatively adding to television and video games, the Internet is simply giving people a more productive activity to replace these.

Without a doubt, the activities people choose, being on-line, spending time talking with friends, enjoying physical activity outdoors, or reading books, should all be part of a balanced lifestyle. If one is on-line so often as to exclude any other activity, if one neglects his or her work, family, or physical health, then a problem exists. There can be no firm rule of thumb as to what amount of time on-line is healthy, but a good way to consider the question is to think about what one is doing on-line, since the activities there vary so widely. Is five hours a day a problem? Perhaps so if the five hours are spent playing boggle (http://boggle.stanford.edu/play.html). But if the time is divided among reading news and literature, writing an on-line publication, playing a game of chess with an opponent on the other side of the world, exploring your interests and hobbies with others, learning about how to do a home repair, and then 20 minutes playing boggle, then perhaps it's not so bad after all.

Addiction to the Internet is becoming recognized as a genuine pathology. Non-profit managers need to be concerned about Internet addiction for several reasons. First, it is increasingly being considered a pathology that results in decreased productivity in the workplace, missed workdays, and employees who are too tired to function after an evening spent in the Ready for Love (or the Non-Profit Managers) chat room. Second, it can afflict *you*. Just as compulsive gambling and obsessions with food, sex, and exercise can become troublesome, so can Internet use.

Among the typical warning signs found posted on the 'Net are:

1. You experience withdrawal symptoms (such as depression, irritability) when you are not on-line, or are constantly thinking about your next on-line session.
2. You spend longer periods surfing than what you intended when you went on-line, and are unsuccessful in cutting back on the time you spend on-line when you try to.
3. You sacrifice time spent on other important pursuits (such as time with your family, work time, sleep time) in order to devote more time to being on-line.
4. You withdraw from other social and family activities in order to be on-line.
5. You neglect your health (such as giving up exercising) in order to have more time to be on-line
6. People such as your family members, close friends, or your boss complain that you are spending too much time on-line.
7. You use the Internet to escape problems with your "real life."

Psychologists are busy at work researching this obviously new health concern. The newspapers are filled with anecdotes of those whose lives were shattered as a result of Internet addiction, or as a result of "meeting" the wrong person in a chat room.

There are lots of humorous Web postings about Internet addiction (such as "you know you are addicted to the Internet when you..."). But serious studies are just being undertaken. One such study attempts to correlate various demographic and personality data with Internet addiction. The results of this study, carried out by Dr. Kimberly Young of the University of Pittsburgh at Bradford, are posted on the Internet at http://www.pit.edu/~ksy/apa.html and is being read, hopefully, by thousands of Internet-dependent people who are checking out the site every hour, day and night, to see if they have anything to worry about.

Among the sites that have information about Internet addiction are:

Center for On-Line Addiction: http://www.pitt.edu/~ksy
Internet Addiction Information: http://www.seanet.com/~gtate/addict.htm
CyberWidows: http://web20.mindlink.net/htc/4_1.html

Pornography and Other Controversial Content On-line

Some of the strongest concerns about the Internet have formed around the topic of on-line pornography and, to a lesser extent, the access to other dangerous or harmful information on-line. Faced with the broad ability to publish text or photos, some have raised this as the greatest, or at least the most tangible, danger of the Internet.

In the months preceding the Supreme Court's decision in *Reno v. the ACLU*, the Internet community demonstrated its single greatest example of solidarity as individual and organizational Web sites carried a familiar blue ribbon image proclaiming the site owner's stance against the infringement of the First Amendment by the *Communications Decency Act.* It should not have been a surprise that those on-line so overwhelmingly opposed the legislation censoring Internet content.

In this decision, Justice Stephens spoke for the majority finding that the Internet should be afforded the same protections as printed publications and should not be censored. As above, much of the debate centered on drawing the right analogy. Printed text has traditionally been limited by the fact that any would-be publisher had to incur the costs of publishing material, and any would be viewer had to incur the cost of purchasing it. With the Internet, the printed word could be made available to all and viewable by all for virtually nothing.

As Justice Stephens noted, the growth of the Internet has not been hampered by fears of this kind of content, but rather has grown at "phenomenal" rates despite it. It is probably true that, like the court, most people view this question as one of balancing the pros and the cons. Can we accept the incredible access to information for the good it brings people knowing that there will be downsides when information is misused? The easiest solution to the issue would be to have our government restrict access to the Internet, to suppress information it deems dangerous to its society. But very few would find this a reasonable solution. So instead, many sought to limit content—an approach that, if implemented, would create a nightmare for policing efforts and for courts trying to discern pornography from art or educational material.

One of the most important reasons why the Court may have ruled in favor of granting the Internet full freedoms of expression was probably the fact that ways are being developed to limit access. Programs for parents to curtail access to unwanted sites exist now and can be expected to improve dramatically in the coming years. Contrary to the perception that one can accidentally stumble upon nude photos (or worse, have them foisted upon them unsolicited), sites containing pornography typically contain a warning at their gateway, a fact Justice Stephens emphasized.

In some ways, this problem, too, is not really brand new to the Internet. Children have often found ways to access magazines and other forms of pornography. The availability on computers, while easier to access, may be more difficult for young people to hide. An offshoot of the current debate has centered on those demanding that libraries utilize blocking software to prevent access to pornography. Libraries have, in most cases, refused to agree to this censorship. Few have considered, however, the impracticality of sitting in a public library viewing pornographic photos on-line while others stroll by.

Privacy On-line

A recent talk show featured another content-based fear of the Internet. It is possible to place a camera or video-cam and to broadcast the image to a Web site, updating it daily or even every few seconds, or to stream the video in. Audio can be similarly streamed in.

Many positive uses of this are apparent. For distance learning, it allows one to view a conference on-line. Video-cams along highways are allowing people to view traffic and to see weather relevant for their travel and driving.

Some uses are more creative and may be highly beneficial, or may raise entirely new issues of concern. One of the more creative is the use of such a camera in daycare centers. Parents will no longer need to have fears about the care their children receive when they can peek in at any moment to see their child. This practice is being used in a number of daycare centers already. Another creative use was Geocities' inventive and popular Hollywood bus stop camera. Broadcasting a bus stop bench where many stars pass allowed people to check in and possibly catch a glimpse of a favorite celebrity.

But then there are the misuses of this idea. One site, for example, was discovered to be linked to a camera placed in a public restroom. Will our tort laws protecting privacy be able to compensate for the potential personal damage this kind of publication can cause? In the past, there were practical limits to the extent of injury from the publication of words or images about an individual. The average person would find it difficult to reach a large audience, and a publication that could do so would tend to be in a better position to compensate the injured in a lawsuit. But now, any person, rich or poor, could have the ability to destroy another's reputation through publication on-line and reach millions of people rather than tens or hundreds.

In addition, the increasing use of cameras on-line brings another development that will likely disconcert people. How will people feel knowing that they are being broadcast to the Internet while they await a bus, even if the image is ordinary?

Conclusion

In surveying the risks and realities of the Internet, there are few easy answers. Certain things seem clear, however. First, the Internet will bring changes. Second, fear of the changes will not stop the Internet from becoming an integral part of mainstream society. Equally certain is that the Internet will deliver immeasurable benefits to all people at the same time that it causes irreparable harm in other cases. One would like to say that time will tell how these balance against one another but, to be honest, even time will probably not be able to answer that question the same for everyone.

As different as the Internet is, in some ways it is quite the same as any other technological advance. Are we better off now with nuclear technology than we were without it? Are we better off with automobile transportation? With electricity? With gunpowder? With fire?

Any technology can be misused. Since we can't avoid the risks by avoiding the technology, the better approach may be to dispassionately assess the real risks and dangers and to address, limit, and alleviate them to the extent possible. This will be an important issue for policy makers, non-profit managers, and many others seeking to make the Internet as valuable as possible, increasing access to all those who might benefit and ensuring that the Internet contains a growing quantity of useful and used resources for people and those who serve people. And we must work to curtail its harmful effects to children, to those whose privacy is violated, to those who experience damaging interrelations through their Internet contact with others and to any person who finds himself or herself failing to balance healthy off-line activities with their Internet activities.

Essay: So What is the Internet Community Really Like?

by Gary B. Grant

The Internet today is probably much more mainstream than most would think, and is becoming more of a melting pot as entry barriers to Internet access fall.

Perhaps in its earlier incarnations, the Internet was largely the realm of a more tightly-knit community of people who shared a strong proficiency with computers. One can sometimes hear the lament in the newsgroups about the number of "newbies" on-line (although, by definition, all of us were "newbies" at one time). Nostalgically, they reminisce about the days when their smaller circle had these forums all to themselves. Some regret the newer developments that make the Internet more user-friendly and, therefore, potentially accessible to all. In days past, the difficulty getting connected served as a screening mechanism ensuring that those on-line were especially sophisticated with computers. Today, almost anyone who wants to can connect to the Internet. The flood gates have opened, for good or bad, and can never be closed.

There is probably, however, still truth to the perception that the Internet is disproportionately white and male, although the gender and race gaps could quickly disappear in coming years. A deeper question, perhaps, is whether the economic gap will close. The Internet is not nearly as accessible for poor individuals and communities, the obvious reason being the cost of computers and on-line services and the view that they are not essential for everyday life, at least at the moment (unlike, for example, a car that may cost as much or more).

Whatever the facts may be regarding race, gender, and similar questions of equity, the Internet is so widely populated that just about anyone can find many others in their particular group on-line, regardless of how you define the term "group." Parents of children with autism can find other such parents in a matter of minutes at Web sites devoted to this topic. Similarly, there are sites for multiracial people, for women in science, even sites for those who are left-handed. There are newsgroups for elderly retired persons, those who enjoy folk-dancing, or for just about every cultural group, from Albanians to Zimbabwenese.

The possible gaps that may exist in the proportions of particular groups on-line may have vital social significance overall, but in terms of the people one encounters when on-line, the fullest possible range is already, for the most part, there and easily accessible for those who wish to seek them out. Moreover, people can limit their connections to these groups and there is no need to wander to open chat rooms. Simply viewing Web sites and reading discussion areas are like wandering neighborhoods invisibly until you choose to reveal yourself by participating. Whenever you wish to, you can again disappear and move away.

How do people "meet" or encounter one another on-line?

To say that you can find any group you are seeking on-line begs the question whether we (or our children, or our organizations) might still be at risk of being "approached" by someone dangerous. Many articulate their fears of child molestation on-line as though being on-line meant a physical presence. Is this warranted? Can one approach, captivate, and harm others through words and images?

There are several ways that people unknown to one another "meet" on-line. One way is for a person to build a Web page that lists his or her e-mail address or other method of contact. With little effort, anyone can obtain a Web page for little or no cost, and include in it comments, intended or not, to elicit response. This is not necessarily the most effective way to contact others. There are literally billions of Web pages on the Internet, and the chances of someone running across yours are minimal without additional efforts to draw attention to it.

Up Close: Hospital and Healthsystem Association of Pennsylvania (http://www.hap2000.org)

John Hope, recently retired from the communications department of the Hospital and Healthsystem Association of Pennsylvania (HAP), was one of the initial Webmasters for the Harrisburg-based association. Currently, he does Internet consulting and training, among other pursuits.

Hope began the HAP Web site in a favorable climate. "There was an amazing amount of support, even more than I had expected," he says. "We had a new, computer-literate president who was interested in using the Internet. So the idea fell on more-receptive ears."

It took about four months to get the site on line, and there were few problems. "We did it all ourselves," says Hope. "We read some books, went to some workshops, and created our own Web site. The biggest mistake we made was underestimating the time commitment needed to keep the page updated daily. It requires more staff resources than we had anticipated."

What other pitfalls would Hope caution other Webmasters about? The biggest mistake page editors make, he says, is not updating the pages often enough. "We saw 'news' on some pages that was six months old," Hope points out. "We decided this was unacceptable for us. There are elements on our page that have to be changed every day. Other than contracting with a server, we do it all in-house."

The in-house efforts were helped along by the newer software. "When we started, we had a text-only Web page. We knew how to code text, but we didn't know how to do tables or graphics," Hope recalls. "We were proud just to be able to put links in. But *FrontPage*™, for example, allows you to put in the graphics and tables very easily without having to concern yourself with the coding, and you can see how it will look immediately."

Finding the right graphics meant balancing the tastes of members and customers. "Our members liked the plain look; it gave them information they wanted," says Hope. "It loaded quickly. They could download or print quickly and then go back to their work. My experience is that people are willing to wait about 30 seconds for a page to load, but not much longer. But our staff colleagues didn't like it because they thought it was too plain."

Some of the organization's expectations about the Web site have been fulfilled: it is accessed by the media and the general public for its daily news summaries of Pennsylvania newspapers, issues updates, promotional material about HAP's educational programs, news releases, policy and position statements, and links. A password-protection area holds memos to CFOs and CEOs, managed care data, and other proprietary information.

The results of other expectations are harder to evaluate. "The goal was to take five years to get our members to the point that they would rely on the Web site rather than on the mail, and it is too early to tell whether five years is long enough," says Hope. "While the site hasn't saved the

Another way to find people is to search for a particular forum or Web site that is indexed in search engines or directories as a place where people who share an interest or characteristic network with one another. Here, people can reach out to others who have elected to be listed or can announce their own Web sites to the particular group. Suppose, for example, that one wished to find others interested in charitable organization fund-raising. It would take about 30 seconds of searching to find lists of these people and their e-mail addresses.

A third way to encounter people who share an interest topic is to become a participant in a newsgroup or mailing list discussion about that topic. In both of these cases, one may begin a association money in terms of mail costs, it has solved another problem. We used to get complaints from some high-level staff that the memos we were sending out to their bosses were not being distributed to them in a timely manner, or at all. This Web site gives these staff members the opportunity to see the memos and get the information they need."

What advice would Hope give to Internet novices? "Talk to some of your peers who are already involved," he suggests. "Find a trainer or a training course and work to overcome your concerns. If you don't, you will be left behind."

On the other hand, Hope notes, this is an area in which you can't expect to have all the answers—or even all the questions—before you start. Recognize that everything is going to change. "The important thing is just to start in—and make changes and adjustments as you go along."

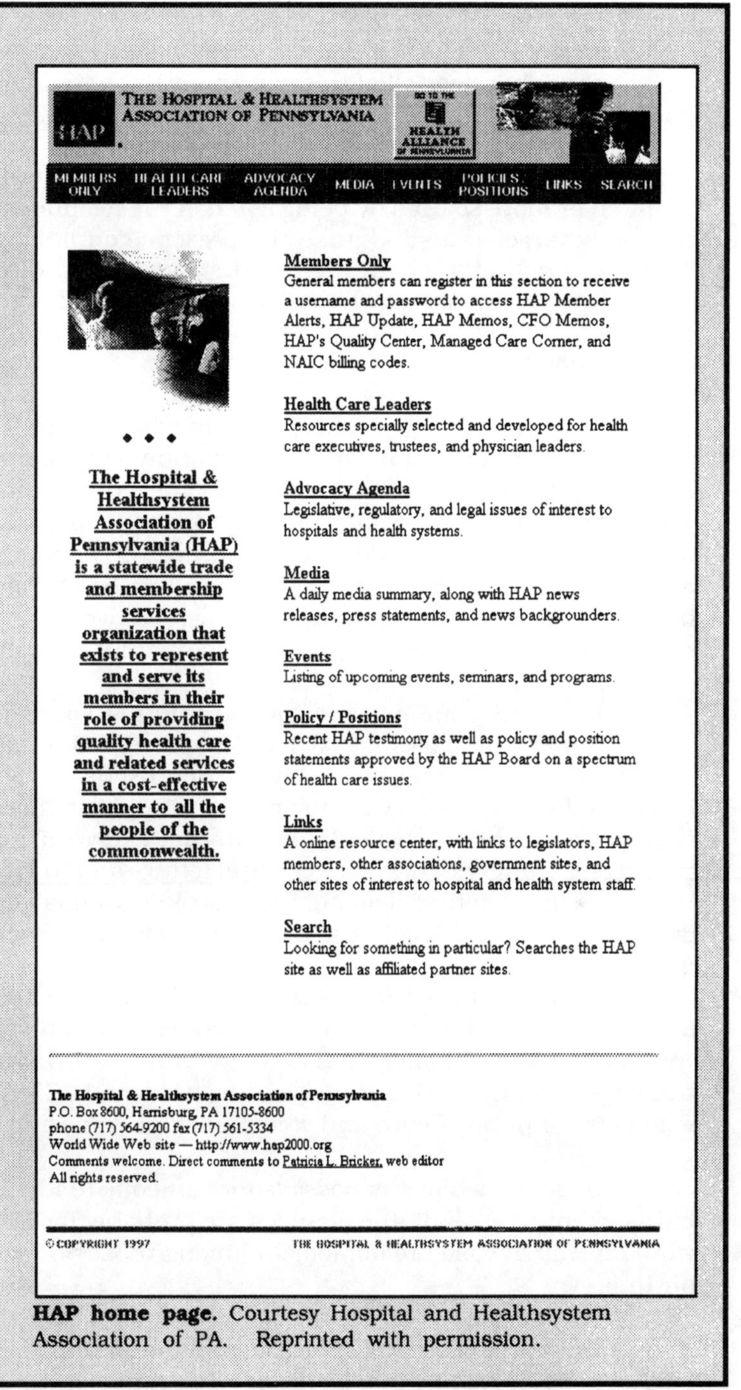

HAP home page. Courtesy Hospital and Healthsystem Association of PA. Reprinted with permission.

dialogue with one person, but must remember that the conversation can be read by anyone else participating unless it is sent only to that person's e-mail address. When responding to the whole group, the message goes to every other participant. Any other participant can respond personally or in the public forum to the writer.

Finally, there are ways in which people can search directories of e-mail addresses or phone/address listings. Anyone whose name is in the phone book may be listed in these sources, even if they are not themselves on-line. Marketers "harvest" e-mail addresses from mailing lists and newsgroups, and send random advertisements to those whose e-mail addresses they obtain.

These can become bothersome and a serious pitfall to e-mail if they continue to grow beyond the handful one might get every week now.

But what does all of this say about the potential of someone reaching out to harm people on-line?

For the most part, those on-line are anonymous by the sheer numbers of people out there—as much or more so than by being listed in the telephone directory. The risk is minuscule of being randomly targeted just because of a presence on-line, whether through a Web site of one's own, listing in another's, or through participation in a discussion forum. This risk might rise to significance if one were deliberately and repeatedly inciting or otherwise annoying others, but even then, there are just far too many people on-line to fear random harassment will befall any single individual.

There may be some exceptions in which there is a legitimate reason to be cautious. You should be careful about what information you make available. Tracking someone's home information by their e-mail address would be tedious and difficult if even possible. So it is probably wise counsel to limit contact information to e-mail addresses only and to never give out home information to those you don't know on-line. In addition, the Internet's convenience for targeting members of a particular group can be used for bad by members of a hate organization as easily as by others of the particular group wishing to network with one another. Again, the key may simply be to make sure not to post personal contact information beyond an e-mail address.

Cautiously limiting the contact information will help ensure that if one is targeted, it is only for e-mail messages, which can be ignored. One can see this potential problem vividly in the newsgroups. For example, a newsgroup for discussion about gay and lesbian issues will frequently be visited by people who wish to provoke angry responses. While the best cure for this is to ignore hateful comments, it typically results instead in a major digression in which almost all the postings are angry banter in all capital letters and in language one would not want their children to read. This of course delights the provoker, who is all the more likely to keep on doing what he or she is doing and ignore the pleas to go elsewhere.

In all of this, it is important to distinguish that the risks are not likely to go beyond inappropriate on-line messages, the sender of which may live hundreds of miles away. Perhaps the worst you might likely find is that you have to change your e-mail address because someone has decided to waste their time sending hate mail. Even this would be rare indeed for any person who is not a public figure and who persists in ignoring the efforts to provoke them.

In short, while it is *possible* for someone to identify and target another on-line for off-line harassment or assault, the chances are probably far less than by other means. Physical threats would be much easier to implement among those one sees in public than among those one meets on-line.

Of course, this still leaves the potential harm, especially to children, who may read foul language or threats from another. In this regard, many of the fears are legitimate. The newsgroups, in particular, are often a place where incivility and anger seem to breed. Most are perfectly harmless and productive communication forums. But parents, teachers, and others should be watchful of them and prepared to deal with the possibility of children reading something inappropriate. Commercial software programs are available that can be set to filter objectionable material.

But once again, this is not a problem unique to the Internet. A parent at a baseball game might be in exactly the same position of having to explain inappropriate, rude, and obnoxious behavior. Few, however, would suggest that this should mean avoiding taking children to the ballpark.

Do people take on different on-line personas?

This debate about the incivility that exists in some discussion areas of the Internet raises a question about how people behave on-line as compared to off-line. Is it possible that people feel a certain freedom to be obnoxious on-line? It would appear that they do. Anonymity and the ability to avoid the consequences may mean that people behave more rudely on-line than they would in real life. At a baseball game, or any other public place, one is limited to some extent in what one says or does by the risk of antagonizing the patrons around him or her, or even being expelled from the stadium. Such limits have not been as present in on-line forums. Although there are numerous cases of people being locked out of a mailing list or newsgroup because of inappropriate behavior, this usually only happens in the very worst cases, and people can often return under a new e-mail address or name.

Interestingly, the Internet can also have the reverse impact on people's personae. There are many examples in which people seem even friendlier on-line than they probably are in face-to-face interactions. Some possible reasons for this might be that for many the new environment makes them especially careful not to offend. They may be aware that there are rules of "netiquette" and a culture on-line of which they are not familiar. In addition, it is easier to be misinterpreted and may require more cautious wording to convey that one is not trying to be offensive, for example, when disagreeing with someone on-line. Thus, for many, there is an added effort to be deferential.

Also, one sees people being particularly open on-line, expressing more of themselves than they might in casual conversation in public. At the same time, for many, there is the reverse effect, in which there is more of an effort to remain concealed and not to be open.

The differences in people's behavior and tone on-line may become an interesting area of study in the future and there seem to be many contradictions. It appears, however, that in many cases, people indeed act differently on-line than they do off-line. What this may suggest for relationships that develop on-line—friendships, professional interactions, or romances—is not at all clear. It is likely that some such relationships will become disappointments when people meet face-to-face; on the other hand, it is also likely that some will not be disappointing at all. There are plenty of examples of both, but to say right now that the good outweighs the bad or vice versa would be clearly premature. Will the Internet lead to a rash of bad relationships or will it instead help people with common interests to meet one another? If the Internet tends to bring people together who share common interests, will the diversity of their friends diminish, or will it expand as people from different continents become more accessible to one another? These are the kinds of questions that we should consider in the next few years.

Essay: The Internet Economy

by Gary B. Grant

Who pays for the Internet

Why are so many private companies providing such useful services for free? Many of the services on the Internet are free and you may be wondering why. You may be amazed when you consider the work it must take to build and maintain a search engine, or to create and expand a directory with a staff of directory makers. It is costly to develop browser software and distribute it. Who is paying for all of this? The Internet economy is an interesting topic, though we will only briefly touch on it here.

Consider television programs. Cable TV costs the viewer, while network television is paid for by advertisers and sponsors. Then there's privately-funded or government-funded programming. These methods are all being explored for the Internet. Companies, more often than not, seek advertisers to fund their pages, and the goal is to make their sites as attractive and useful as possible to you and others, because the frequency of your visits will ultimately determine how marketable their sites are as Internet "billboard" spots.

How and Why Businesses Advertise on Web Sites

By "billboard," we mean just this. You will see many sites on the Internet that include one or more boxes or "banners" across the screen representing other sites, companies, and their products or services. You can click these banners to move to the advertisers' sites and ultimately (the advertising company hopes) purchase something. In other words, the "free sites" such as search engines, directories, and others form a partnership with the Internet business sites (those that offer you information about their products and how to order them).

For a business advertising on the Internet, this kind of exposure might be critical, especially since people are not likely to bookmark or visit with frequency its site unless they have some particular pre-existing interest in it. People are also used to buying goods and services from sources other than the Internet and may not go searching/shopping here for the products they want to buy. However, it's not hard to imagine that if you are in the market for a car, and happen to see a banner for Toyota, you might click to it briefly, temporarily distracting yourself from whatever you are doing, to learn more about the Toyota company. Toyota would obviously love this opportunity to give you basic information (especially pictures), so that you may become a knowledgeable buyer, to impress you with the cutting edge design of its Web page so that you have greater confidence in the company, to demonstrate all the wonderful continued connection you can have with the company through its Web site once you purchase their car and, in the end, increase the likelihood that you will purchase its product.

Even if you don't visit the business advertised on a Web site, the banner itself can be its own commercial, complete with moving graphics and other eye-catching designs which, if well done, can not only make you remember the business's name, but perhaps even communicate something of its character.

How much can a site actually earn by selling advertising space? In April 1996, the *Chicago Tribune* reported rates for major search engines in the area of $20,000 to $50,000 for every million times that people click to the banner ad. Sites that are free to the public can still be enormously valuable companies when they begin selling stock openly. Yahoo! by the end of its first day on the market was worth $848 million at $43/share. Not bad for a project that began as an Internet diversion for two graduate students at Stanford just a few years ago.

Other Methods of Supporting Internet Service Sites

This system of paying for free sites by selling advertising space is not the only example of "giveaways" on the Internet. There is also a wonderful free-distribution system for attracting people to particular software. For example, browsers have been, and continue to be, easy to come by. Netscape was long given away free as were competitors such as Mosaic. Netscape won the popularity contest here and became the browser of choice for some 80% of the Internet viewing population. Having done so, it now sells for a modest cost and continues to be free for educational uses. Its current competition comes from Microsoft, which is investing a significant amount of its vast resources to develop and give its "Internet Explorer" browser away in an effort to grapple away some of that market before, we suspect, it sells some advanced version down the road.

There are many alternative systems for funding software. In some cases, you are trusted to be honest and pay for the item beyond a particular free-trial period of use, such as 30 days. In other cases, the software is programmed to disable itself after that time. In still other cases, the software can be tested, but is limited in some way, and if you find it useful, then you will need to pay to have the software upgraded to its full potential. Of course, some software is simply free, or "freeware." Sometimes this is done because the product's creator wants to make a name for himself or herself, and therefore gives it away to establish a reputation in the field.

Again, there are parallels to this on Internet sites, too. Some will give you a portion of their features, but make other important services accessible to only paying members or they will give you a trial period, but cut you off if you do not join. HandsNet is a good example of this. HandsNet is a leading full-service Internet provider and information resource to the human services sector. Any member of the Internet public can browse HandsNet's Web site and find files and other material of use to the non-profit advocacy community. But in order to access the entire site, membership is charged which, as of press time, is $300 ($180 for students and grass-roots membership organizations with budgets less than $100,000 annually), for those who access the service via the Internet.

Still others may give away their entire service for now, but may begin at a later date to implement a payment system, for example, when they become established as the best in their category, the most popular, or the only site providing a particular service.

One reason for these various permanent or temporary "giveaway" systems is that the Internet is working through questions of how to transfer money from the user to the provider of services. Many accept credit card payments, but some users are reluctant to pass these numbers through the Internet. Caution here is based on the fact that the communications may not be technically secure. Concern also arises because anyone could create a false site to attract consumers, and it might be difficult to track them down should they use your card for unauthorized purchases. On the other hand, if you are careful to restrict purchases to reputable sites (many of which provide for encryption of your credit card data), the risk really falls on the card company and not the user, and may not be greater than using a card over the phone or giving it to a server (yes, this word does have another meaning) at a restaurant.

Even given the current ability to use credit cards for electronic transfers of money, the problem many are trying to solve is how to charge small amounts, such as the pennies and nickels one might be willing to pay for a search engine or other service. If, or should we say when, developers build into the Internet a way to charge for small amounts, we might see the most popular search engines and other services collecting their money from the user. For now, this is not possible (at least on a large scale) and so the public benefits freely. You may, however, begin to see things like "electronic money" become popular that would provide a way to transfer dollars into Internet cash that can be billed by a service provider. This already exists, albeit on a small scale.

Another way that Internet sites support themselves is by charging users a membership fee. Joining is required to access certain parts of the Web site. So, for example, once you have joined as a member, you are given an access code required to see publicly restricted parts of the site. An example of this is the electric library (http://www.elibrary.com/), an enormous database of articles from publications that can be accessed by the Internet, but used only if you are a paying member. These sites, however, are rare. Do not worry about "accidentally" entering one. You cannot be charged or billed without your knowledge and agreement. Some charging sites may offer particular information as a "sample" of their content, or allow free trial memberships to allow you to test them out first, so you can be encouraged to visit any of them without hesitation about the possible costs.

In short, the Internet economy today is in a state of experimentation, and what it will be in the future is unclear. Will the majority of useful services and features be free with the costs funded by advertising (as we see on public television), or will we be charged for every service as used (such as we are when we use our phones), or instead, will we have to sign on to memberships in every useful site paying annually for their services? Perhaps it will work more like cable TV, with our Internet providers charging rates or "packages" that include accessibility to some useful sites, but not to others.

Understanding the Internet economy is a part of understanding what it is, what it can do, and what it will become. And it is hard to imagine the Internet "industry" not becoming a major part of our economy with hundreds of billions of dollars in direct and indirect revenue some day soon. It is quite unclear how (or if) the Internet will serve to improve business. One thing that seems clear, however, is that the business of the Internet will only thrive if it is profitable. This is to say that not everything that can be done via the Internet and that is useful to someone will be done if it produces insufficient revenue. Thus, the economic issues have an effect on the content of the Internet. Consider what this will mean. Will it mean that the distribution of pornography, access to gambling on-line, and commercialism will be the bread and butter of the Internet, making it merely a convenient vehicle for economic exploitation? Or will other, perhaps more altruistic, sites also generate enough attraction to be economically valuable, for example, voting, educational information, and access to social services?

In addition to the content, the economic issues will likely have an impact on accessibility. Will the Internet become a resource primarily available and used by the advantaged in our society, serving perhaps to widen the gap between the rich and the poor? Or will it instead be universally accessible, helping to narrow the gap so that some of the same advantages and access to resources are available to all instead of only the wealthy?

For example, will populations that might most benefit from the educationally enriching opportunities, the access to resources, and the empowerment of greater communications be excluded from the Internet as being beyond their financial means, or will they be included as a way to improve their lives and overcome the disadvantage of poverty? In what cases should the government fund Internet projects?

Today, a computer is considered a luxury item, and many would find it hard to imagine it as a necessity. Will that be the case tomorrow? Why not? A stripped down Internet-ready version could perhaps in a few years, through mass production, be purchased for a few hundred dollars. Will the government set up a program to provide "Internet stamps" to finance hardware, software, and Internet Service Provider fees for those who are "income challenged"? Farfetched as it may seem, government may step in with tax credits, subsidies, and loans to promote a goal of universal Internet access. The economic and educational benefits to the nation may justify this. One thing is certain to us: The Internet is not the Hoola-hoop of the end of the 20th century. In some form, everyone will have a stake in its development.

All of these questions show the importance of having all of us involved in thinking about the Internet economy. Those who manage non-profit organizations should have a strong interest in making sure that economic factors do not serve as the only guide to the Internet's direction, but that social policy is also weighed into it. As the conscience of our communities, we are also in a position to advocate, as appropriate, for Internet services, Internet freedoms, and Internet rights and responsibilities on behalf of the public we serve, and our communities.

For these reasons, keep a watchful eye on the direction of the Internet in all of its forms, whether economic, or otherwise. It is here that you have something of great value to offer the Internet, even if you are a technological novice yourself.

Essay: That's It?

By *Robert Tell*

"That's it?" is the typical response when I show someone the World Wide Web for the first time. They have come to catch a glimpse of the Information Superhighway, that rumored, incredible convergence of information, technology, and art that is the beginning of a new world order, but instead they find themselves looking at a picture of a student's dog in Ohio. Just as typical is open-mouthed awe with seeing a Web site (particularly one that is designed attractively) for the first time, using a "graphical user interface" (GUI) browser like Netscape, compared to a text-based browser. And where else might you expect to find the entire text of a U.S. Supreme Court opinion that was handed down yesterday? Certainly not in your morning paper.

The Web can be a phantasmagoria of sight and sounds (can smell be technologically possible?) or can be rather anticlimactic. When you heard about the Web for the first time, it may have sounded like the ultimate reference tool where you could look up any fact and get all the latest news, and, in many cases, it's true—you can. At least if you know where to look.

The Web is completely disorganized. Eventually, you will find the information that you want, but before you do, you will have to read boring and tedious descriptions of people you don't really care about. Of course, that's after waiting a couple of minutes for a very large picture to download. The problem with the Web is that anyone can create a page that's accessible to millions with about as much effort as it's taking me to write this. Any crank has an instant platform to inflict his or her particular and sometimes twisted view of reality on the rest of us.

Cyberspace is a mirror of the society that developed and uses it. It has crime and virtue, deception and genuineness, love and hate, passion and indifference, heroism and cowardice. And it is a rare day that I spend a few hours surfing the Internet that I don't find at least one posting that puts a smile on my face.

This is the Web's problem, but it is also its strength. Whatever your passion or cause, you can create a page that is accessible to an incredible number of people. The Web is the Digital Age's printing press, and just as Thomas Paine provoked the colonies with *Common Sense*, an individual can provoke "the Web" with his or her own digital manifesto. Rumors (such as the many about viruses, true and imagined) and conspiracy theories (for example, what caused the crash of TWA Flight 800) flourish on the Web. And jokes that took months to saturate through the fabric of society after a first airing on Letterman now take days.

Some large corporations and agencies have put together some really impressive Web sites. But there are sites equally as impressive that have been put together by individuals or small groups. This raises one word of caution about the legitimacy of the information you read on the Web and the importance of knowing your source and its reputation for dependability and accuracy.

As you wander the Web, it is not always apparent whether a particular page has been put together by a large organization or an individual. In fact, the Web is really driven by individuals. Companies are scrambling to set up Web pages, while individuals all over the world have well-established pages that incorporate all of the latest features and technology. In this respect, particularly, the Web has the potential to be a great equalizer. For the first time, an individual can present his or her own views on an equal footing with large organizations.

The Web is therefore both an opportunity and a responsibility for non-profit managers. It is a new tool for advocating and educating. It's also a new arena in which many voices are still being left unheard. Non-profit managers can utilize the Web not only to better their work, but also to speak for those who don't—yet—have access to the Web. The Internet may well be the beginning of a new world order, and non-profit organizations that, perhaps more than any other types of business organizations, are on the front lines of meeting human service needs must make sure that it becomes even more inclusive.

So, the next time you set out to wander the Web and you start to think to yourself, "That's it?" say instead, "That's it!"

"I'm advertising my new business on the Web. For $25 an hour, I'll come to your house, lick your face, listen intently, wag my tail and be your best friend."

Appendix A

General Internet Tips & Netiquette

1. Periodically delete your Web browser's caché file. If you are not sure how to do this, read the documentation that came with the browser software, or ask your Internet Service Provider.
2. Don't send e-mail that you would be embarrassed to see on the front page of the *New York Times*.
3. Routinely and frequently scan your hard drive for viruses.
4. Don't, even jokingly, use the Internet to make threats, slander (or libel) others, spread rumors, or use in a manner that violates the law.
5. Do not use obscene, abusive, or threatening language in your e-mail messages and other postings.
6. Do not send chain messages.
7. Do not broadcast an e-mail message to hundreds of people who are not likely to appreciate receiving it.
8. Do not post blatantly commercial messages on the Internet.
9. Don't post the work of others (including their personal e-mail messages) without obtaining their permission, or obtaining a license to do so.
10. Don't post a response to a question to an entire mailing list when an e-mail to the poser of the question is more appropriate.
11. Do not "flame" (send insulting and/or abusive messages) on the Internet or respond to those that do.
12. If you are on vacation or otherwise off-line for an extended period of time, unsubscribe from your mailing lists, unless you have space in your mailbox for thousands of messages and the time to read them.
13. If you are unsubscribing or subscribing, make sure you are doing so to the correct address rather than to the list itself. Save the instructions on how to unsubscribe, and follow them.
14. Never send e-mail under someone else's name/account without their knowledge and authorization.
15. Use sarcasm and humor sparingly; it doesn't usually translate well in a text-only environment.
16. Don't use your business e-mail account for personal use.
17. If you send out broadcast e-mail to your own personal list and someone asks to be deleted from your list, honor that request and don't take it personally.
18. If you have "call waiting" service, make sure you have disabled it before going on-line.

Appendix B
How to Set Up Your Own WWW Page

Commercial services are available to design and administer World Wide Web pages for a fee. With a minimum of technical background, you can do your own. The software that is used to create Web pages ranges from free software available by downloading from the Internet, to simple HTML editors available commercially, to WYSIWYG ("what you see is what you get") programs like Microsoft® *Front Page* or Adobe *Pagemill*, to even high end professional programs. If you know the HTML codes to insert, you can even prepare a World Wide Web page entirely in Windows Notepad or other programs that create ASCII files, which consist entirely of text characters.

Among the types of information that can be found on typical World Wide Web pages of non-profits are:

- newsletters
- annual reports
- press releases
- brochures
- how to contribute or volunteer
- financial data
- action alerts
- job openings
- information about board and staff members
- publications
- upcoming conferences and seminars
- product catalogs and order forms
- the organization's e-mail address, and
- links to other organizational and government-based home pages related to the mission and purpose of the organization

Step 1. Identify your server.

Before setting up the page, it is helpful to decide which server to use. The server is the computer where your Web site files physically reside. It should be accessible 24 hours a day. There are several choices:

1. *In-house server.* If you work at a university, there will likely be a server available for you to use through the campus computing center. Likewise, if you work for a large non-profit organization, there may be resources to set up an in-house computer as a Web server.

2. *An on-line service.* Most commercial services, such as America OnLine (AOL), now offer their subscribers space for a small Web site, included in the subscription price.

3. *Internet Service Provider.* Many local and national Internet service providers offer home pages for their subscribers. There may be an additional fee, or the Web space may be included in the Internet access account fee.

4. *Web-hosting services.* These are companies that specialize in "renting" Web space on their servers, often at reasonable prices. Many of these companies advertise in the back of *NetGuide* and other computer magazines. Some commercial (and non-commercial) organizations offer non-profit organizations free or reduced-fee space for home pages.

Some of the issues you need to resolve include the cost, limits on how many bytes are allowed for the Web site files, the process by which the files are updated (can you do this yourself from a remote computer, or do you upload the file to your ISP and the ISP puts it on-line when he or she gets around to it?), and whether the server provides you with a way to determine the number of "hits" and other statistics.

Some of the other issues you should consider when choosing a server include limits on commercial use, whether the server supports encryption software, whether access and availability is reasonable, extras offered such as site counters and site search engines, and the availability of experienced technical support.

There are many organizations that provide free space for non-profit organizations, or do so for a modest charge. There are directories available on the Internet that list hundreds of these. We suggest:

The Contact Center: http://www.contact.org/orgs/frspace.htm and
Peter Scott (Northern Lights Internet Solutions): http://www.lights.com/freenet

Step 2. Determine the Content and WWW Design

What are you trying to communicate, and who is your audience? Are you willing to sacrifice the time required for users to access your page in exchange for lots of flashy graphics? Do you need to use animation, lots of color, and breathtaking graphics to attract visitors, or is plain vanilla information enough? What is the purpose of the site? To attract clients or members? To get new donors? To recruit volunteers? To provide a public service? All of the above?

If you create a site, consider whether others would want to visit it and why. Are you creating a site to ask for donations for your organization? If that is all, then do not be too surprised if you get few visitors. This is not to say that you cannot and should not seek donations on your Web site. You have to be a bit subtle about it. You perhaps need to include information resources that are beneficial to the visitor.

Typically, you will start with a home page that serves as a table of contents, with your logo, address, telephone number, e-mail address, and links to other Web pages—maybe one for each of the above purposes. To give you a head start on a constructive and efficient design, look at the pages of other organizations that you find attractive and effective. Then look at the source code, or HTML code, of those pages to see how they achieved the effect that you liked. Software, such as Web Fetch or Wing Flyer, is designed to capture all of the HTML source code that created a page (but beware, these files may be copyrighted). Even without this software, the HTML file of every page you view with your browser is captured byte for byte in a file in the caché subdirectory of your communications program's directory. Since HTML is compatible with ASCII (which is the basis for text files), you can view these files in Windows® Notepad or any word processing program. Simply open up the file in either of these programs.

If you are using Netscape Navigator as your browser, you can open the View menu and click on "Document Source" to see the coding for any page.

Step 3. Convert your files to HTML.

Inexpensive (or even free) software is available to convert conventional document files to HTML format. You also can do it manually by placing HTML codes where they belong.

Each HTML file should include the following:

```
<HTML>
<HEAD><TITLE>Insert title here</TITLE></HEAD>
<BODY>insert rest of page here</BODY>
</HTML>
```

As you can see, HTML codes often are in pairs. There is a code at the beginning and a code at the end of words to which the code is applied. The beginning code is enclosed by an open caret and closed caret. The code at the end is enclosed by an open caret followed by a forward slash, and ends with a closed caret.

Background colors can be changed from the default white by placing codes within the <body> code. For example, using Body Bgcolor=A5 2A 2A will make the background brown.

Headings can be sized by adding the tag <hx>insert text here</hx>, where x is a positive whole number from 1 to 6 (small to large).

Paragraph/line breaks. A line break code (<br>) will start the text that follows on a new line without adding space above or below the line. A paragraph break code (<p>) will place the text that follows this code on a new line, with a space between the previous line and the new line, making a new paragraph. There is no need to put a line break at the end of each line within a paragraph—the lines will automatically wrap. The line break is used when you need a "hard return" after a partial line, such as in an address or a poem.

Other commonly used text codes include:

<center>insert text to be centered </center>
<b>insert text to be made bold</b>
<I>insert text to be italicized</I>
<font color="RGB" Size=n>insert text to have a font or color change
<Font> where RGB is the color code and n is a number between -7 and 7 which is greater or less than the baseline font size.
<blockquote>insert text here to be indented from both margins</blockquote>
<HR> creates a horizontal line
<HR WIDTH=X% Align=Y SIZE=Z> creates a line where x is the % proportion of page width, Y is the position (left, center or right), and Z is the thickness of the line.

Ordered lists are sequentially numbered items. The list is begun and ended by <OL>insert items to be listed</OL>. Each item that is part of the list is enclosed by the tag <LI>insert item</ LI>. Using this tag places a number in front of each item.

Unnumbered lists are bulleted items. The list is begun and ended by <UL>insert items to be bulleted</UL>. Each item that is to be preceded by a bullet is tagged in the same way as an ordered list.

Links

As we discussed before, there are several basic kinds of links that appear on Web pages. Here is how some of these look in HTML code:

Links to a local file. This is a link to a file within the same directory (and within the same Web site) being linked from. It appears on the browser in a different color than other text. The tag for accomplishing this in the body of text is:

<A HREF="name of file.html">the text that you want to appear on the page</A>

Links to other HTML pages:
<A HREF="http://fullURL">name of page</A>
This type of link sends the viewer to another Web page, which can be within the same Web site or part of another site.

Links to e-mail:
<A HREF="MAILTO:gary.grobman@paonline.com">Send mail to Gary</A>
This type of link provides a form for the viewer to send e-mail to you or someone else in your organization.

Links to graphics files:
<IMG SRC "nameofgraphicsfile.GIF" height=xxx width=yyy> where x and y are integers
This type of link puts a graphic on the Web page.

You can put together an attractive Web page without being any more sophisticated than using the above tags. For the more adventurous, there are languages other than HTML, such as JAVA, which is used to provide animations on your page.

There are plenty of reference books on how to design and construct a WWW page, and there are also lots of Web sites that explain the basics, including:

The Contact Center (http://www.contact.org/tools/computer.htm)

There are also sites for World Wide Web clip art and CGI scripts (used as templates for guest books, counters, surveys, and other forms for your pages). Among them are:

A+ Art (http://aplusart.simplenet.com/aplusart/index.html)
Here, you can download copyright-free icons, bullets, animations, clip art, backgrounds, and bars.

Nuthin' But Links (http://pages.prodigy.com/bombadil/advanced.htm)

There are links to sites here where you can find HTML tutorials, Web page graphics, animated GIFs, tools for determining colors, JAVA resources, CGI scripts, counters, guest books, and almost anything else you may need to build and enhance the attractiveness of your Web site.

Barry's Clip Art Server (http://www.barrysclipart.com/)

This site has a searchable and indexed database of hundreds of downloadable, copyright-free images.

The following pages show a sample simple World Wide Web home page, and the HTML code that generated that page.

My Non-Profit Organization Home Page

(Insert Logo Here) ***This page was last updated: September 12, 1997***

Gary Grobman, Chairman
Gary Grant, Executive Director

The mission of My Non-Profit is to help non-profit organizations create simple World Wide Web pages.

Member agencies are:

- Organization 1
- Organization 2
- Organization 3
- Organization 4
- Organization 5
- Organization 6
- Organization 7
- Organization 8
- Organization 9
- Organization 10

My Non-Profit Organization publishes a number of publications, among which are the following:

1. My Non-Profit Organization brochure
2. My Non-Profit Organization FY 1998-99 Annual Report
3. My Non-Profit Organization Newsletter (August 1998)
4. My Non-Profit Organization Legislative Alert
5. My Non-Profit Organization Action Alert
6. How To Help My Non-Profit Accomplish Its Mission

- *Links Useful to Non-Profit Organizations:*

The Internet Nonprofit Center

Yahoo Internet search engine

Lycos Internet Search Engine

Library of Congress

The Foundation Center

The White House

Independent Sector

Handsnet

Contact My Non-Profit at:

My Non-Profit
2353 184th Avenue
Harrisburg, PA 17113
tel: (555) 888-1111
fax: (555) 888-1112

Send an e-mail message to My Non-Profit's Chairman, Gary Grobman

Send an e-mail message to My Non-Profit's Executive Director, Gary Grant

The URL for this page is: http://user.aol.com/garygpjc/nonproft.htm

copyright © 1997 by My Non-Profit

The following is the HTML file which created the sample home page which appears on page 121.

```
<HTML>
<HEAD><H1>My Non-Profit Organization Home Page</H1>
<TITLE>My Non-Profit Organization Home Page </TITLE>
</HEAD>
<BODY><IMG ALIGN=bottom SRC="logo.gif"><P>(Insert Logo Here)
<I><B>This page was last updated: September 12, 1997</B></I>
<P>
<center>Gary Grobman, Chairman<BR>
Gary Grant, Executive Director<P></center>
The mission of My Non-Profit is to help non-profit organizations create simple World Wide Web pages.<P>
Member agencies are:<P>
<UL>
<LI> Organization 1
<LI> Organization 2
<LI> Organization 3
<LI> Organization 4
<LI> Organization 5
<LI> Organization 6
<LI> Organization 7
<LI> Organization 8
<LI> Organization 9
<LI> Organization 10
</UL>
<p>
My Non-Profit Organization publishes a number of publications, among which are the following:<P>
<OL>
<LI><A HREF="brochure2.htm">My Non-Profit Organization brochure</A>
<LI><A HREF="annrepot2.htm">My Non-Profit Organization FY 1998-99 Annual Report</A>
<LI><A HREF="newsltr2.htm">My Non-Profit Organization Newsletter (August 1998)</A>
<LI><A HREF="choice2.htm"> My Non-Profit Organization Legislative Alert</A>
<LI><A HREF="exempt2.htm"> My Non-Profit Organization Action Alert</A>
<LI><A HREF="contribt.htm"> How To Help My Non-Profit Accomplish Its Mission</A>
</OL>
<HR>
<LI><I>Links Useful to Non-Profit Organizations:</I>
</UL>
<ol>
<P>
<A HREF="http://www.nonprofits.org">The Internet Nonprofit Center</A><p>
<A HREF="http://www.yahoo.com/">Yahoo Internet search engine</A><P>
<P>
<A HREF="http://www/lycos.cs.cmu.edu/">Lycos Internet Search Engine</A><P>
<A HREF="http://lcweb.loc.gov/homepage/lhp.html">Library of Congress</A><P>
<A HREF="http://www.fdncenter.org">The Foundation Center</A><P>
<A HREF="http://www.whitehouse.gov/">The White House</A><P>
<A HREF="http://www.indepsec.org">Independent Sector</A><P>
<A HREF="http://www.handsnet.org"/>Handsnet</A>
</ol><HR><P>
Contact My Non-Profit at:<p>
<I> My Non-Profit</I><BR>
<I>2353 184th Avenue</I><BR>
<I>Harrisburg, PA 17113</I><BR>
tel: (555) 888-1111<BR>
fax: (555) 888-1112<BR>
<A HREF="mailto:gary.grobman@paonline.com"><p>
Send an e-mail message to My Non-Profit's Chairman, Gary Grobman</A><p>
<A HREF="mailto: g-grant@uchicago.edu"><p>
Send an e-mail message to My Non-Profit's Executive Director, Gary Grant</A>
<P>
The URL for this page is: http://user.aol.com/garygpjc/nonproft.htm<P>
<P>
copyright &#169; 1997 by My Non-Profit </BODY>
</HTML>
```

Tips for Non-Profit Web Page Design

1. Frequently update the material on your site and make the content useful. Regardless of how "cool" your site looks, people won't return unless there is new information there on a regular basis.

2. Keep the design simple. People value their time, and graphics and special effects slow down browsers. Those who want to continually use your site don't want to have to search around each time because the design changes frequently.

3. Market what you are good at. If your organization's niche is in child advocacy, make your Web site the one-stop shopping place to find all of the information related to children, and don't stray too far from that.

4. If your organization depends on membership revenue, don't give out everything on your Web site. What is the incentive for individuals to become members if they receive the services for free just by logging in to your site?

5. Don't put information on the Web that you would be embarrassed to find on the front page of your local newspaper. For example, if you are calling for advocacy on a certain bill, don't disclose the strategy of the legislative coalition with which you are working.

6. Don't be shy about providing plenty of links to related organizations, including your statewide and national affiliates, and government sources of information. It is polite to request permission first from these sites, and virtually all of them will be thrilled to have as many links to their site as possible. It also enables them to keep a record of those who link to their sites, which is useful in case they change their URL which, now that virtual domains have become common (see page 124), is not unusual.

7. Don't put everything on your home page. Use it as a Table of Contents and introduction rather than as the body of the Web site. Use links to take your site's visitors to internal files, such as brochure, newsletter, message from the President, advocacy corner, board member list, and other files.

8. Place a text line on the home page letting viewers know when the page was last updated.

9. Place links at the bottom of each Web page to return to the home page and to send e-mail to the Webmaster (or executive director) of the organization.

10. Provide a place on the home page for a link to a text-only version of your pages. If you are using sophisticated animations or frames, the page may be inaccessible to those using outdated browsers.

11. Simplify your domain name as much as you can (see page 124).

12. Publicize your site on all of the popular search engines. Point your browser to these search engines (see page 84) for information on how to register your site.

13. Make sure that you do not post material that is copyrighted by others without obtaining written permission, and be sure to place a copyright notice on your own material on your Web site (see page 90).

Domain Names

Every computer connected to the Internet has a unique Internet Protocol (IP) address. These addresses look like four numbers, separated by a period (207.44.25.233, for example). When you connect to another computer over the Internet, your computer needs to know the IP. However, IPs are too difficult to remember, for the most part. A system has been developed to provide more memorable addresses, called domain names. Once you get used to this system, domain names become easy to remember. In addition, you can tell a lot from the domain name—the type of organization, the geographical location, and often the name of the user. A domain name is the part of the Internet address after the "@" sign. For example, our personal e-mail addresses are: gary.grobman@paonline.com and g-grant@uchicago.edu. Paonline and the University of Chicago are our respective Internet Service Providers (ISPs), ".com" indicates that it is a commercial provider, and ".edu" indicates an academic provider. However, we could, for a fee, have one of these changed to: gary.grobman@Npinternethandbook.com for purposes of getting e-mail messages and orders relating to this book, assuming no one else has taken the domain name "Npinternethandbook" already.

Most domain name suffixes tell you something about the type of organization, and the last extension often indicates the country code (see page 32).

Obtaining a Domain Name

Let's say you are setting up a Web site, and your Web space is being provided by a company called "Yourweb." YourWeb is a reseller for space on a server at "Myweb." Your site's URL may look like this:

http://www.myweb.com/~yourweb/yourorganization/home.html

If YourWeb allows its customers to have "virtual domain" space, your site's URL could be shortened to the easier to remember and more distinctive:

http://www.yourorganization.org

There are registration fees charged for setting up virtual domains, in addition to the fee for connecting to the Internet charged by your Internet Service Provider. Many organizations find the cost well worth it. Domain names are registered through the Internet Information Center (InterNIC). There is a $100 registration fee for the first two years and $50 annually after that, in addition to the fees charged by your provider(s).

Applications must be submitted electronically, by filling out a template on the World Wide Web site of InterNIC (http://www.rs.internic.net) or by FTP to the text version (ftp.rs.internic.net). If you do the latter, log on as anonymous and use "guest" as the password. You will need your name and address, the domain name you want to use (e.g., yourname.org) and the primary and secondary server Internet protocol number, which you can obtain from your ISP or Web space provider. Names are assigned on a first-come, first-served basis and are checked for prior use and for whether they are in some way objectionable. If this sounds too complicated, check with your server; many will do all of this work for an additional fee.

Appendix C

State Home Pages on the World Wide Web

Alabama
http://alaweb.asc.edu

Alaska
http://www.state.ak.us

Arizona
http://www.state.az.us

Arkansas
http://www.state.ar.us

California
http://www.state.ca.us

Colorado
http://www.state.co.us

Connecticut
http://www.state.ct.us

Delaware
http://www.state.de.us

District of Columbia
http://www.dchomepage.net/dcmain

Florida
http://www.state.fl.us

Georgia
http://www.state.ga.us

Hawaii
http://www.state.hi.us

Idaho
http://www.state.id.us

Illinois
http://www.state.il.us

Indiana
http://www.state.in.us

Iowa
http://www.state.ia.us

Kansas
http://www.state.ks.us

Kentucky
http://www.state.ky.us

Louisiana
http://www.state.la.us

Maine
http://www.state.me.us

Maryland
http://www.state.md.us

Massachusetts
http://www.state.ma.us

Michigan
http://www.migov.state.mi.us/

Minnesota
http://www.state.mn.us

Mississippi
http://www.state.ms.us

Missouri
http://www.state.mo.us

Montana
http://www.mt.us

Nebraska
http://www.state.ne.us

Nevada
http://www.state.nv.us

New Hampshire
http://www.state.nh.us

New Jersey
http://www.state.nj.us

New Mexico
http://www.state.nm.us

New York
http://www.state.ny.us

North Carolina
http://www.state.nc.us

North Dakota
http://www.state.nd.us

Ohio
http://www.state.oh.us

Oklahoma
http://www.state.ok.us

Oregon
http://www.state.or.us

Pennsylvania
http://www.state.pa.us

Rhode Island
http://www.state.ri.us

South Carolina
http://www.state.sc.us

South Dakota
http://www.state.sd.us

Tennessee
http://www.state.tn.us

Texas
http://www.state.tx.us

Utah
http://www.state.ut.us

Vermont
http://www.state.vt.us

Virginia
http://www.state.va.us

Washington
http://www.state.wa.us

West Virginia
http://www.state.wv.us

Wisconsin
http://www.state.wi.us

Wyoming
http://www.state.wy.us

Appendix D
A Short Course on Copyright Issues

Copyright owners are granted the exclusive rights to reproduce a work, to modify it (such as by creating what is termed a "derivative" work), to distribute it, and to perform or otherwise show it to the public. A copyright is a government-sanctioned legal right (referenced in the U.S. Constitution in Article I, Section 8) for the creator of a work to maintain the exclusive right to copies and/or publication of that work. It is federal law, and thus the rights associated with copyrights do not vary among the states. The work must be something tangible and creative. Thus, it can't be an idea, nor can it be a collection of facts (although if the way a collection of facts is put together is itself creative, then this compilation can be eligible for copyright protection). But it can be a photograph, a Usenet posting, a piece of art, or this book. No special registration is required for a work to be copyrighted. You can't legally take photographs or cartoons from magazines without prior permission and scan them for use in your organization's Web page.

This legal protection is bestowed automatically on every work created in the United States after April 1, 1989. This means that even if you see a document on a Web site (or anywhere else) that lacks the copyright symbol, it is still copyright-protected, unless the creator explicitly states that the work is intended to be in the public domain.

There are, are course, legal advantages to formally registering a work with the Copyright Office (with a $20 fee), and registration is necessary in the event that you want to recover economic damages from copyright infringement.

A copyright lasts until 50 years after the work's creator dies. This means that you could post the entire set of Shakespeare's plays on a Web page (as has been done) and not have to worry about copyright infringement.

Prior to the ratification of the North American Free Trade Agreement and the Uruguay Round Agreements Act (P.L. 103-465), once a work was in the public domain, the creator could never regain the copyright rights. These two documents provided some exceptions.

It makes sense to use a copyright symbol on works you want protected, although in theory, this is not really necessary. This is done by putting on the work a © (insert year of copyright) by (insert name of creator). If you are truly risk-averse concerning the work, you should register it with the Copyright Office.

You can be charged with infringement whether you use a work for commercial or non-commercial purposes, although the purpose could affect the damages that could be recovered from you by the creator of the work.

Copyright protection is not absolute. For example, under the "fair use" doctrine, a person may, without permission, make limited use of portions of a work. This often occurs in quoting one book for use in another, or making copies of part of a work to distribute in schools, for example. This doctrine, as interpreted by the Register of Copyrights in a 1961 report, permits limited use of copyrighted material used in the "quotation of excerpts in a review or criticism for purposes of illustration or comment; quotation of short passages in a scholarly or technical work, for illustration or clarification of the author's observations; use in a parody of some of the content of the work parodied; summary of an address or article, with brief quotations, in a news report; reproduction by a library of a portion of a work to replace part of a damaged copy; reproduction by a teacher or student of a small part of a work to illustrate a lesson; reproduction of a work in legislative or judicial proceedings or reports; incidental and fortuitous reproduction, in a newsreel or broadcast, of a work located in the scene of an event being reported."

In most cases, the quote or excerpt must be attributed to the creator, and must be such that the commercial value of the work is not harmed.

Public domain

This term refers to works that are not protected by copyright. It includes works created before copyright protection existed, works created by government employees in the scope of their employment, works once protected by copyright that has since expired, simple facts and figures, and works that the creator permits to be in the public domain.

For the most part, creators of works desire to have their works seen by as many people as possible. If you want to put something on your Web site that is the work of another person, it makes sense to simply ask him or her for permission (but get this in writing, even if it is an e-mail message response). If the creator is not willing to grant permission for free, the offer of a few dollars may make the difference. If it is an article written by a college professor, it certainly has a better chance of getting free permission than if the work was written by a free-lance writer who makes a living from, in part, electronic distribution of his or her work.

When in doubt, ask. Copyright infringement law is changing; what once was restricted to the civil damages arena is slowly evolving to the criminal arena, and some violations are likely to be felonies by the time you read this. Even if you win a case, the risk is time, legal resources, and a lot of sleepless nights.

Up Close: Hyde Park/Kenwood Community Conference (http://www.hydepark.org/)

One effective example of building support for a non-profit through the Internet is reflected in the fledgling efforts of The Hyde Park/Kenwood Community Conference. At present, the conference—maintained by a community organization—doesn't seek contributions on-line. As a local group, it has a narrow reach, and people in the community wouldn't have a reason to visit the site unless they were already involved in the organization.

Hyde Park/Kenwood obtained free server space donated by a company, Ganymede Inc., which is recognized at the Web site.

With this server space, the organization offers to establish a "beginning" Web site for any non-profit or business member as a part of membership. Small-budget non-profits can have a Web site built by the organization's volunteer designers at no cost; all others pay a small fee. Businesses and organizations with existing Web sites can join as "link" members, supporting the organization and in return being linked to its directory.

Free consultation is provided to members seeking to develop more elaborate Web sites. Through these services, and by organizing a community directory, HP/KCC helps organize a Web site where community members and potential visitors can access existing on-line information and resources in a single place.

In addition, over time, Hyde Park/Kenwood is using the Web site to enhance its own mission—improving the quality of life in the community and increasing participation by all community members in the decisions, policies, and issues that affect them.

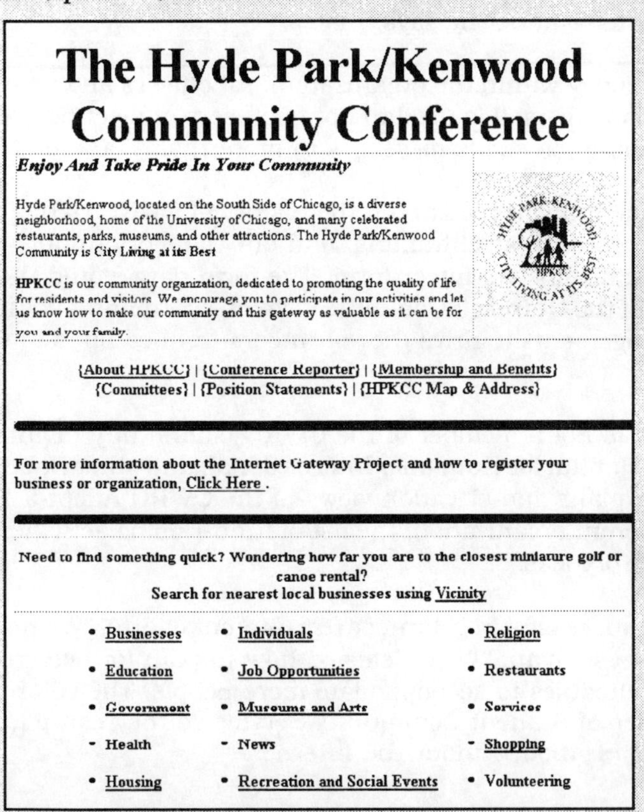

Hyde Park/Kenwood Community Conference home page.
Courtesy HP/KCC. Reprinted with permission.

Up Close: Habitat for Humanity-Case Western Reserve University Chapter (http://www.cwru.edu/orgs/ habhum/homc.html)

Patrick W. Glynn, a full-time student, is the Publicity Committee chair and Web Site Maintainer for Case Western Reserve University's Habitat for Humanity chapter. The site, which logs almost 150 hits daily, was the brainchild of David Kaelber, now a liaison for Greater Cleveland Habitat for Humanity, who was a top officer of the CWRU chapter at the time.

Kaelber began the site in February 1995. Case Western Reserve University provides free server space for recognized student organizations, so startup costs were minimal.

"CWRU provides free high-speed Internet access for students from their dormitories," says Glynn. "Since CWRU is a very 'wired' campus, most students have computers in their rooms. Consequently, our Web site and e-mai listserver have become central tools for publicizing events and attracting new volunteers."

During the academic year, Glynn updates the Web site from his dorm room once weekly or more often. "It's convenient and easy," he says. "I usually update the on-line schedule within a few hours of returning to my room from an event. Through FTP, I can continue to make changes from my home in Northern Virginia although CWRU is in Cleveland."

Glynn is currently analyzing the usage statistics to determine which documents are accessed most frequently The results will assist in long-term planning of the site's content. "I plan to scan in more photos of volunteers working at the Habitat for Humanity construction site and participating in other events to 'personalize' th organization for Web site visitors," he says.

The site enhances efficiency within the organization. All officers and nearly all volunteers of the organizatio have Internet connections. E-mail is used to notify officers of meetings, and volunteers of special events an group meetings. A mailing list sends messages to more than 700 e-mail addresses.

On the Web site, a student might read about the history of CWRU Habitat for Humanity, look at photograph of other students working with steel framing, find out that "drywalling" is on the construction schedule fc Saturday, or fill out an on-line volunteer form. The form data would then be automatically e-mailed to th appropriate members of the Outreach Committee, which coordinates volunteers. It would also go to an office who would make arrangements to drive the volunteers from campus to the construction site in a universit van.

A Web site visitor who is not a member of the CWRU community might find the links to Greater Clevelan Habitat for Humanity, Habitat for Humanity International, and other Habitat-related pages useful. Or he or sh might look at the floor plans and elevation views of the CWRU Adopt-a-House. If the visitor is from anoth Habitat group or a different organization, the list of fund-raising activities and amounts raised through the might be a good source of ideas.

The site has been very successful in volunteer recruitment efforts. "We now have so many volunteers, we hav to turn some away," says Glynn. "We've learned how to plan for overcrowding at the construction site ar reconsider our work schedules to accommodate more people. The volunteers we have to turn away we ref to the university's Office of Student Community Service so they can participate in other projects. Frankly, can't imagine this organization without the Internet."

Please note our new URL: http://www.cwru.edu/orgs/habhum/home.html

Habitat for Humanity

Case Western Reserve University • Habitat for Humanity Campus Chapter
10900 Euclid Avenue • Cleveland, Ohio 44106-7103

No Java(TM) Version of this Page

Events Calendar

INFORMATION	GET INVOLVED!	ARCHIVES
Introduction	How?	Wall of Fame
Work Schedule	Register for e-mail list	Pictures
Meeting Minutes	**Sign up to Volunteer!**	CWRU Adopt-A-House I
Officers	Contact Us	CWRU Adopt-A-House II

CWRU Office of Student Community Service
Habitat for Humanity International
Greater Cleveland Habitat for Humanity
Don't live in Cleveland? Find a Habitat for Humanity Affiliate Near You!
Habitat for Humanity Home(page)s Around the World
Habitat for Humanity Gift Shop

 Search CWRU HFH web site

 Statistics for CWRU HFH web site

31 August 1997

ACADEMICS | DEPARTMENTS | COMPUTING | CAMPUS LIFE | LIBRARIES | INDEX
WELCOME! | ADMISSIONS | ALUMNI | CLEVELAND | NEWS | DIRECTORY | SEARCH

Patrick Glynn (pwg@po.cwru.edu) -- About this server -- Copyright 1994-97 CWRU -- Unauthorized use prohibited

Case Western Reserve University Chapter, Habitat for Humanity home page. Courtesy Case Western Reserve University Chapter, Habitat for Humanity. Reprinted with permission.

PART 2

Reviews of Web Sites of Interest to Non-Profit Organizations

"Warning: If you keep your web browser at Hot Site Of The Day for too long, your computer may overheat. If this happens, link immediately to Cool Site Of The Day."

INTERNET NON-PROFIT URL LISTINGS AND REVIEWS

Note: *Unattributed quotes within these reviews that describe the purpose of organizations are taken from these organizations' Web sites.*

A. Our top 20 sites of specific and general interest to non-profit organizations (in alphabetical order):

Chronicle of Philanthropy
http://www.philanthropy.com

The site provides highlights from this publication, which is the trade journal for America's charitable community. The tabloid format biweekly is the number one source for charity leaders, fund-raisers and grant makers, and the Web site provides more than just a taste of what its subscribers receive in snail mail every two weeks. The site is updated every other week at 9 a.m. on the Monday before the issue date, and job announcements are updated on the Monday following that. The principal categories of this site are gifts and grants, fund-raising, managing non-profit groups, and technology. Each of these headings is further divided by a news summary, workshops and seminars, and deadlines. Also on the site are front page news stories, a news summary, conferences, Internet resources, products and services, and jobs. Most of the articles consist of one-sentence summaries but are still useful, particularly if you don't have the $69 in your budget to subscribe to the publication for a year. The "Jobs" button transports you to a searchable database of hundreds of positions available. In some respects, this searchability makes the Internet version of the *Chronicle* more useful than the conventional version. There is also a handy directory of "Products and Services."

The Contact Center's IdeaList
http://www.idealist.org/tools/tools.htm

This site is a great resource. It contains a searchable database of 10,000 non-profit organizations (you can click on a form to add your organization to the database), a page on "Computing and the

Internet" with links to free and low cost servers, publications on Web site development, HTML tutorials, and a list of organizations that offer free products and services to charities. The "Tools for Nonprofits" button transports you to the *Computing and the Internet* page, *Employment and Internship Opportunities*, and *Fundraising*. The fund-raising page includes application forms for several grants and a "Proposal Writing Short Course." There are plenty of links to other organizations, although they are not attractively organized. The directory is organized geographically and by the organizations' areas of focus. Non-profits that ask to be included in the directory are requested to make a $25 voluntary contribution, but otherwise the site is free.

The Council of Better Business Bureau's Philanthropic Advisory Service
http://www.bbb.org

The mission of the Better Business Bureau (BBB) is to "promote and foster the highest ethical relationship between businesses and the public." This site has a searchable database, as well as a resource library of publications and other files with links to other organizations. There are on-line complaint forms, files relating to marketplace ethics, "Standards for Charitable Solicitation," a Code of Advertising, and a directory of local BBB Councils. The "Reports on the Most Asked-About Charities" (124 of them as of September 1997) provide in detail how they meet the standards of the Council's Standards for Charitable Solicitation. Also included is information about the charity's programs, governance, budgets, staff, and sources of funding. There are alerts about the latest scams. We found this site interesting, if not fascinating. Put this on your "must visit" list.

Council on Foundations
http://www.cof.org

The Council on Foundations, founded in 1949, is a non-profit membership organization of approximately 1,500 grant-making foundations and corporations whose members control $139 billion in assets. The site has a Community Foundation Locator, which includes a map of the United States that permits you to identify the name and location of approximately 300 of the 400 community foundations that are COF members. Clicking on the *Headlines* icon links to Legislative and Public Policy Watch issue papers (unfortunately the one we found was almost a year out-of-date). The site offers information about the Council's useful, but pricey, publications. Most of the files are directly useful to foundations, but should be of interest to those who seek grants from them as well. At the time of this review, there were files entitled "Developing a Travel Policy," "First Steps in Starting a Foundation," and "Foundations and Lobbying: Safe Ways to Affect Public Policy," for example. The site is searchable, and has been redesigned since our initial review.

The Foundation Center
http://fdncenter.org/

The Foundation Center is an independent non-profit information clearinghouse established in 1956. The Center's mission is "to foster public understanding of the foundation field by collecting, organizing, analyzing, and disseminating information on foundations, corporate giving, and related subjects." It is the recipient of *NetGuide's Gold Site* award and several other prestigious accolades. Our only complaint is that there are large files for its graphics, so the pages tend to load more slowly than most others. But they must have heard us kvetching, because unobtrusively, there is a place to click for the "no frills" low bandwidth site, which makes the pages fly like an arrow. If you are looking for grants, this site may be the number one resource on the 'Net (look under "Grantmaker Information"). You can perform searches (by subject or geographic keyword) relating to foundations and corporate and charitable grantmakers and get links to these organizations. The Foundation Center has information on more than 40,000 grantmaking foundations and corporate programs in its database. Subscribers can access this on-line. In addition, there are links to more than 180 foundations with Web sites.

Click on the home page's "Reference Desk" and see: "Welcome to the Foundation Center's Electronic Reference Desk. This is the section of our site where we answer your questions about foundations, nonprofit resources, and our own services." Almost as friendly as our neighborhood librarian. The Reference Desk has three components: a list of frequently asked questions, an On-line Librarian, and a comprehensive directory of links.

The FAQ (Frequently Asked Questions) file answers 26 general questions of interest with not only good information but also links to additional resources on the WWW (such as "Where can I find information on volunteerism?"). There are questions and answers that directly relate to the Foundation Center, and many more of general interest to grantseekers.

Links at the reference desk are organized by the categories of: General Resources, Nonprofit Resources, Nonprofit Resources by Program Area, International Resources, Philanthropy Resources, Nonprofit Management, Nonprofit Fundraising, and Government Resources.

Also on the site is an abridged version of The Foundation Center's *Grants Classification Manual and Thesaurus*, (Internet Edition) and e-mail access to *Philanthropy News Digest*, the Foundation Center's award-winning on-line publication. This publication includes abstracts of philanthropy-related articles and feature stories. Current and back issues are available at this site.

Among other files are a Prospect Worksheet, a Proposal Writing Short Course, a Glossary, and Common Grant Application Forms. If we were giving out awards, this would get the highest one. Also, in order to assist small foundations in getting started on the Web, the Foundation Center provides Web space and assistance in building a Web page.

Goodwill Industries of America
http://www.goodwill.org/

Goodwill Industries is one of the world's largest providers of employment and training services for people with disabilities and barriers to employment. The searchable site links to its local affiliates, non-profit information sources, other charities, government offices, organizations and offices related to disabilities, and computer/Internet technical assistance and information. The president is well-known—Fred Grandy, who was a Gopher Server on *The Love Boat*. One of the most useful pages on the Internet is Goodwill's Estate Planning Menu. The Goodwill Industries Estate Planning Web site provides information on each of scores of topics of interest to fund-raisers, including, for example, those with the headings of Federal Estate Tax, Living Revocable Trust, Charitable Remainder Trust, Power of Attorney, and additional topics that serve as a veritable encyclopedia for charitable fund-raisers and their donors.

GuideStar
http://www.guidestar.org

GuideStar, administered by the Williamsburg, VA-based Philanthropic Research, Inc., publishes comprehensive reports about individual American charities. Its purpose is "to bring the actors in the philanthropic and nonprofit communities closer together through the use of information and communication technologies. GuideStar collects and analyzes operating and financial data from the IRS Form 990 and from voluntary submissions from the charities themselves." The database consists of more than 600,000 reports on individual charities, and the site is colorful, accessible, and well-designed. The database can be searched, at no charge, by any number of parameters, such as name, location, or type of charity. This is simply the best site on the 'Net for finding financial information about charities. Charities can provide their reports and update them on-line at no charge. The site also includes links of interest to charities, and essays about philanthropy via the "GuideStar Forum" button.

HandsNet (see page 66)
http://www.handsnet.org

Founded in 1987, HandsNet links 5,000 public interest and human services organizations using the Internet to promote collaboration, advocacy, and information-sharing by the sector. The public pages are updated daily, and the members only pages are considered to be the most valuable around for non-profits that engage in advocacy. The organization offers a free trial membership for 30 days. The subscription fee is much less for organizations that choose to access the service through the Internet site rather than through a separate dial-up service. The site's Action Alerts provide lots of government links, state-of-the-art information on current issues (most of which is provided by member organizations whose niche includes that particular public policy issue), capsule summaries, sources to find more information about the issue, sample advocacy letters, and information about new legislation. The pages are colorful with excellent graphics, but there is no sacrifice on substantive content. The *Weekly Digest* includes samples from hundreds of policy, program, and resource articles posted by members. The "Welfare Watch" button is a must-click for those interested in this hot issue, as it leads to information on the latest developments including public policy alerts, analyses, notices of new bills, rules and regulations, legislative studies and reports, new programs, *Federal Register* notices, funding information, and daily summaries of newspaper and wire services articles. The site also links to the Training and Resource Center, whose mission is to "provide leadership in helping human services organizations use new information technologies to embrace communication, information sharing and collaboration." If your organization can afford it (the basic annual membership fee is $300), joining should be a top priority. You will be returning several times each day, not only to access information, but to meet and begin collaborations with others.

Independent Sector (see pages 72-73)
http://www.indepsec.org

Founded in 1980, Independent Sector is a national coalition of 800 voluntary organizations, foundations, and corporate-giving programs that encourages philanthropy, volunteering, and citizen action. The site begins modestly with a simple home page with nine buttons: Members, Leadership, Research, Advocacy, What's New, Feedback, GIVE 5, About IS, and Links. The members-only links require a password, but there is plenty of useful material for non-members. The Leadership button links to documents on ethics and accountability, including a "Political Checklist of Accountability." While the Research button links to publications (most of which are for sale), there is also a file called "Did You Know" that has useful and informative general information about the non-profit sector, with links to other organizations that can provide more information. The Advocacy link takes you to press releases, public policy analyses, and useful links to government relations publications such as lobbying guides, information about permissible political activity by tax-exempt organizations, justification of the charitable tax exemption, and summaries of the new lobbying law. The Links button is a good place to start for finding other resources. The links are categorized by Advocacy and Public Policy, Philanthropic Research, Non-Profit Management, General Nonprofit Resources, and Other. The What's New button, at the time of this review, contained speeches about the sector, which we found current and useful. We recommend that every charity visit this site, which is in the process of being totally redesigned as we go to press, at least once a month.

The Internet Nonprofit Center
http://www.nonprofits.org

This site has been available since 1994 and was initially sponsored by the American Institute of Philanthropy. It has spun off as an independent non-profit corporation. The home page boasts that it has "information on more nonprofits than any other site in the world!" This is not hyperbole. It is clearly one of the most comprehensive and esthetically pleasing Internet Web sites for non-profits. The home page is divided into four sections:

Gallery of Organizations—features a non-profit locator to find almost any charity in the United States, a site for home pages of many non-profits, and information on how new non-profits can join.

Library—includes publications and data about non-profits and the non-profit sector compiled by third parties, and also includes files of ethical standards published by the National Charities Information Bureau and the New York Philanthropic Advisory Services organization.

Parlor—links to a site for live "chat," back issues of *Non-Profit News*, files on how to prepare World Wide Web pages, and how to find free or reduced space to post non-profit home pages.

Heliport—provides links to other Internet sites useful to non-profits.

MAP Blast
http://www.mapblast.com

Vicinity Corporation is the sponsor of this free mapping service. MapBlast! allows you to create, customize, and save easy-to-read digital maps pinpointing almost any location within the United States (except Alaska). You specify the location and MapBlast! launches the map. The resulting map can be zoomed in for detail, zoomed out for more geographical area to appear, and printed out. The maps include landmarks and can be e-mailed to anyone with a simple click of the mouse and filling out a form. The applications for non-profit organizations range from letting people know where your office is for a meeting to providing your staff with a helpful guide in navigating for home visits. The site's management permits its maps to be viewed and printed out for personal, non-commercial use. Read the license agreement for details. The Webmaster encourages you to *Save* the map, which provides you automatically with an HTML fragment to insert into your home Web page's files. "When you copy it to your Website, it will display your map and provide a hotlink to the Vicinity MapBlast! server, so you and your users can jump into the map and look around," promotes part of the MapBlast! page. The server says that the company is in the process of acquiring international maps. Detailed road maps are expected to be available by the time you read this. Of the more than 300 sites considered and/or reviewed for this book, this is the one that actually got an audible "cool" from us.

Meta-Index of Nonprofit Organizations
http://www.philanthropy-journal.org/plhome/plmeta.htm

This award-winning site was featured in America OnLine's Web Diner's *Best of the Non-profit Web*. It consists of hundreds of links to other non-profit organization home pages, as well as those of government, political parties, and international organizations.

Minnesota Council of Nonprofits **(see page 98)**
http://www.mncn.org

While much of this site is targeted to the needs of Minnesota non-profits (such as local grant information), it is an excellent resource for all. There is a *Non-profit Job Board* and a *Non-profit's Yellow Pages*. There are numerous and useful links to outside organizations that make this site an excellent resource for those interested in grants, foundations, government information, and general information useful to non-profits. The site also boasts a New Federalism Web page featuring topical discussion on welfare reform. MCNP can take pride that its site gives the major national non-profit advocacy organizations a run for their money in staking a claim to being the best gateway for valuable and current information, particularly with respect to how to start a new organization.

National Center for Nonprofit Boards
http://www.ncnb.org/home.html

The National Center for Nonprofit Boards (NCNB), is "the only nonprofit organization dedicated to building stronger nonprofit boards and stronger nonprofit organizations." This site has an FAQ (the answers to some of the questions, in our judgment, take a middle road on many controversial issues faced by boards, thus not satisfying anyone), an on-line form to raise additional questions to its Board Information Center with no charge (or access its 800 number), information about publications and membership, and information about the organization's workshops and courses. We recommend everyone involved in a non-profit read this FAQ, because even if it doesn't satisfactorily answer the questions, it raises the right questions and gives the pros and cons of various strategies to find an answer.

The NonProfit Gateway Network
http://www.nonprofit.gov

We were told about this site, initially dubbed the *U.S. Nonprofit Advisor,* during a visit to the White House in late 1996 to meet with the director of the White House Office of Public Liaison, Doris Matsui. We get the impression that this site will be perpetually under construction and will become much more useful in the near future. This site's strength lies in its convenient and user-friendly links to federal departments and agencies—executive, legislative, and judicial— and an easy-to-use guide to access publications of importance to non-profits, such as the *Federal Register,* the *Catalog of Federal Domestic Assistance,* and access to the General Services Administration. The home page has a search form that permits more than 300,000 federal government Web pages to be searched by keyword or phrase. A search of the term "Independent Sector" did not get a single hit, to our chagrin. But the term "unrelated business income tax" did register, albeit modestly. The White House Office of Public Liaison has assigned one person in each Cabinet Department and in many independent agencies to serve as an official Federal "Nonprofit Liaison" and serve on the Task Force that created the site. We'll go out on a limb and include this in our top 20, and hope the White House doesn't disappoint us with its plans to make this site the gateway of choice for the national non-profit community.

Nonprofit GENIE of the Support Center for Nonprofit Management
http://www.supportcenter.org/sf/genie.html

The Support Center for Nonprofit Management "is a consulting and training organization with a regional focus and a national reach. Through consulting, workshops, publications, and special management programs, we seek to help non-profits utilize the best management tools and concepts to help them best serve their communities." This site features the G.E.N.I.E., (Global Electronic Nonprofit Information Express), with a frequently asked non-profit questions file focusing on fund-raising, financial management, strategic planning, and board development. The answers are comprehensive; there are 15 answers to questions about strategic planning alone. What makes this site particularly valuable is that permission is given for copying and distribution of these files, provided the copyright notice is included. This page has a link to the on-line newsletter *Food for Thought* with (mostly) San Francisco Bay Area information of interest to non-profits. The "Marketplace of Ideas" page has links to book reviews categorized by usefulness to each of 12 non-profit job titles, a monthly interview with a local grantsmaker, a page devoted to fund-raising software and other software that is non-profit specific (see Technology Forum area on this site), and lots of national, regional, and local links to government and private organizations.

Up Close: Microsoft® Network

"Build it and they will come." Perhaps that advice was applicable to constructing a baseball stadium for ghosts but, at least to this point, it has not applied in the area of on-line services designed to appeal to non-profit organizations. Microsoft® in 1995 entered the competition for your on-line dollar by establishing an on-line service that was almost guaranteed to be successful as a result of its integration, both from a marketing and technical standpoint, with its Windows® operating system.

By the time you read this, millions of computers will have been sold with Microsoft® Network built into the operating system. After a free trial period, it could be accessed with very competitive rates.

For non-profits, the material available on this service promised to be worthwhile. One advantage over the market's leader for on-line services, America OnLine (AOL), was that non-profits could find the content they were looking for. The infrastructure for non-profit content on MSN is first rate. There are colorful icons, and the information is organized attractively. Enter MSN Classics at the main menu screen, click on Public Affairs, and then "NonLine Non-Profit Network." A menu of 12 icons appears: NonLine Non-Profit Management, Employment Center, Non-Profit Information Resources, Publications and Resources, State by State, Federal Assistance, CancerNet, Federal Register, Charity Watch, NonLine on the Net, Internet Newsgroups, and NonLine National Information.

Other than those areas that are links to World Wide Web sites that would be prospering with traffic with or without it, MSN's non-profit area is moribund. Most forum areas have either no messages, or messages and files from two individuals that were placed in 1995 and 1996. There was good information here at the time. MSN gave a party and nobody came. Our view is that MSN made a good faith effort to provide content that non-profits need. Perhaps this site "peaked" too early, and we hope they try again in a year or two when the critical mass of subscribers with an interest in non-profit matters is reached.

Many of the areas show evidence that two attempts were made, one in each of its first two years, to spike this area with useful files, and to encourage non-profit organizations to make this site their home for networking.

It may take several years before Microsoft®'s marketing genius (or anti-competitive practices, according to some of its critics, including many in the U.S. Justice Department's Anti-Trust Division) finds a way to significantly eat into AOL's dominance in the on-line service industry.

In August of 1997, Microsoft bought a $150 million stake in Apple Computers, the innovative chief competitor of Bill Gates' computer conglomerate, as well. Will bushels of Apples have the Microsoft® Internet Explorer at their core? Don't be surprised, and this could give a boost to traffic on MSN.

Putnam Barber's Page on Nonprofit Resources
http://www.eskimo.com/~pbarber

This is one of the most useful sites for non-profits. Included is a bulletin called *Information for Nonprofits* about developments affecting the sector and information about new Web sites of interest (and links to them). The Nonprofit Files FAQ (Frequently Asked Questions) is a must visit for the non-profit novice and the expert as well. This is the FAQ file that accompanies the most popular non-profit newsgroup, soc.org.nonprofit. There are loads of useful documents, including articles on how to start a new non-profit, advice about board and management, non-profit organization marketing, resources for volunteerism, and on-line resources of interest to non-profits. Our

Up Close: America OnLine (AOL)

"Welcome! You've Got Mail!" We haven't gotten tired of the friendly voice that makes that announcement each time we log on (assuming there is e-mail in our e-mail box). For many, it is welcoming enough to not get a busy signal, and that has been only one of many complaints subscribers have had about AOL, the chief provider (10 million subscribers and climbing) of on-line services. Another complaint is the incessant bombardment of commercial messages and offers appearing on your screen and in your e-mail. We feel that it has been only lately (1997) that this has gotten to the point of being more than annoying. Yet AOL is the on-line service of choice for those interested in non-profit issues (or virtually any other issue, for that matter). If you can't find it or people interested in it on AOL, you probably won't find it on any of the other major on-line services. But even if it is on AOL, it may not be so easy to find. Like the Internet itself, AOL has the problem of being wonderfully disorganized. For example, if you are interested in finding the area related to non-profit organizations, you might logically think that using the keyword "non-profit," with or without the hyphen, might help you find it. Not! Basically, you find things on AOL by asking people who know the answer through experience.

We recommend two AOL sites of general interest to non-profits. The first is ServeNet (keyword: SERVEnet), which includes the Civic Involvement System at the "access.point" area (which was not functional at the time of our review, but which is directly accessible on the World Wide Web at: http://www.accesspoint.com). ServeNet has some content of usefulness to non-profits (such as a grants guide), but we did not feel there was much here of value that couldn't be found on the WWW for free. What we did find useful was the area called *Community Matters* (although it was not accessible at the time we were going to press). Here you can find forums, chats, and other interactive places for non-profit managers to network and seek advice (and give advice) on almost every conceivable subject. You can also click on Community News and find a searchable database of news and feature articles about public policy issues. For example, click on "Hunger and Poverty" and find more than 450 matches on a search for "non-profit" and "nonprofit."

favorite was "What Use is the Internet to a Nonprofit Organization (NPO)?" It is divided into 21 topics, such as volunteer resources, community fund-raising, marketing, and non-profit applications of the Internet.

Research-It!
http://www.itools.com/research-it/research-it.html

This site is like having your own research librarian 24-hours/day in your computer room, only this one knows how to conjugate French verbs and doesn't say "shhhhhh" when you talk. The site scrolls to forms that permit searches to find word meanings, spellings, and translations to and from almost two-dozen languages. There is a thesaurus, a quotation finder, a biographical dictionary, stock quotes, maps, a rhyming dictionary, acronym dictionary, a place to look up telephone numbers, and scores of other useful reference materials that individually can be found throughout the Internet but not, to our knowledge, at a single site. As one of the promotional lines on the site says about itself, why not "Give it a whirl!"

Switchboard
www.switchboard.com

This is one of the most useful sites on the Web and, not unexpectedly, has become one of the most linked-to sites (more than 15,000 links to it from other Web sites and counting). What can it do? Type in a name of a company, hit the search button, wait a few seconds, and the name, address, and telephone number of the company appear. Click on the map icon, and a color map of the company's location appears, which can be zoomed in or zoomed out. Trying to read the address of someone who scrawls illegibly? Type in as much data as you can read and let a computer do the rest. Why pay $100 or more for those CD-ROMs with telephone book data when you can have free access to (as we write this) 106 million residential listings and 11 million business listings? Our advice is to bookmark this site immediately!

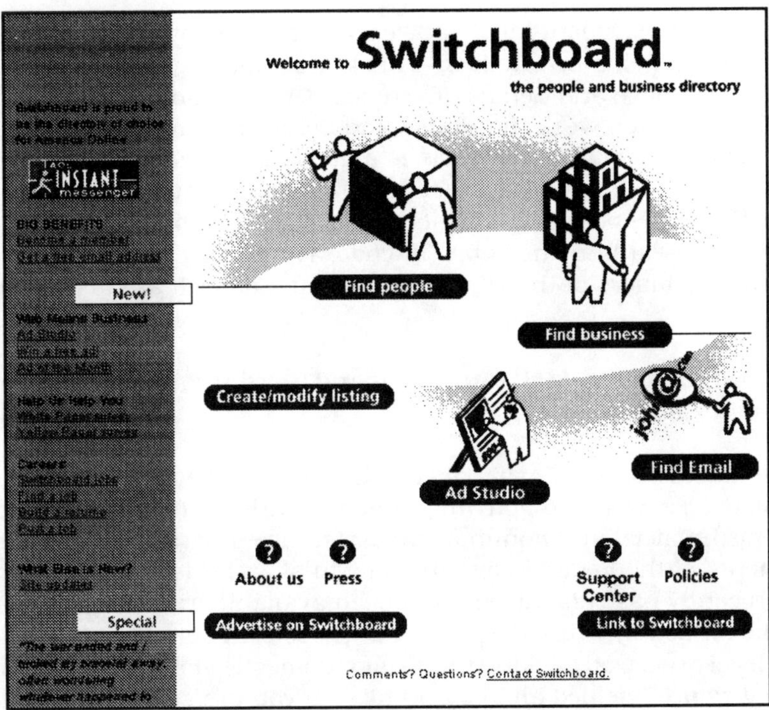

Switchboard home page. Reprinted with permission.

Yahoo! (see page 92)
http://www.yahoo.com/

Yahoo! is both a search engine and a directory. If you are trying to find something on the Internet, Yahoo! provides a one-two punch, and automatically searches Alta Vista if a search of Yahoo! does not turn up much. With news, weather, sports, people finder, maps, and other services, this site is simply one of the best for finding information on the Internet.

B. Government Sites

CapWeb
http://www.capweb.net/

While not an official government site, Capweb was created by two Capitol Hill staffers, and is hosted by Net.Capitol, Inc., a private firm. This is a terrific site for finding out what is happening each day in the U.S. House and Senate. There are general Congressional directory files (many of them searchable), and each week the House and Senate's committee schedules are posted. This site even posts hearing cancellations. This is a good site to visit before heading for Capitol Hill, and a good place to check for your member of Congress's room number, telephone/fax numbers, picture, bio, and the names of senior staff members, too. If you don't know who your Congressperson is, you can perform a search using your ZIP code. There is a convenient form for sending e-mail messages to many members of the House and Senate, as well as tips for making your message effective.

Catalog of Federal Domestic Assistance (General Services Administration)
http://www.gsa.gov/fdac/

"The Catalog of Federal Domestic Assistance (FDAC) is a government-wide compendium of Federal programs, projects, services, and activities which provide assistance or benefits to the American public. It contains financial and nonfinancial assistance programs administered by departments and establishments of the Federal government." In short, it is the "Bible" for government grant seekers. Only recently has this information been available free of charge, and the fact that it is searchable makes it doubly attractive to all but those commercial providers who used to charge steeply for this level of access. Seeking funds for a domestic violence program? Our search on the term "domestic violence" yielded almost 100 hits. If you are seeking federal funds for your non-profit, there is no better place to start than at this site.

Corporation for National Service
http://www.cns.gov/

"The Corporation for National Service is a public-private-nonprofit partnership that oversees and evaluates three national service initiatives: AmeriCorps (a 'domestic Peace Corps' with 25,000 members engaged in a year of service in return for an educational scholarship), National Senior Service Corps (with a half-million older Americans serving as Foster Grandparents, Senior Companions, and RSVP volunteers), and Learn & Serve America (which provides models and resources for teachers integrating service projects into the classroom curriculum of over 750,000 students from kindergarten through college)." The site has information about grant awards and grant availability from the Corporation, news affecting its programs, press releases, and the on-line version of *National Service News* (which is also available automatically in your e-mail by subscribing to its mailing list). You can apply on-line for an AmeriCorps position. Click on "Resources" and find useful publications relating to citizen service, and links to related organizations, including state, national, and community service commissions, and general non-profit organizations/resources. This is an attractive site and a must-visit place for those interested in citizen service issues.

Council of State Governments
http://www.csg.org/

"The Council of State Governments is a national, nonpartisan organization that champions excellence and innovation in state government. Founded in 1933, CSG serves all three branches of government through leadership education, research and information services." Surf to this site, and the latest index of issue alerts flashes before your eyes like an electronic billboard at Times Square. You can find files of suggested state legislation, the full text of the organization's monthly publication *State Government News* (put on-line three months after the issue comes out to regular subscribers), issue alerts (for example, one was on-line about the tobacco company settlement with the states within five days of the deal being consummated), and press releases. Need to know the political composition of the state house for each state? It's all here, as well as a list of each House and Senate member, district number, and political affiliation.

Department of Labor
http://www.dol.gov

Right on the home page, you can click on the button "minimum wage" and see useful information about this issue, including a map of the United States showing which states have higher, the same, or lower minimum wage requirements than the federal law. Click on the state and get detailed information. There is a "What Employers Need to Know" file giving information about changes to the Fair Labor Standards Act enacted in 1996. There are plenty of files on the 1996 welfare reform law, which can be accessed from the home page by clicking on the "welfare to work" button. If you are an employer, this is a good site to browse periodically for information about new rules and regulations affecting the workplace.

The Federal Register On-line via the Government Printing Office (GPO)
http://www.access.gpo.gov/su_docs/aces/aces140.html

This site contains the entire *Federal Register*, which is the official federal government publication for agency and department rules and regulations published during 1995, 1996 and 1997 (to date). Here, you can search these databases for the particular document(s) you need, including information about federal grants. Before 1995, this service cost $375 to use. It is publicly available now at no cost. The *Federal Register* includes all published documents from federal agencies, including new regulations, administrative orders, requests for comments and (important for fund-raising purposes) Notices of Funding Availability (NOFAs). Every federal grant is released through a NOFA, which contains all pertinent information on the grant program such as program descriptions, eligibility criteria, submission deadlines, and descriptions on how to obtain application kits.

Fedix Opportunity Alert
http://nscp.fie.com/wincgi/fed/all/any/any/foa/any/keywords.exe/Menu

This is another site that provides a free automated and regular search of federal agency research funding opportunities in your particular areas of interest. Participating agencies include the Department of Energy, Department of Transportation, National Institutes of Health, Agency for International Development, Department of Veterans Affairs, and Environmental Protection Agency, among others. This site is a product of the Federal Information Exchange (http://Web.fie.com/). Here you can register to receive free e-mail delivering information about research and education funding opportunities in your area of interest by selecting key words on an on-line form.

FedWorld
http://www.fedworld.gov/

FedWorld is a site administered by the National Technical Information Service Technology Administration, U.S. Department of Commerce. It is a shopping mall for government information, providing access to 15,000 files, more than 100 government agencies' databases, and even hourly updates of satellite photos of the east and west coasts of the U.S. You can search abstracts of government reports and order many by credit card. Our search using the term "nonprofit" turned up two files, but a search on the word "tobacco" turned up 26 files. This is a good place to browse for studies, reports, and publications involving your organization's niche.

Internal Revenue Service
http://www.irs.ustreas.gov/prod/cover.html

At a minimum, this is a useful site for non-profits simply as a source for IRS forms. And as a bonus, this site is strewn with useful files, advice, and news—for example,Tax Stats, Tax Info For You, Tax Info For Business, Electronic Services, Taxpayer Help & Ed, Tax Regs In English, IRS Newsstand, Forms & Pubs, What's Hot, Meet the Commissioner, Comments & Help, and a Site Tree. About six months ago, we left a question on the comments and help form and never got an answer (but we didn't get audited, either). There are on-line publications and documents explaining the latest developments. This site is not as stodgy as you might expect from a government agency with the IRS's reputation. In fact, we found this to be one of the most colorful, informative, and user-friendly government sites on the 'Net. We actually found it fun to visit. Access the *Digital Daily* (the home page newsletter format), and find out how many days there are until April 15! The site is searchable, as well. Also, hidden in "Tax Stats," are hundreds of useful files, including the IRS Master List of 501(c) organizations. You can download these files and search for organizations similar to yours.

Internet Law Library (The U.S. House of Representatives)
http://law.house.gov:80/

Administered by the U.S. House of Representatives' Law Revision Counsel Office, this is an excellent, useful site for legal information, and includes a searchable *Code of Federal Regulations, U.S. Code,* information about treaties and foreign laws, and almost 9,000 links that are of great value to the legal community (if only marginally of value to the non-profit community). Looking for current or historical court opinions? They may be scattered at sites all over the 'Net, but you can find links to hundreds of important cases here. This site is coordinated with the Library of Congress's Thomas database and contains additional information on the Web sites of all members of Congress, congressional committees, and commissions.

Library of Congress
http://www.loc.gov/

"The Library of Congress's mission is to make its resources available and useful to the Congress and the American people and to sustain and preserve a universal collection of knowledge and creativity for future generations." The agency doesn't harm its reputation for successfully achieving this mission with this Web site, which is one of the most fascinating we have found. When Thomas Jefferson founded the Library in 1800, even with his genius he would have had trouble envisioning the grandeur and magnificence of how it would evolve into what the Library of Congress is today, both physically and on-line. The Library of Congress Web site's usefulness to non-profit organizations is much more than Thomas (see page 147). The Library has more than 110 million items in its collection, and you can find out about millions of them by performing searches based at this site. The Web site itself is searchable as well. There are, for example, 1,800 full-text newspapers and periodicals available for viewing in the Newspaper and Periodical Reading Room (this is just one of 20 such reading rooms with on-line access), and academic and professional journals as well. Spend an hour or spend a day at this site, but it is time well-spent.

National Archives and Records Administration (NARA)
http://www.nara.gov/

Several NARA publications periodically accessed by experienced non-profit organization staff are available on-line, including the *Federal Register; U.S. Government Manual*, the *Privacy Act Issuances*

Compilation; Public Laws, and the *Code of Federal Regulations. The Government Information Locator Service* (GILS) at this site has a searchable database of information about NARA information resources with links to other sources of government information.

National Governors Association
http://www.nga.org

"As the only bipartisan organization of, by, and for the nation's Governors, NGA provides a forum for Governors to exchange views and experiences. NGA also provides assistance in solving state-focused problems, information on state innovations and practices, and bipartisan forum for Governors to establish, influence, and implement policy on national issues." The site is colorful, animated, and provides good source material on public policy issues, including NGA position papers (more than 100 when we last checked), and a page devoted to welfare reform that includes statistics, studies, reports, and other valuable primary source material. When the NGA speaks on public policy issues, the White House and Congress listen. And if you engage in advocacy on public policy issues, so should you.

The NIH Grants Page
http://www.nih.gov/grants/

This is the source for learning more about current funding opportunities from the National Institutes of Health or for subscribing to the NIH Guide via e-mail. This URL takes you to NIH pages on grants, contracts, and an NIH *Guide for Grants and Contracts.* The *Guide* is the official document for announcing the availability of NIH funds for biomedical and behavioral research and research training and general policy and administrative information. The grants page, administered by the Office of Extramural Research, is both searchable (a search on the term "AIDS" yielded 55 hits) and indexed, and is attractively designed. The grants page is also a home for CRISP (Computer Retrieval of Information on Scientific Projects), a biomedical database system containing information on research projects and programs supported by the Department of Health and Human Services.

Thomas (Legislative Info)
http://thomas.loc.gov

The Library of Congress has a well-organized and extensive site directing you through the morass of federal government agencies and departments. "Thomas" is a specific project through which much of this is done. Using the Thomas database, you can access the text and other information on bills currently receiving or expected to receive floor action in Congress. Bills are usually available within 48 hours of their introduction. Virtually any other bills' and amendments' text and other information can be found. You can read the *Congressional Record* here. Most, though not all, committee reports are available. You can find many historical documents, from the *Federalist Papers* to the *Bill of Rights*, along with background information. There are also useful educational files about the legislative process, how bills are enacted into laws, and similar civics lessons.

U. S. Census Bureau
http://www.census.gov/

The U.S. population increases by one person every 12 seconds. How did we know? We watched the projection of the U.S. population increase by clicking on a population clock linked to the home page of the U.S. Census Bureau. There is a clock for the world population, as well. This searchable Web site is "user-friendly" and fun. In fact, there is a file accessed from the home page called "Just for Fun" that features the Census Bureau's Map Stats, an interactive site that presents statistical profiles for states, congressional districts, and counties as well as detailed maps for counties. Click on your state on a colorful map of the U.S., and link to a map of your state, divided by counties. Click on a county, and view a map that permits you to zoom in and identify thousands of important features. These maps may be downloaded as GIF files (suitable for Web pages). Being on this site is like visiting the Smithsonian—you don't know what to look at first. The page claims to be "your source for social, demographic, and economic information." And it is. There is a cornucopia of information of use to virtually any non-profit, including economic indicators, statistics relating to your client base, radio broadcasts, and videoclips. So much Web site and so little time! Is there useful material at the Census Bureau site? More than we can count!

U.S. Code
http://www.law.cornell.edu/uscode

This site is a service of the Legal Information Institute, a part of the Cornell Law School. This searchable database permits you to access the *U.S. Code*, the entire codified body of federal law that has been enacted up to the most recent printing of the Government Printing Office's CD-ROM (which is perhaps 18 months out-of-date at any one time). This site also provides guidance on finding current information (such as using the Library of Congress's Thomas database). Each of the 50 titles of the U.S. Code is available for searching, using a form that permits you to search by a particular section, a popular name, or by keyword. We tried a search using the word "nonprofit" in Title 13 and it delivered the appropriate "hit." The Institute's site also hosts a page on recent and historic Supreme Court decisions, historical legal documents, and many other databases of interest to the legal community.

The U.S. House of Representatives Homepage
http://www.house.gov/

This colorful and functional home page links to pages that provide the schedule of bills to be considered each week (updated each session day), the current order of business on the House Floor (including a minute-by-minute account of each motion and other action), an annual schedule of dates when Congress is in session (great for planning those Washington lobby days!), holidays when there are no sessions, a target date for when Congress will adjourn, and files about the legislative process. There are plenty of related links on the home page, including links to leadership offices, the Library of Congress's Thomas, C-Span, and the Internet Law Library (see page 146). You can even take a virtual guided tour of the U.S. Capitol from here. There are links to each of the House's 18 standing committees and the Joint Economic Committee. ***Note:*** *A new, companion site is available at: http://clerkweb.house.gov*

The U. S. Senate Homepage
http://www.senate.gov/

The Senate's home page is more compact and better organized than its House counterpart, but has basically the same information. Click on the "Legislative Activities" button and view information about bills, the Senate's schedule, committee meetings and hearings, and related links. There are files concerning nominations and treaties (one difference between the House's and Senate's Constitutionally mandated duties). "Learning About the Senate" takes you to files about the Senate's history, a virtual tour of the Senate, and a glossary of Senate terms. There are lots of related links, and the entire site is searchable. There are individual pages for Senate Committees and Senate members.

U.S. Supreme Court Decisions from 1930-1975
http://www.fedworld.gov/supcourt

This site accesses the full text of 7,407 U.S. Supreme Court decisions from 1937 to 1975. Decisions are available as ASCII text files. The database can be searched by title or by full text search engine.

The White House
http://www.whitehouse.gov/

This site offers information about the President and Vice President and other resources that might be helpful to you such as *The Interactive Citizens Handbook*, which contains a link to the Government Information Locator Service (GILS) and other pointers; *The White House Virtual Library*, which contains White House papers, audio versions of speeches, and executive orders; Commonly Requested Services, which offers quick information most frequently requested; and *The Briefing Room*, which provides updated daily information on what is happening at the White House as well as a link to federal statistics.

C. Advocacy Sites

Children

Children Now
http://www.childrennow.org

The mission of Children Now is to "promote pioneering solutions to improve the lives of America's children." This site includes poll data, child welfare data, briefings, articles, calls to action, and sample letters to policy makers. There is also a listserv mailing list to receive regular updates from Children Now. Volunteer opportunities and state information is also available at this animated site.

Children's Defense Fund
http://www.tmn.com/cdf/

Children's Defense Fund home page. Reprinted with permission.

The Children's Defense Fund, founded in 1973, is perhaps the most visible and powerful national children's advocacy organization. The mission of the CDF is to "provide a strong and effective voice for all the children of America, who cannot vote, lobby, or speak for themselves." If your organization has anything to do with children, this is a must site to visit daily. The information is frequently updated. When you click on the "Issues" button, you see a page with five innocuous-sounding headings. Click on one (they relate to education, health care, welfare, crime/safety, and morality issues), and you are taken to a page that has up-to-date issue papers, bills of interest, and an FAQ that provides statistics and descriptions of the problems facing kids. There are great files such as "10 Things You Can Do to Help Children," which includes information about how to make donations to the organization. There is a chart depicting the cost of raising a child to the age of 18. There is information about internships, CDF publications for purchase, the text of articles by founder and president Marian Wright Edelman, and hundreds of other useful and interesting files. CDF's Web site is also used to teach actual and potential child advocates about what they can do in their own communities and what actions are needed to protect children from violence, sickness, and the effects of poverty. The format and design are professional and pleasant. This is simply a great site and a worthy format to imitate.

Child Welfare League of America
http://www.cwla.org/

The Child Welfare League of America is "the nation's oldest and largest organization devoted entirely to the well-being of America's vulnerable children and their families." CWLA uses the Web site to link member agencies—organizations that are part of its network of organizations supporting its mission. In doing so, the site provides, in effect, an on-line petition representing supporting organizations, as well as a practical communication network among the member agencies. There are links to the agency's publications, consulting services, membership, upcoming conferences, and how to make donations and purchase the organization's products.

KidsCampaigns (Benton Foundation)
http://www.kidscampaign.org/

KidsCampaigns is "the information, knowledge and action center for adults who want to make their communities work for kids." There is a vast amount of information here relating to on-line advocacy. The principal interactive efforts carried out on-line include some of those found in Interact for Kids. Here you can sign the guestbook and begin receiving an e-mail newsletter informing you of breaking news. Augmenting these newsletters is an e-mail discussion group for people working on behalf of children. Even one-time visitors are urged to share their stories with Benton about their efforts relating to working for children. Article submissions are encouraged for possible inclusion on the Web site.

The National Association of Homes and Services for Children (NAHSC)
http://www.nahsc.org/

The National Association of Homes and Services for Children (NAHSC) "advocates for at-risk children and families and the private nonprofit organizations that serve them." This site links to member agencies and offers these agencies their own Web sites for assisting in their advocacy efforts. In doing this, NAHSC proactively creates an on-line community and network for advocacy. There are buttons to click on to access files on advocacy, education, publications, links to member agencies, and more.

Community Organizing

Alliance for National Renewal
http://www.ncl.org

This National Civic League program includes the participation of more than 180 community-building organizations, including the American Association of Retired Persons, Habitat for Humanity, and the Points of Light Foundation. The site includes an e-zine called *The Kitchen Table*, and a "Community Stories" index of articles about what is taking place in local communities, indexed by 10 different categories (e,g, children, youth, and families). The site is searchable, and there is information about publications.

CivicNet
http://www.tmn.com/civicnet/

This is a project of the Center for Civic Networking (http://www.civic.net:2401/ccn.html), an organization providing civic networking services for other organizations. There was an on-line event scheduled for May 22 to June 30, 1997, which aimed to help inspire participants and provide practical tools for community building, especially through the use of the Internet. The event was structured much the same as any traditional conference. Participation was restricted to registrants (at a $50 fee), and activities included exhibitions on products and services, discussion forums, speaker presentations, workshops, and breakout groups. Even posters and papers were available for participants.

Environmental Advocacy

20/20 Vision
http://www.2020vision.org/

The mission of 20/20 Vision is "protecting the environment and promoting peace through grassroots action." The site is used to recruit individuals who want to be involved but who have little time to determine where their efforts are most needed or what they should do. Those completing a questionnaire are sent a postcard each month detailing 20 minutes' worth of recommended activity, based on their specific Congressional districts. Recommendations come from national and local policy analysts. Most actions involve letter-writing. Every six months, a report is sent to participants. Success stories are shared on-line. Those not wishing to join can still visit to read about actions needed that require little time commitment to do. 20/20 Vision also includes a very good collection of activist resources, *Tools for Grassroots Activists*. These resources include: *Using Cyberspace: Activism On-line — An introduction to Internet Resources* and links to FAQs and interesting and informative sites; *Tips for Grassroots Activists* — a simple "how-to" course in writing a letter or making a phone call to a key policy maker; *Beating the Bureaucracy — A guide for contacting and influencing the United States Government Administrative branch*; *Pursuing the Press* — a series of three documents focusing on writing Op-Ed pieces, writing Letters to the Editor, and having a voice in talk radio; and *Tips to Help Your Office be Green!* — first published in the Spring, 1995, issue of *Who Cares* (see page 184). This guide will help you save the planet, energy, and money in your workplace.

Environmental Working Group
http://www.ewg.org/

The Environmental Working Group is "a nonprofit environmental research organization based in Washington, DC (whose goal is to) provide the public with new, locally relevant information on environmental issues in their own states, home towns and neighborhoods." This site is an information-intensive one useful for local advocates for environmental issues. The site breaks down anti-environmental actions state-by-state and includes campaign contribution information for each member of Congress, alerts, and other reports helpful to advocates in each state. Using this site, an advocate for the environment can learn exactly which local facilities are discharging toxic waste into the water, which drinking water systems have shown the greatest number of health violations, and how many permits were issued related to the filling of wetlands.

The International Rivers Network
http://www.irn.org

The IRN specializes in human rights and environmental protection. Its *Join the Fight* link also includes a form allowing individuals, organizations, and institutions to sign up for one-, two-, or three-year memberships at rates ranging from $35 to $300. Members receive a subscription to the organization's newsletter. Payment can be by billing or by credit card (through an unsecured form). Alternatively, interested individuals can request a free one-year subscription to the newsletter. Volunteers with special skills are also sought at this site.

League of Conservation Voters
http://www.lcv.org/

The League of Conservation Voters (LCV) is "an independent political watchdog organization for all people who care about the environment. Unique in the environmental community, LCV is the only group to devote itself full-time to educating voters and winning elections on behalf of the environment." Calling itself the non-partisan political arm of the environmental movement, the League uses its site to recognize and reward members of Congress who vote for pro-environmental legislation and to bring to account those who do not. Making use of a clickable environmental scorecard, the site allows activists to find their elected representatives—and their votes on key environmental issues. Also through a clickable map, the site gives background on legislation and links to Congress. Posted at the site are LCV's letters to Congress describing its positions on current issues and giving all activists an example of what they can say in their own letters.

National Wildlife Federation
http://www.nwf.org/

The National Wildlife Federation "focuses its work on five core area environmental issues: Endangered Habitats, Wetlands, Sustainable Communities, Land Stewardship, and Water Quality." This colorful site contains a toolkit for activists telling how to write a letter to a legislator, a press release or a letter to the editor; how to organize a rally, raise money, run a petition drive, or do a talk radio show; and how to lobby, hold a news conference, arrange a town meeting, and more. The site also contains an EnviroHotline for information and news relevant to legislative efforts relating to environmental concerns. There is even an area where visitors can hear the sounds of the animals whose protection the organization seeks to ensure—a nice hook for attracting support.

Natural Resources Defense Council
http://www.igc.org/nrdc/

The NRDC pursues a wide range of environmental issues and concerns, ranging from protecting endangered species to pollution prevention and preserving environmental resources. The bulk of NRDC's site is used for full-text articles for advocates and others, providing a wealth of data and information in the form of fact sheets, analysis, opinion pieces, guides, histories, updates, and findings. The site personalizes the environmental issues and incorporates a connection with children. Visitors can view pictures and poems written by children. Thus, for example, one can see Lauren K's picture of a whale and read her priorities: "Whales are too precious. To put a salt factory in their clear waters." Not only does this serve to educate young people about environmental issues and to build their spirit of advocacy, but it brings home the importance of the organization's efforts for protecting the future of the world we pass on to our children. For adults and children to respond to such issues, there is an on-line petition that allows you to sign your name at the end of a letter to the president of Mitsubishi, Inc., asking that the company not build a salt factory in waters used by whales. Individuals can print, sign, and mail a similar letter to the President of Mexico about his country's participation in the proposed project. Similar advocacy pages can be found here on a wide variety of issues. The site is also used to keep advocates up to date with a legislative bulletin, which can also be subscribed to by e-mail. There is even a place for people to share their views, which are then posted at the e-Amicus portion of the site.

Wisconsin Stewardships Network
http://www.wsn.org/

The Wisconsin Stewardships Network's mission is "to build a cooperative environmental network that recaptures and strengthens Wisconsin's stewardship ethic for the betterment of its people and natural resources." This site, which has frames, non-frames, and text-only versions, is a great example of local organizing on the Web, demonstrating one of the most exciting benefits of the Internet—the fact that organizations at any size and level can make and use a well-designed Web site. This multi-purpose site includes chat and discussion pages where experts answer citizen questions, a calendar to which anyone can post events, local and national media links, sample letters-to-the-editor, alerts, and more. Community groups can learn about, and apply for, small grants described at the site. The site also features a map of the state, which individuals can use by clicking any county, to find local resources, news, and contact persons.

Gay and Lesbian Rights

The Human Rights Campaign
http://www.hrc.org

The Human Rights Campaign advocates for equal rights for lesbians and gay men. This is the nation's largest organization fighting for equal civil rights for lesbians and gay men. HRC's was one of the first sites on the Web to allow readers to find their members of Congress and send them e-mail by simply entering their ZIP codes. HRC goes one step further and gives you the members' biographical information and their voting records on gay and lesbian issues—thus making it easy to tailor your e-mail message for the individual member of Congress. The site also contains other "hands on" resources making it easy for advocates to get involved—these include: an extensive list of events that can be held on "National Coming Out Day" and, in 1997, a Web form to order on-line an "Ellen" house party kit (to watch the coming out of television comedienne Ellen Degeneres' sit-com character, and raise money for HRC). HRC reported that the number of house parties registered via the Web equaled the number received from all of its field organizers combined—the Web ended up being an easier and quicker method for reaching advocates nationwide.

The National Gay and Lesbian Task Force (NGLTF)
http://www.ngltf.org

The National Gay and Lesbian Task Force (NGLTF) is "a leading progressive civil rights organization that has supported grassroots organizing and advocacy since 1973." Its professionally-designed site offers a comprehensive on-line database of state-by-state legislation affecting the gay community. The database can be searched by state, type of legislation (e.g. civil rights, hate crimes, health), or by disposition (e.g., signed into law, vetoed by governor, died in committee). This is a good example of an organization taking advantage of the Web to provide local advocates with improved access to resources that were previously available only in a more cumbersome paper version.

Health Care and Mental Health Advocacy

The Arc Homepage
http://TheArc.org/welcome.html

The Association of Retarded Citizens is "the country's largest voluntary organization committed to the welfare of all children and adults with mental retardation and their families." Its site includes numerous fact sheets on mental retardation, position papers and a discussion board for posting inquiries. The Arc's semi-monthly government affairs report is published on-line in full text, and the weekly *Capitol Insider* newsletter is a terrific source of legislative information. Point Survey rated this site among the top 5% of all social services sites. We agree.

Bazelon Center for Mental Health Law
http://www.bazelon.org/

The Bazelon Center is "the leading national legal advocate for people with mental illness and mental retardation." This organization seeks reform in the areas of housing, health care, and support services. The Center's site features action alerts describing legislative updates and proposals. The site also contains a large volume of substantive information on advocacy in this area. It also contains resources and text of the Americans with Disabilities Act (http://www.bazelon.org/ada.html).

Families USA
http://www.familiesusa.org

Families USA "advocates high-quality, affordable health and long term care for all Americans." The site has plenty of articles and reports on Medicaid, Medicare, managed care, and consumer protection issues relating to health care. The design is not particularly pleasing, but the information appears to be the best in the field, although obviously viewed through a prism of progressive ideology. Managed care companies are likely to find the information hazardous to their health. There are hundreds of health care-related links, and these are well-organized. If you are involved in health care issues, go right to the "Health Policy Links" file, and bookmark it immediately.

Family Violence Prevention Fund
http:www.fvpf.org/fund/

The Family Violence Prevention Fund is "a national non-profit organization that focuses on domestic violence education, prevention and public policy reform." Those advocates interested in domestic violence issues can sign up here on an e-mail list to receive news, or read news or statistical information about family violence as well as personal stories from victims, people who have taken action against domestic violence, and children and family members exposed to violent domestic relationships. The organization uses its site to promote its public education campaign and its slogan: "There's No Excuse for Domestic Violence." It does this through advertising shirts and bumper stickers and by posting quotes from its celebrity sponsor, actor Danny Glover, on-line. There is a wealth of training and educational information for people in a variety of settings. Another creative use of the Web site is to provide a celebrity watch that details stories of family violence committed by celebrities, juxtaposed by ways other celebrities are fighting or increasing awareness of domestic violence. This section includes news of domestic violence information broadcast in radio and television programs. The site also features a quiz to test your knowledge of domestic violence facts. FVP Fund provides articles detailing action steps concerned individuals can take to influence policies relating to family violence. The *What You Can Do* page gives information on how to talk with victims of domestic violence, educate others, and keep informed about domestic violence. Also, the FVP collects information from its site through an on-line survey, which it uses to learn about visitors and their concerns, the level of their involvement, and how useful they find the information provided by the organization.

Join Together On-line
http://www.jointogether.org/

Join Together On-line is "a national resource center and meeting place for communities working to reduce substance abuse (illicit drugs, excessive alcohol & tobacco) and gun violence." This is a comprehensive, professionally-designed, colorful, and informative site, with plenty of useful information, advocacy tips, electronic discussion lists, funding sources, and more. Join Together uses its site in just about all of the major ways an advocacy organization can. It is interactive, encouraging all communities and organizations serving their communities to share their stories (both successes and failures) with others. One unique on-line advocacy effort Join Together co-sponsors with cable television's HBO and funded by the Robert Wood Johnson Foundation is its *Faces of Addiction*. This public education site provides background information leading into a televised program on the topic of drug abuse. Using multimedia, the site complements substantive information with personal accounts of the effects of drugs, tobacco, alcohol and their impact on family violence, workplace success, health, and safety. Links to organizations and on-line resources for getting help are provided.

Kickbutt.org
http://www.kickbutt.org/

The purpose of this organization is "to learn all about the dangers and health risks of tobacco, about the sneaky tactics the tobacco industry uses to peddle their stuff, and how you can act through government to make our country a safer and healthier place." In addition to providing relevant facts and strategy resources for activism, this site includes a section for smoking out specific policy makers to urge them to vote in favor of legislation designed to curb tobacco use. You must be a member of kickbutt.org to take advantage of the site but, according to its Webmaster, "Registration is free, easy, and confidential."

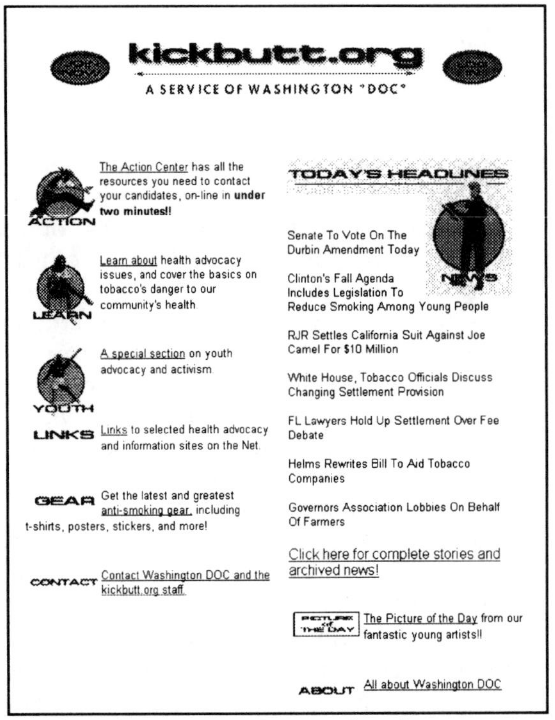

Kickbutt home page. Reprinted with permission.

Civil Rights, Human Rights, and Peace Advocacy

American Civil Liberties Union
http://www.aclu.org

The ACLU is "a 275,000-member, nonprofit, nonpartisan, public interest organization devoted to protecting basic civil liberties for all Americans." Within this colorful, meaty, and searchable site, the ACLU posts its organizational positions on everything relating to basic constitutional freedom, including church/state separation, death penalty, free speech, reproductive rights, racial harmony, workplace rights, student rights, voting rights, women's rights, gay and lesbian rights, and lots more. Additionally, you can e-mail your Congressional representative or take a Free Exercise of Religion non-credit course via America OnLine (AOL). You can even become a card-carrying member of the organization on-line. This site has received almost every major Web site award, and deservedly so.

Amnesty International
http://www.amnesty.org/

Amnesty International "is concerned solely with the protection of human rights... regardless of either the ideology of the government or the beliefs of the victims." Its site contains press releases, articles, and briefings from this organization. It includes actions you can take in promoting human rights and combating human rights violations. On-line activity includes a place where visitors and members can find out how and what to write to named countries found to be committing human rights violations. Place your mouse over one of the page's buttons and an explanation appears of what happens if you click there. Nice touch!

The Electronic Activist
http:www.berkshire.net/~ifas/activist

The Electronic Activist is part of the Web site of the Institute for First Amendment Studies. Founded in 1984, IFAS is "a non-profit educational and research organization focusing solely on the activities of the radical Religious Right." This site is an e-mail address directory of members of Congress, state government officials, and media entities, categorized by state, in addition to a federal/national file. You can use its Zipper program to obtain the name of your member of Congress and Senators by searching under your ZIP code, and you can send an e-mail message to every member of the House and Senate (provided it is less than 5,000 bytes long). There is a searchable database, which can tell you about key votes in the House and Senate.

PeaceAction of Washington (State)
http://www.scn.org/ip/peaceact/

Peace Action of Washington "is more than 13,000 dedicated individuals who work together in a grassroots effort to bring peace—internationally, in our communities, and in our own lives." This site is a good example of how a local affiliate of a large national organization is able to use the Internet to rally its members and provide them with easy access to information on key issues, and the means to act on it. It includes contact information for local members of Congress and links to their biographies and voting records.

Women and Gender Issues

The American Association of University Women
http://www.aauw.org

The AAUW is "a national organization that promotes education and equity for all women and girls." This colorful, well-designed site, has information about the organization's public policy guiding principles, legislative priorities, voter education efforts, a way to contact your members of Congress, action alerts, subscription information for its monthly public policy newsletter, and Congressional voting records on issues of importance to AAUW, all accessed by clicking on the green "issues" icon. The research icon gives you abstracts of AAUW research papers and how to purchase the full versions. Click on "resources" and connect to files relating to Gender Equity Resources for K-12 Teachers, Education Efforts, Voting Records, and information about the organization's legal advocacy programs. There is a button to click for information about fellowships and grants, and a generous supply (22 at the time of this review) of related Web links. The site appears to be updated frequently and is a good place to start if you are doing research on issues of importance to women.

The Feminist Majority
http://www.feminist.org

The Feminist Majority's mission is to work "in a variety of ways toward social, economic, and political justice and equity for women." This site is a well-rounded model for advocacy by a diverse group. The organization was founded in 1987 by Eleanor Smeal and Peg Yorkin. Today, some 150,000 concerned women and men who firmly believe that women deserve political, economic, and social equality have joined The Feminist Majority. The site is a good example of a lot of information assembled in a very user-friendly fashion, making it easy for advocates to get current and archival information and to act on their interests. It contains a list of action steps people can take to help the cause, including options for joining feminist student and faculty networks, and the ability to submit information to an events calendar and share viewpoints in an ongoing census of public opinion on feminism. It has a collection of women's issues mailing lists; job banks; a site for posting research questions and answers; and a page to help advocates find and contact their members of Congress by entering their state of residence, name of members, or ZIP code.

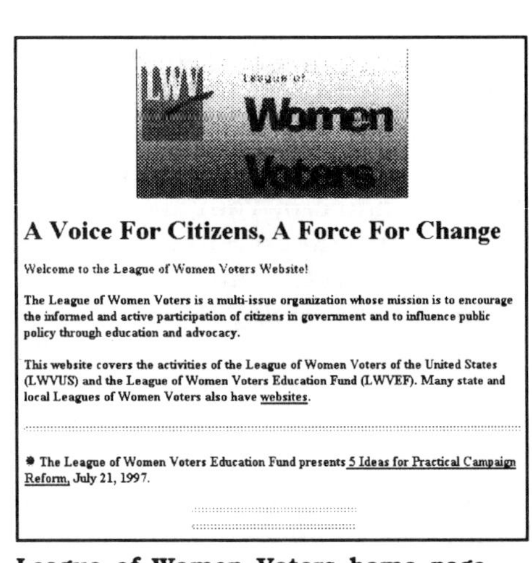

League of Women Voters home page. Reprinted with permission.

League of Women Voters
http://www.lwv.org

The mission of the League of Women Voters, founded in 1920, is "to encourage the informed and active participation of citizens in government and to influence public policy through education and advocacy." There are the usual files on how to join, how to contribute, programs administered by the organization and how to purchase League publications. The legislative priorities pages have up-to-date advocacy information on certain public policy issues that most general interest non-profit organizations would have no problem with supporting. The "League Action Line" button links to a Legislative Action Center, which includes schedules for the House and Senate, Legislative Alerts, Congressional e-mail lists with automated forms for e-mailing members of Congress, and a guide to the 105th Congress with biographies, photos, committee assignments, and the names of key staff members. Among the key staff included are not only the top staff director and legislative assistant but also the current appointments secretary. Put your ZIP code in an on-line form, and find out who represents you in Congress. There is also a first rate primer on tips and information about lobbying members of Congress, called "Tell It To Washington." Before you head for the Capitol, head here first!

National Abortion and Reproductive Rights Action League (NARAL)
http://www.naral.org

NARAL's mission is to promote "reproductive freedom and dignity for women and their families." Its site is another well-organized and focused site with a great deal of content on-line. In terms of on-line advocacy, there are some particularly nice touches. One is the ability to test legislators. One section asks how you would have voted on recent legislation and then presents how your legislators actually voted. Another feature is a clickable map listing all NARAL state affiliates and providing e-mail links, as well as the state status on reproductive rights and sex education. Third, there is a wonderfully comprehensive media contact list providing e-mail and Web links to the national TV networks (and all of their state affiliates on-line), the national news magazines, and a link to another site where you can search for your local newspapers and magazines. Another section includes shared stories of the site's visitors' experiences relating to the difficult choices involved in abortions.

Women Leaders On-line (WLO) Women Organizing for Change
http://www.wlo.org/

The purpose of WLO is "to build a powerful network of one million women and men to improve women's lives." This site was the first and largest women's advocacy group created on the Internet. The award-winning site is a wealth of women's information, with interactive e-mail lists, a feminist faxnet, lots of alerts, and various newsletters, feature stories, and even a humor page (with a unique and interesting "Family Values Flow Chart" that is a hyper-linked poignant joke/political statement). The site contains a lot of information and ways to get involved—both important for building an on-line movement.

Miscellaneous

AFL-CIO's LaborWeb
http://www.aflcio.org/

The AFL-CIO represents "the interests of labor, organizing and advocacy on behalf of workers." Besides using the Web site to make numerous documents, policy statements, and news available, there is a *Stand Up On-line* (http://www.standup.westlake.com/) section which allows visitors to review pre-composed letters to legislators and, if they agree, enter their ZIP code to get a list of their legislators and to indicate if they want a document sent in their name to a legislator via either fax or e-mail. If readers wish, they may compose their own letters for the same forms of distribution. This is a most convenient service for any advocate. Another on-line advocacy use by the AFL-CIO is the inclusion of a boycott listing of those businesses currently in dispute with the organization. Visitors can obtain more information about the particular dispute in each case. There is also a section on women's issues in the workforce, including a survey used to determine the conditions in the workplace for women.

American Public Health Association
http://www.apha.org/

This organizational site has sections for Legislation and Advocacy; News and Publications; Science, Practice, and Policy; and Public Health and Resources. The legislation and advocacy page includes on-line copies of testimonies, action alerts, and an on-line "pledge" form that visitors can use to pledge to do advocacy on the organization's issues. The news and publications section has news releases and information on the *American Journal of Public Health.* Science, Practice, and Policy includes information on fields of public health and the public health and resources section has links to other sites.

American Public Health Association home page. Reprinted with permission.

Corporate Watch
http://www.corpwatch.org

Corporate Watch "is designed to provide you—every day Internet users, activists, journalists and policy makers—with an array of tools that you can use to investigate and analyze corporate activity. We are committed to exposing corporate greed by documenting the social, political, economic and environmental impacts of these transnational giants." This site provides an interesting use of the Web and mailing lists to provide information on corporate activities. There are resources here for learning how to conduct research on corporations. The site awards a monthly "Greenwash Award" publicizing commercial advertising that it finds nefarious and misleading, relating to the effects particular corporations have on the environment. It provides global news and action alerts about corporate activity and wrongdoing. Corporate Watch is also concerned about maintaining public ownership of the Internet.

Disability Rights Activist
http://www.teleport.com/~abarhydt/

This is the place to go for advocacy information relating to disability issues. New action alerts are posted almost daily, and the latest court decisions, press releases, regulations, and news are posted here. This award-winning site does not have a lot of fancy graphics, icons, or maps, but has good, solid, and current information. When we reviewed the site, there were 13 current Action Alerts posted, giving a succinct summary of a public policy issue, the current status, what action was requested by the organization, and links to more information. This is how it should be done!

HungerWeb (see page 68)
http://www.hunger.brown.edu/Departments/World_Hunger_Program/

"The aim of this site is to help prevent and eradicate hunger by facilitating the free exchange of ideas and information regarding the causes of, and solutions to, hunger. It contains primary information, made available by the World Hunger Program—the prime sponsor of this site—and its partners, as well as links to other sites where information of relevance to hunger can be found." The World Hunger Program is part of the Watson Institute of International Studies at Brown University. The site is indexed, and has a file accessed from the home page introducing the issues of hunger and malnutrition. The pages are organized under the general headings of *Research* (institutions, research results, and major hunger-related data sources), *Field Work* (non-governmental organizations, UN agencies, situation updates, and reference materials), *Advocacy and Policy* (organizations and materials, upcoming legislation), and *Education and Training* (training materials for hunger education at all levels). Little information is provided on these pages other than links to organizations with pages that have valuable material. Some substantive material (particularly on international hunger issues) was available from the World Hunger Program Web site (http://www.hunger.brown.edu/Departments/World_Hunger_Program /hungerWeb/WHP/ overview.html).

Impact On-line
http://www.impactonline.org/

Impact On-line (IOL), founded in 1994, is a non-profit organization that uses the Web to connect volunteers with non-profit organizations who need them. Potential volunteers can find out about volunteer opportunities and research non-profits in their communities. Any non-profit organization can create its own free Web page and list immediate volunteer needs. This searchable site is flashy and the winner of many prestigious awards. And, in our opinion, there is as much steak as sizzle. The site has information about its program on Virtual Volunteering, which targets the development of volunteer activities that can be completed over the Internet. Although the pilot program for virtual volunteering is currently restricted to San Francisco and Philadelphia, there are plans to expand it to more cities. This is an idea that can really catch on, and by the time you read this, this program may be "virtually" everywhere.

InterAction
http://www.interaction.org/

InterAction is the nation's largest coalition of private relief and development agencies. With 150 non-profit organizations, it advocates for humanitarian assistance to the world's needy. Its membership list is a Who's Who of international relief organizations, many of whom have their own Web sites, which are linked to Interaction's. *PC Computing Magazine* awarded this professionally designed, colorful site as one of the *Best 1001 Websites on the Internet* (among other awards bestowed on it). There is information about volunteer opportunities and, for a modest subscription fee, a newsletter detailing job opportunities at international organizations. There are publications, information relating to advocacy with legislative alerts and updates on international aid issues, an events calendar, program links, and *A Guide to Appropriate Giving* with tips on how and what to donate to international relief organizations. There are lots of useful links, the information is frequently updated, the Web site is searchable, and it is one of the most well done Web sites we found.

The Interfaith Working Group
http://www.libertynet.org/~iwg/

The mission of the Interfaith Working Group is to "inform the public of the diversity of religious opinion on social issues where it is not widely recognized by providing a voice and a forum for religious organizations, congregations and clergy in the Philadelphia area who support gay rights, reproductive freedom, and the separation of church and state." This site provides a gathering place for religious organizations and individuals committed to religious diversity. The site lists participating member organizations and individuals. Relevant interfaith and other events are listed, alerts are posted (helpful not only for showing your network what you're actually doing, but also good templates for others to use in preparing such letters for the first time), and an on-line record of organizational letters sent (http://www.libertynet.org/~iwg/letters.html). A nice feature of this site is its *Member Pulpit* (http://www.libertynet.org/~iwg/forum.html), which gives cyber-air time to members to discuss their views and experiences. The site includes a searchable list of progressive interfaith organizations, which helps advocates tap in to local like-minded individuals. There is also an e-mail list visitors can join to stay in touch.

Internet Democrats
http://www.us.net/indc/indem.htm

Internet Democrats is "an independent on-line community seeking a more participatory democracy." This example of political advocacy is a site formed several years ago to get as many Democratic activists on-line as possible. Its founders initially offered free Web pages to other Democratic organizations, but now the site focuses more on lessons of Web advocacy. The site provides an interesting list of 10 examples of Internet activism (http://www.us.net/indc/activis.htm), a large number of articles on on-line advocacy, and even offers an on-line course on the subject. The site is a good example of how a very small operation can use the Web to get its message across.

National Coalition for the Homeless
http://NCH.ari.net

The National Coalition for the Homeless is a national advocacy network of homeless persons, activists, service providers, and others committed to ending homelessness through public education, policy advocacy, grassroots organizing, and technical assistance. This professionally-designed site contains a bibliographic database on homelessness, housing, and poverty; five directories of people, organizations, and Web sites working on these issues (including a national directory of street newspapers); and information about coalition projects, action alerts, a file called Facts About Homelessness, and a Legislation and Policy page. That page has up-to-date welfare reform information, lots of action alerts, and links to other advocacy resources.

We the People (An Unofficial Republican Homepage)
http://www.netrunner.net/~covers/republic/

If you prefer elephants to donkeys, this site is a funkier and more lively place to visit compared to the official Web site of the GOP. There is lively commentary, a large collection of links, and a decent search engine. The site's many Internet awards are well-deserved. If you are conservative in both political philosophy and Web design, try the stodgier, but snazzy official GOP Web site at http://www.mc.org.

D. General Research Source Sites

Acronyms
http://www.ucc.ie/cgi-bin/acronyms/acro.html

This award-winning site (Magellan 4-Star Site, and a top 5% award) boasts a searchable database of (as of this writing) almost 16,000 acronyms. This site also provides a convenient way to electronically submit new acronyms to the database. We submitted the Association of Committees of Reform Organizations Never Yielding to Mindlessness.

AT&T 1-800 information
http://www.tollfree.att.net

This is a searchable database of more than 150,000 toll free numbers for commercial businesses and organizations. But don't expect to find any of AT&T's national competitors here (we tried a search using the word "sprint" and "MCI" and came up empty). We found the "dead tree" paper version of this publication free on our doorstep, with a $24.95 cover price.

Bartlett's Book of Quotations
http://www.columbia.edu/acis/bartleby/bartlett/

This site is a part of Project Bartleby, administered by Columbia University. What makes it particularly useful to non-profits is a searchable database of quotations, not just those available from Bartlett's, but from many other sources. For example, a search on the word "taxes" resulted in not just the well-known Ben Franklin quote of "but in this world, nothing is certain but death and taxes," but more than 30 additional matches. For speaking engagement preparation or spicing up the newsletter or legislative testimony, this is a useful and engaging site to explore. And you can quote us on that!

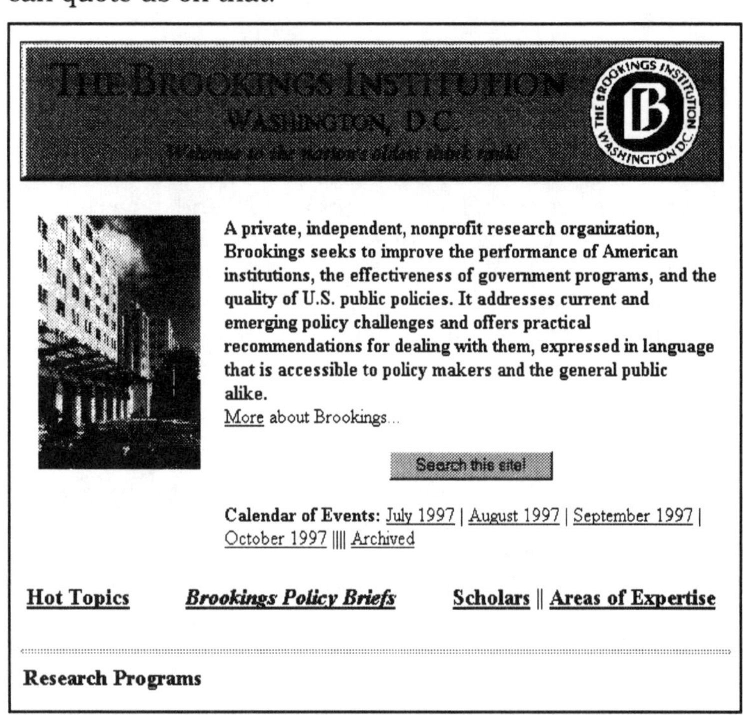

The Brookings Institution home page. Reprinted with permission.

The Brookings Institution
http://www.brook.edu

The Brookings Institution, founded in 1916, is the United States' oldest think tank. Among the features of this searchable site are full-text policy papers (there were 15 when the site was reviewed), Congressional testimony, op-ed articles, conference notices, and information about the organization's publications. This is a useful site to browse (and perform a search) if you are preparing to give testimony on a current public policy issue.

CIA World Fact Book
http://www.odci.gov/cia/publications/pubs.html

This is a great place to start for researching countries you are planning to visit. If you are engaging in international business dealings, providing grants to foreign organizations, or just curious about the structure of the new government in Zaire, this site is a treasure-trove of information about geography, climate, economy, and political stability. Among the files you can spy on this site are *The World Factbook 1996; The 1995 Factbook on Intelligence; Chiefs of State and Cabinet Members of Foreign Governments* (which appears to be updated each week); *Handbook of International Economic Statistics, 1996*; and *CIA Maps and Publications Released to the Public.* There is a searchable database for the site.

Database America
http://www.lookupUSA.com/

Among other useful free databases, this site includes a "reverse lookup" directory. You can find a name and address when all you have is a telephone number.

Encyclopaedia Britannica
http://www.eb.com/

A free trial offer provides seven consecutive days of free access to the 32-volume industry standard "plus thousands of newly added articles, graphics, and related Internet links." An FAQ file explains the offer. Unlike most on-line services, you do not have to worry that you will be charged in the event that you decide not to subscribe and forget to let them know. The subscription cost is $12.50/month or $150/year as of September 1997.

The Gallup Organization
http://www.gallup.com/

This is a commercial site of the Gallup Organization, perhaps the best commercial polling service in the United States (at least according to one recent Gallup Poll!). It includes press releases about publicly available poll results, averaging about five such polls each month. This is a good site to browse when looking for general topics that are on the public's mind and for identifying public trends. The information from these press releases provides free and verifiable speech filler material. The site also has on-line polls for visitors. Our favorite question was "What percentage of the time do you lie to pollsters?" Not!

General Sources of Women's Legal and Public Information Policy
http://asa.ugl.lib.umich.edu:80/chdocs/womenpolicy/legpol.html

This guide was compiled by Lydia Potthoff and Tom Turner of the School of Information and Library Studies, University of Michigan, Ann Arbor. *The Legal and Public Policy Information Guide* contains links to legal and public policy information from the United States Federal Government, the United Nations, several international organizations, and links to Internet resource guides. Although copyrighted in 1994, there are still working links to useful sites.

Internet Public Library
http://ipl.sils.umich.edu/

The Internet Public Library is the first public library of the Internet, founded in 1995 and run by real librarians. The IPL began in a graduate seminar in the School of Information and Library Studies at the University of Michigan. It has a budget of almost a half-million dollars, mostly from grants from the Mellon and Kellogg foundations. Its database, entitled *Stately Knowledge: Facts about the United States*(http://www.ipl.org/youth/stateknow/), is billed by the site as "a fact-filled and fun-to-use resource for students, teachers, parents and anyone interested in finding out more details about the United States and Washington D.C." There are pages loaded with information for each state, and a page loaded with, for the most part, offbeat trivia. There are useful state-related links as well. The library maintains a collection of network-based ready reference works and responds to reference queries. And the best thing is, you don't get "shuushhed" for screaming "Cool Site!"

Project Gutenberg
http://www.promo.net/pg/

Project Gutenberg was started in 1971 with the goal of making available in ASCII format the complete text of books that are in the public domain, either as a result of copyrights having expired or having the rights donated by the works' creators. In addition to the usual classics one might expect, you can also find useful books about the Internet. Books may be searched by author or title. As this was being written (September 1997) the site had just added its 1,036th title. This Web site can be very useful to non-profit organization staff who need to research important historical documents and books when the library is closed. Imagine how the inventor of the printing press would have reacted to seeing the World Wide Web through Netscape Navigator!

The Quotations Page (Michael Moncur's Collection of Quotations)
http://www.starlingtech.com/quotes/

The site includes files on Quotes of the Day, Random Quotations, Quotes of the Week, Search for a Quotation (with a 1,500 quote database), Contribute a Quotation, Quotation Links, and an FAQ file.

University of Chicago's Department of Humanities Dictionaries
http://www.lib.uchicago.edu/LibInfo/Law/dict.html

Included at this site are links to the *World Wide Legal Information Association Legal Dictionary, Oxford English Dictionary, English Language Dictionaries, Roget's Thesaurus of English Words and Phrases* (based on the text of the 1911 edition from Project Gutenberg), *Bartlett's Familiar Quotations* (based on the 9th edition, 1901), *Notable Citizens of Planet Earth* biographical dictionary containing information on more than 18,000 prominent people, and the *Dictionary of PC Hardware and Data Communications Terms.* Why buy the commercial CD-ROM of these texts when you can get them free for a click of the mouse at your bookmark?

ZIP Code Information
http://www.usps.gov/ncsc/lookups/lookup_zip+4.html

Enter an address and find the ZIP code from the US Postal Service. The search also tells you the Carrier Route, County, 09 and Check Digit information.

E. Foundation-related Sites

Regional Grantmaker Associations/Coalitions/Networks

Associated Grantmakers of Massachusetts
http://www.agmconnect.org

Associated Grantmakers of Massachusetts was founded in 1970. Its mission is "to support and advance effective and responsible philanthropy throughout the Commonwealth." The home page is similar to Independent Sector's—filling one computer screen and having nine buttons. Included on the site (by clicking on the Library Services button) is a series of seven "tip sheets" providing technical information for those who wish to start a non-profit in Massachusetts or find sources for grants. For example, there is a sample letter of inquiry one might send to a grantmaker. The Market Place button links to files concerning publications and other products for sale by the organization. There is a member list with links to their home pages where they exist, an events calendar, and a *What's New This Week* button that updates not only new additions to the Web sites but new additions to the Web sites of its members and counterpart organizations around the country. The Links button provides the Web sites for regional media outlets, local academic centers with an interest in non-profits, government links, links to grantmakers, resource pages of interest to non-profits, hundreds of Massachusetts non-profit organizations, and regional grantsmaker associations.

Coordinating Council for Foundations
http://www.hartnet.org/ccf/

The Coordinating Council For Foundations is a membership association of Hartford-area grantmaking institutions, including public, private, and operating foundations, as well as corporate foundations and giving programs. The Council's mission is to promote effective philanthropy. The site includes links (only five to national non-profit resources), information about its membership, publications, and a common application form. One useful file, "Ways to Give," explains different ways to participate in philanthropy, from setting up one's own foundation to establishing a Charitable Remainder Trust. There is a page set aside for news provided by members, but there was nothing there at the time of this review.

Council of Michigan Foundations
http://www.novagate.com/~cmf

The Council of Michigan Foundations is "an association of more than 360 foundations and corporations which make grants for charitable purposes. As a membership organization, our mission is to enhance, to improve, and to increase philanthropy in Michigan." There are five buttons: About CMF, What's New, Visit Our Colleagues (which, in addition to members, has a modest supply of links to government and national non-profit resources), Programs, and Publications. The latter is of general interest, because many of the publications are both free and of interest to non-profits regardless of location.

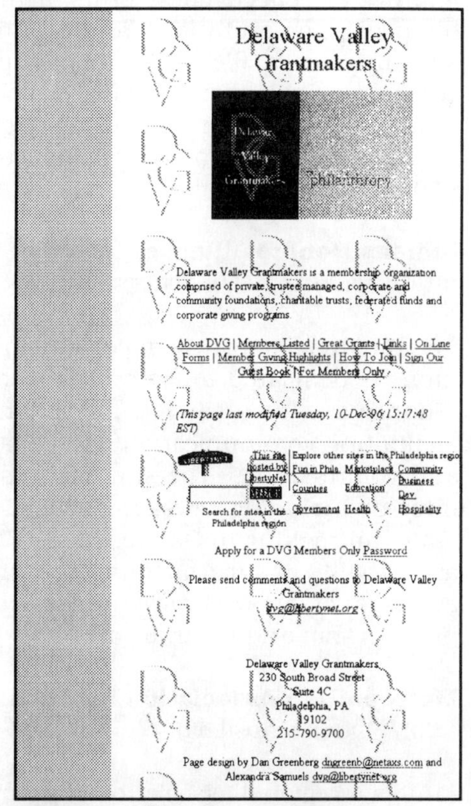

Delaware Valley Grantmakers home page. Reprinted with permission.

Delaware Valley Grantmakers (see previous page)
http://www.libertynet.org/~dvg/

Delaware Valley Grantmakers is a regional (chiefly PA, NJ, and DE) membership organization comprised of private, trustee managed, corporate and community foundations, charitable trusts, federated funds, and corporate giving programs. The site includes a Common Grant Application Form that is accepted by 46 of its grantmaker members. The site includes a generous number of links to Internet resources of interest to non-profits, both from the Delaware Valley Region and nationally.

Donor Forum of Chicago
http://www.uic.edu/~dbmaint/donors94.html

The site features the 1994 *Philanthropic Database* of the Metro Chicago Information Center and the UIC Academic Computer Center. This database is searchable by foundation, beneficiary type, grant purpose, by support type, and by recipient (there are more than 3,000 recipients in the database). The site is a terrific place to start for grantsmanship—for identifying what foundations make grants in the fields of interest, for researching who your competitors are for getting these grants, and for brainstorming about developing programs locally that may parallel pilot programs elsewhere.

Grantmakers of Western Pennsylvania
http://www.telerama.com/~gwp/

"Grantmakers of Western Pennsylvania is an association of grantmaking organizations—foundations, corporations, and charitable trusts—of all sizes and purposes. Its mission is to improve the effectiveness of its members in the philanthropic community to meet the needs of the people, organizations, and communities of Western Pennsylvania." This simply-constructed site includes a file on membership benefits, information about upcoming conferences and seminars, a calendar of events (which was several months out-of-date at the time of our review), links to its counterpart regional grantmaker associations, mission statement, links to its membership, a common grant application form used by its members, and the organization's values statement.

Indiana Donors Alliance
http://www.in.net/indonors

The Indiana Donors Alliance, a membership association serving Indiana's grantmaking community, "is dedicated to fostering responsible and creative philanthropy for the public good. The Alliance acts as a catalyst for philanthropic action by providing information and education, by facilitating communication and collaboration, and by encouraging new opportunities for giving and volunteering." The site has lots of publications, documents, and files of general national interest, including newsletter articles from past issues that provide sound legal information, such as "Grantmaking to Organizations NOT Exempt Under Internal Revenue Code Section 501(c)(3)" and legal guidance on filing the annual 990 tax return. This is one of the better regional grantmaker sites to browse and learn something you didn't know before. The site includes on-line membership and order forms.

Metropolitan Association for Philanthropy (St. Louis Area)
http://www.mapstl.org

MAP is a regional association of grantmakers in metropolitan St. Louis, serving both donors and donees "to facilitate more effective philanthropy in the St. Louis region." The site has links to national and regional non-profit and grantsmanship resources, information about its Foundation

Center-sponsored library collection, and information about publications, many of which are available for free.

New York Regional Association of Grantmakers
http://www.nyrag.org

The New York Regional Association of Grantmakers "is a nonprofit membership association of donors in the tristate area. Its mission is to promote and support effective philanthropy and concerted action for the public good." This is a colorful, professionally-designed and wonderfully constructed site, but it is not particularly useful compared to its counterpart regional organizations. The calendar of events wasn't up-to-date, there were no general files of interest, and most of the documents related to internal aspects of the organization. One internal document we did find interesting was NYRAG's policy statement on diversity and inclusiveness, which could serve as a model for non-profits in general who wrestle with this controversial issue.

Foundations

AT&T Foundation
http://www.att.com/foundation/

The AT&T Foundation "is the principal instrument for AT&T philanthropy in the United States and throughout the world." The AT&T Foundation awards grants in the program areas of Arts and Culture, Education, Health and Human Services, International, and Community Services. Included is information about the foundation, the requirements for grant eligibility, and a file describing highlights of its grant program going back to 1984. Each of the program areas has a page that includes general information and links to some of the foundation's grantees.

Ben and Jerry's Foundation
http://www.benjerry.com/index.html

The scoop about Ben and Jerry's Foundation is that it was established in 1985 and makes competitive grants to non-profit organizations throughout the United States "which facilitate progressive social change, by addressing the underlying conditions of societal or environmental problems." Among the files you can access at this searchable site are descriptions of grant recipients for each calendar quarter, foundation guidelines, foundation tips, annual reports, links, and a creative series of pages for kids ("Fun Stuff") with games, puzzles, multi-media (check out "Ice Cream Rap") and craft ideas.

Benton Foundation
http://www.benton.org

We found this to be one of the most attractive sites of a private foundation, and the Webmaster indicates that there will be a major redesign to the site soon. Benton is a private foundation, based in Washington, DC, that was founded in 1981 by Charles Benton, the son of U.S. Senator William Benton, who was the founder of Benton & Bowles and owner of the Encyclopedia Britannica. Its mission is "to promote communications tools, applications, and policies in the public interest." This is a searchable, attractively designed site (as one would expect, since Charles Benton is the owner of a large communications company). There are links to pages of major programs of the Foundation that have been set up with their own domain names, including the KidsCampaign (see page 151), the Open Studio Arts-On-line, and Destination Democracy (campaign finance reform). The Communications Policy & Practice pages include information relating to communications policy, the Telecommunications Act of 1996, regulation of the communications industry, and a "policy toolkit" that includes a fascinating FAQ about how to follow what's going on with the Federal Communications Commission and participate in the policy debate. There are hundreds of links to other organizations, foundations, and those who are interested in telecommunications policy. The site has lots of reports and other documents relating to the telecommunications industry from a consumer's point of view. The site also includes a form to subscribe to one of two Foundation-administered mailing lists on telecommunications policy and (we wish all lists had this feature) includes sample postings.

Carnegie Corporation of NY
http://www.carnegie.org

Carnegie Corporation of New York was created by Andrew Carnegie in 1911 "to promote the advancement and diffusion of knowledge and understanding." The Corporation's capital fund, originally donated at a value of about $135 million, had a market value of $1.37 billion on December 31, 1996. The Web site includes files of recent grants, publications, press releases, and links. No frills here.

Global Fund for Women
http://www.igc.apc.org/gfw/

The Global Fund for Women is an international organization, established in 1987, that focuses on female human rights. It supports issues as diverse as literacy, domestic violence, economic autonomy, and the international trafficking of women. The site has an on-line pledge form, a grant request sheet that serves as an application for grants (but cannot be filled out on-line), information about the group's programs, and an informative FAQ.

Robert Wood Johnson Foundation
http://www.rwjf.org

The Robert Wood Johnson Foundation, based in Princeton, NJ, is the nation's largest philanthropy devoted exclusively to health and health care. The site includes publications explaining the guidelines for applying for grants, annual reports, information about data collections, the foundation's newsletter, information about its current programs, and nearly a dozen publications, reports, and studies.

George Lucas Education Foundation
http://glef.org/welcome.html

Established in 1991 by the famous and successful filmmaker, this Foundation does not provide grants or scholarships but promotes education, "especially those (activities) that integrate technology with teaching and learning." The site includes sound files and movie files that would be of interest to educational institutions.

John D. & Catherine T. MacArthur Foundation
http://www.macfdn.org

The John D. and Catherine T. MacArthur Foundation is a private, independent grantmaking institution "dedicated to helping groups and individuals to improve the human condition." The "Hot Links" button brings up hundreds of organizations and institutions who are current or former recipients of foundation grants, and links to them. This searchable site includes links to related organizations and non-profit resources, grant information resources, and information about the foundation's programs. And you don't need to be a genius to figure out how to navigate through this site (although if you are one, these folks may have an unsolicited large check in the mail to you).

Mitsubishi Electric America Foundation
http://www.hri.com/MEA/meafhome.html

The mission of the Mitsubishi Electric America Foundation is "to contribute to the greater good of society by assisting young Americans with disabilities, through education and other means, to lead fuller and more productive lives." The site has an on-line guidelines brochure explaining how to apply for a grant, and files with information about current grant recipients with summaries of the projects being funded. The foundation also operates the *MEA Volunteer Project of the Year Award* program, funded by contributions from MEA executives, to encourage and recognize employee volunteerism and community involvement.

David & Lucile Packard Foundation
http://www.packfound.org/packhome.htm

The David and Lucile Packard Foundation was created in 1964 by David Packard, co-founder of the Hewlett-Packard Company, and his wife, Lucile. Grant recipients are principally universities, national institutions, community groups, youth agencies, family planning centers, and hospitals. The site includes guidelines for qualifying for a grant, the procedures for making an application, the foundation's annual report, and information about foundation programs and priorities. The site also includes the electronic version of the free publication *The Future of Children*, published three times a year by The Center for the Future of Children. The full text can be downloaded here (an Acrobat reader is required, available free at this site and hundreds of other sites on the 'Net).

Pew Charitable Trusts
http://www.pewtrusts.com/

The Pew Charitable Trusts, based in Philadelphia, is a national philanthropy established 49 years ago that seeks to "encourage individual development and personal achievement, cross-disciplinary problem solving and innovative, practical approaches to meeting the changing needs of a global community." Each year, the Trusts make grants of about $180 million to between 400 and 500 nonprofit organizations. The site includes guidelines for obtaining a grant and the procedures to submit an application, information about recent grants and programs, and organizational press releases.

Rockefeller Brothers Fund (see page 60)
http://www.rbf.org/rbf

The Rockefeller Brothers Fund is a private, philanthropic foundation created in 1940. At the end of 1995, the foundation's assets were $400 million. The Fund's major objective is "to improve the well-being of all people through support of efforts in the United States and abroad that contribute ideas, develop leaders, and encourage institutions in the transition to global interdependence." One of the program interests is to promote and sustain a vital non-profit sector, both nationally and internationally. Files on the site include information about grants awarded by the foundation, grant application procedures, publications (such as the annual report, grant guidelines, and papers/reports), and foundation programs.

Harry Singer Foundation (see page 52)
http://www.singerfoundation.org

The Foundation was founded in 1987 for the purpose of promoting an increase in public involvement in public policy. The site provides information about the donation of public policy books to institutions, essay contests, and social studies workbooks.

Surdna Foundation
http://www.igc.apc.org/surdna/

Surdna Foundation, Inc. was established in 1917 by John E. Andrus, a businessman and investor who served as Mayor of Yonkers, New York, and as a member of Congress. Surdna's grantmaking activities are concentrated in four programmatic areas: environment, community revitalization, effective citizenry, and the arts. Included on the page is a file discussing guidelines for applying for grants and restrictions concerning them. The foundation does not generally fund individuals, capital campaigns, or building construction. A description of this foundation's approach to grantmaking, general information about the foundation (including its trustees, officers and staff), grantmaking program areas of interest, and guidelines for making application for funding can be accessed from links at the home page.

F. Charity Sites

Top 40 Charities

How are mainstream charities using the Internet to promote their organizations? The following are capsule reviews of the Web sites of the top 40 charities (using 1995 data), as ranked by the Internet Nonprofit Center (see page 138). Use these summaries to identify sites where you can obtain useful information and get ideas for designing your own site.

ALSAC/St. Jude Children's Hospital
http://www.stjude.org/

Memphis's St. Jude Children's Research Hospital focuses on the research and treatment of catastrophic diseases in children, primarily pediatric cancers. Its Web site is searchable, includes a virtual museum giving the history of the facility, has a secure order form to make donations (which was not working on our browser), scores of useful links to related private and government organizations, plenty of pages/files providing general health/disease information, and a plethora of frequently updated, packed information in a pleasing, accessible format, which encourages people who are interested in medical research to return to the page again and again. This is a good place to start for plain English explanations of scores of major diseases.

American Cancer Society
http://www.cancer.org

This site brags about having received so many awards. It is not particularly because of the design (pedestrian by any standard), but the quality of the information. The site's FAQ is done well. There is an entire section of the page devoted to a volunteer recruitment pilot program, involving four state chapters at the time this was written. Obviously, this is the place to start for information on what is perhaps America's most dreaded disease.

American Heart Association
http://www.amhrt.org/

Included on this searchable Web site is a button which links to AHA's database of news media releases and advisories with Reuters Health Information Services. This is *the* site for information about cardiovascular disease, prevention, and clinical cardiology.

American Lung Association
http://www.lungusa.org/

The American Lung Association is the largest organization in this country fighting lung disease, including asthma, emphysema, and lung cancer. Information can be found on the site about making donations and the tax advantages of doing so. There are plans to permit donations to be made on-line on secure forms. The home page has a cute animation of a pair of lungs in the process of breathing. The pages are searchable (the term "asthma" turned up matches in hundreds of files), and include

American Heart Association home page.
Reprinted with permission.

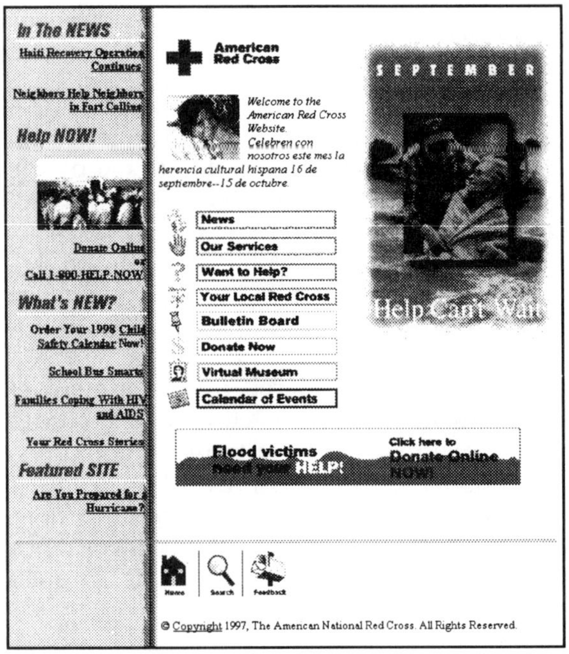

American Red Cross home page. Reprinted with permission.

information about important legislation pending on Capitol Hill, articles from associated medical journals that are re-edited to make them more understandable to the public, and association press releases. According to the site itself, "The ALA Web site contains 82 separate documents related to lung health, ALA news articles, medical and legislative updates, and more than 40 fact sheets." Knowing that all of this information was available for free and with just the click of a mouse made us breathe easier.

American Red Cross
http://www.redcross.org/

This searchable site has the latest news concerning natural disasters and general/world news relating to natural and man-made disasters. Included in the site is a virtual museum giving the history of the agency. The colorful graphics, world-class design, and good information make it worthy of return visits. There is plenty of information concerning how to donate to the organization, including forms to make secure credit card transactions. This site sets the standard for charitable organization Web sites.

AmeriCares Foundation
http://www.charity.org/americ.html

AmeriCares is a private, international non-profit disaster relief and humanitarian aid organization. The pages are simple, consisting of little about the organization, and including lots of links to other disaster/humanitiarian relief agencies, categorized by children, hunger relief, education, medical care, refugees/disaster relief, and jobs/economic aid.

Big Brothers Big Sisters of America
http://www.bbbs.org

"The mission of Big Brothers Big Sisters of America is to make a positive difference in the lives of children and youth, primarily through a professionally supported One-to-One relationship with a caring adult, and to assist them in achieving their highest potential as they grow to become confident, competent, and caring individuals, by providing committed volunteers, national leadership and standards of excellence." This frame-supported site (with text version) is simply designed, and is functional, with links to information about the organization, press releases, studies about the effectiveness of the organization's programs, an on-line donation form, and links to local agencies.

Boys and Girls Clubs of America
http://www.bgca.org/index1.html

"The Boys and Girls Club Movement is a nationwide affiliation of local, autonomous organizations and Boys and Girls Clubs of America working to help youth of all backgrounds, with special concern for those from disadvantaged circumstances, develop the qualities needed to become responsible citizens and leaders." This frame-supported site includes video and audio clips of Denzel Washington speaking on behalf of the organization and a YouthWeb area of web sites that have been built by Boys and Girls Clubs. There are pages devoted to the organization's programs, an entire page lauding the corporate sponsors of BGCA, and lots of interestingly-designed pages.

Boy Scouts of America
http://www.bsa.scouting.org/

This site is geared more toward encouraging scouting and activities for youth, rather than toward promoting the organization itself, seeking donations and volunteers, and the usual mission statements and annual reports. The site promotes BSA's magazines and official gear, and it is relatively boring. We expect the Boy Scouts to be better prepared for what the Web can offer.

Campus Crusade for Christ
http://www.ccci.org

Included is a searchable Web site, in both English and Spanish versions. You can download and listen to RealAudio files, or the entire two-hour film "Jesus." There is not much in the way of appeals for donations here.

Catholic Charities USA
http://www.catholiccharitiesusa.org/

Catholic Charities USA is the largest private network of social service organizations in the United States. The section relating to Capitol Hill testimony and news releases is a good source for those interested in material relating to social services advocacy. New material has been added on the latest welfare reform law. A button labeled "Our Opinion" includes speeches and remarks by organization officials at various conferences and press conferences.

Catholic Relief Services
http://www.catholicrelief.org

Catholic Relief Services was founded in 1943 by the Catholic Bishops of the United States. "In over 80 countries throughout Africa, Asia, Europe and Latin America, Catholic Relief Services (CRS) serves the poor by providing emergency and long-term assistance based on need, not creed, race or nationality." When we visited in July 1997, the Web site was under construction and was a single page, with a few links to outside organizations. The page gave information about the mission of the organization, how to contribute, and the history of the organization. According to the counter, the site averaged fewer than 10 visitors per day during the previous year.

Christian Broadcasting Network
http://www.cbn.org/

CBN's mission is "to prepare the United States of America, the nations of the Middle East, the Far East, South America and other nations of the world for the coming of Jesus Christ and the establishment of the kingdom of God on earth." And, perhaps, in cyberspace as well. The site has an on-line pledge form, links to organizations that share CBN's values, and information about its programs. There are scripture references for counselors dealing with common problems and on-line Bible tracts.

Christian Children's Fund
http://www.charity.org/ccf.html

The Christian Children's Fund is one of the largest independent child care and development organizations. The site is simple, providing links to related organizations and to local affiliates.

Council of Jewish Federations
http://jewishfedna.org/

The Council of Jewish Federations is the continental association of 189 Jewish Federations, the local community fund-raising and social service/education management organizations of the Jewish community. Included on the site is The North American Jewish Data Bank, established by the Council of Jewish Federations and the Center for Jewish Studies of the Graduate School and University Center of the City of New York. Its primary role is to act as the repository for computer-based population and survey data on Jewish communities in the United States and Canada. The "Other Jewish Websites" button is a link to hundreds of Jewish organizations around the world.

Focus on the Family (James Dobson)
corrdpt@fotf.org (e-mail only)

Gifts-In-Kind International
http://www.giftsinkind.org

Gifts In Kind International is "the leading charity in the field of product philanthropy, helping companies donate product efficiently and effectively to charities and schools in your home town and around the world." The site includes files on the benefits of making donations, how to qualify for receiving donations, a list of local coordinating agencies that process donation requests (typically local United Ways), an on-line donation request application form, and detailed information about nine specialized programs administered by the organization, which addresses needs ranging from housing for the homeless to recycling technology. The site is simple and well-organized, getting you where you want to be without unnecessary clicks.

Girl Scouts of the USA
http://www.gsusa.org/

The Girl Scouts is the largest voluntary organization in the world for girls. Information is available at this site about affiliates, Girl Scout cookies, publications, awards, history of the organization, information about making donations, and how to become one of the 800,000 Girl Scout volunteers. The site includes an animated publications section and links to local affiliates that have Web pages of their own.

Goodwill Industries (see page 137)
http://www.goodwill.org

Habitat for Humanity International
http://www.habitat.org/

Habitat for Humanity International is a non-profit, ecumenical Christian housing ministry dedicated to eliminating substandard housing and homelessness. Best known for former President Jimmy Carter's active participation (one file on the site tells the story of his involvement), the organization has an on-line store/catalog (orders are taken by an 800 number rather than on-line), a "news" site of organization press releases, and a searchable database of organizational affiliates. This site also solicits donations and provides information about volunteer opportunities. It is a pleasant, functional site, with additional versions in Spanish and French.

Institute of International Education
http://www.iie.org

IIE provides programs and services to promote international cooperation on business, diplomacy, the environment, hunger, and arms control through education. It conducts statistical and policy research and provides information on international study. The site has a simple, colorful, inviting design. There is not a lot of substance other than information about programs, membership, board, mission, and programs, and other internal organizational matters. You can search listings of more than 4,000 academic year or short-term study abroad programs and obtain information about many of the 240 different international education programs administered by the organization.

International Planned Parenthood Federation
http://www.ippf.org/

International Planned Parenthood is the largest voluntary organization in the world concerned with family planning and sexual and reproductive health. Included on the site is a file called "The Need for Family Planning," which justifies the activities of the organization; information about making contributions and what each contribution amount can purchase; links to related international /national government and private related organizations; and information about, and excerpts from, IPPF publications. Also included are organizational governing documents and the organization's strategic plan. This is one of the few national charities that have their entire strategic plans on the Internet. This document is useful to those organizations thinking about putting one together themselves. The latest files from the "current news and information" were more than two months out-of-date, which gives the impression that the site is not updated regularly.

Larry Jones International Ministries/Feed the Children
http://www.feedthechildren.org/

Feed the Children is an international, non-profit Christian relief organization. It has a state-of-the-art Web site, with information about donations prominent, including a secure on-line form. It is colorful and inviting. There are pictures of hungry kids beckoning you to contribute.

MAP International
http://map.org/

MAP International is a non-profit Christian relief and development organization. Included at the site is a World Health Library, which serves as a developing library of Internet resources on selected world health topics. Its World Health Emergencies file provides updates on the most urgent humanitarian and disease emergencies around the globe, including links to the best Internet sites that track the emergencies. Its "World Health Discussion" contains a listing of e-mail discussion lists on international health topics, with instructions about how to subscribe (and unsubscribe). There is a *Health & Hope Webzine.* The "Get Involved" button leads to a form which lets the site send you publications, financial information, information about contributions and volunteering, and how to participate in the organization's projects and programs.

March of Dimes Birth Defects
http://www.modimes.org/

The March of Dimes is a non-profit organization dedicated to reducing birth defects and infant mortality. Established in 1938 by President Franklin Delano Roosevelt to put an end to polio, the organization accomplished this mission within 20 years with Dr. Jonas Salk's development of the polio vaccine. Among the documents that can be accessed from the home page *are March of Dimes history*, the *March of Dimes today, pregnancy and childbirth, birth defects, the March of Dimes chapter nearest you*, and *volunteering for the March of Dimes*. There is plenty of statistical information on this site, and files about birth defects, educational programs, and organizational press releases. This is the best site on the Web for information about birth defects. It is one of the few sites that offer much of their information in Spanish and English. An on-line form is provided for making donations via credit card (there does not seem to be a secure form at this time), and plenty of other files related to fund-raising, donations, and volunteering to raise money. The site is searchable and has a wealth of information in both English and Spanish versions.

Metropolitan Museum of NY
http://www.metmuseum.org/

The Metropolitan Museum of Art is one of the largest and best-known art museums in the world. This site is designed to give visitors an overview of the collections on display in the Museum's galleries. Also on this site is a Floor Plan; information on services for visitors; a Calendar offering a detailed current listing of special exhibitions, concerts, lectures, films, and other Museum activities; and a Gift and Book Shop, with more than 100 of the institution's best-selling items for sale. This site is simply wonderful and can serve as the model for museums. There is membership information, on-line encryption for purchasing from museum shops, a generous taste of the exhibits, news about the museum, detailed information about most of the museum's holdings, and an innovative educational section for children, adults, and teachers. There are files that tell you everything you would want to know about the facility. Visiting this site will not replace visiting the place in reality, but museums should look at this site for hints on how to do an effective Web site that will encourage return visits.

Muscular Dystrophy Association
http://www.mdausa.org/

The Muscular Dystrophy Association "is the definitive source for news and information about 40 neuromuscular diseases, MDA research and services available to adults and children with neuromuscular diseases and their families." The site has a secure on-line pledge form and information about volunteering and how to make donations of durable medical equipment. There is a link to an on-line "ask the experts" bulletin board run by the organization. There are more extensive files about the diseases being fought by the organization than were available when we first visited in May 1997. You can even hear an audio message from Jerry Lewis promoting the Labor Day Weekend MDA telethon.

National Association for the Exchange of Industrial Resources
http://www.misslink.net/naeir/

The Illinois-based National Association for the Exchange of Industrial Resources is "a nonprofit organization that collects and processes donations of new, top quality merchandise from American corporations, then redistributes those goods to qualified schools and nonprofits across the United States." The home page links to two files—how 501(c)(3)s can join the organization and receive benefits, and how companies can make tax-deductible donations. The organization issues catalogs every 10 weeks. Charities order from them (and average about $2,000 worth of supplies) and pay shipping and handling costs in addition to a fee for each catalog, which averages about $100 each. The site has forms to request information packets for both prospective donors and donees.

National Easter Seal Society
http://www.seals.com

Founded in 1919, Easter Seals is a nationwide network of 109 affiliate societies operating programs to serve the disabled and their families. There are lots of links to disability-related sites.

Nature Conservancy
http://www.tnc.org

The Nature Conservancy is a national environmental organization that seeks to preserve nature by purchasing and preserving endangered and water habitats. This colorful, professionally-designed site is worth visiting, provided your browser supports frames and you have a fast modem. The site is searchable and has more than 20 audio and video clips and more than 300 nature photos. Click on "What's News" and see an interactive feature story from the latest *Nature Conservancy* magazine. Each Wednesday, a trivia quiz is posted on biodiversity, and the winner receives Conservancy merchandise—a creative gimmick to encourage return visitors. Fill out an on-line survey and receive a free Nature Conservancy screen saver program. There is a Calendar of Events, and a Library containing organizational publications, including an index of past *Nature Conservancy* issues. You can sign up or renew membership, volunteer, purchase merchandise, contribute money or materials, and even "adopt a bison or an acre of rain forest." A secure credit card order form is provided on-line. This site is state-of-the-art and fun to browse.

Project Hope/People to People Health
http://www.projhope.org

Project HOPE (Health Opportunities for People Everywhere), established in 1958, is an international health education foundation providing health policy research and analysis, training for health care professionals, and consultations in health systems planning and development. HOPE was originally known for the *S.S. HOPE,* the world's first peacetime hospital ship, which had its maiden voyage in 1960. The site is searchable, and there is a form for making donations on-line, including credit card donations. Web surfers can go to a "quick jump" feature where they can scroll through the names of the states and foreign countries that have Project Hope programs/projects, and launch a page about what is happening there. Included is a link to the Project HOPE Center for Health Affairs (CHA), founded in 1981, a non-profit health policy research organization that provides research and policy analysis on both United States and foreign health systems. Recently added to the CHA site is the Project HOPE Walsh Center for Rural Health Affairs, which conducts research on issues affecting health care in rural America. Also on this site is the journal called *Health Affairs* with a searchable database, which yields the table of contents from past issues, rather than the text of the articles themselves.

Public Broadcasting Service
http://www.pbs.org/

This site is searchable and has information relating to programs produced by PBS. There is often useful material for educators who are using various PBS specials as learning aids. One of the more fascinating parts of this site, and one that is useful to non-profit executives, is a section that provides transcripts of the *On-line NewsHour* (what used to be known as the *MacNeil-Lehrer Report* before Robin MacNeil retired) and RealAudio of the past week's programs, on demand. For those checking out the future of the World Wide Web, this is a good place to find a demo of it (assuming your computer software communications package supports this). A search on the term "non-profit" turned up more than 50 documents in the program's archives, none of the references more than a year old. The term "managed care," by contrast, yielded 1,187 documents. This is one of the best sites produced by broadcast media and, considering the in-depth nature of the programming, particularly its public policy offerings, one of the most valuable as well. If you are researching a public policy issue, it is worth the trip to this site to check out what's available.

Salvation Army
http://www.salvationarmy.org/

The Salvation Army is an international humanitarian and social service organization administered by the evangelical part of the Universal Christian Church. The site's design is impressive—

certainly not second-hand. This site has a Clipart Gallery in the Salvation Army Resources section with hundreds of pieces of downloadable clipart, including cartoons, that are in the public domain. The site is a good source of material for news relating to natural disasters—the Salvation Army is always on the scene. It includes the expected sectarian messages, but it is tastefully done and not offensive to those who do not share the religious fervor of the organization's members and leadership.

Second Harvest
http://www.secondharvest.org/

Founded in 1979, Second Harvest is the largest domestic hunger relief organization in the United States, providing nearly a billion pounds of food each year to the needy. The site includes a newsletter, an events calendar, and information about how to make donations. The design could be improved upon—it is one of the few Web pages we've encountered that requires scrolling from left to right (at least on our monitor), as well as down. The "Legislative" section under "Issues and Events" includes an electronic newsletter, updated every two weeks, on issues of importance to food banks. There is good information concerning natural disasters. The "Action Alerts" explain each issue targeted for advocacy and include what actions are requested. Also on the site is the quarterly magazine *Second Harvest Update.*

Shriners Hospital for Crippled Children
http://www.mn-mason.org/shriners.html

Shriners Hospitals for Children is a network of 22 pediatric specialty hospitals that provide free medical care for youngsters under 18 years of age. (This site is for the Minnesota chapter).

United Jewish Appeal
http://www.uja.org

The UJA Federation Annual Campaign represents 151 local Jewish federations and a network of 450 independent communities in the United States that raise funds in partnership with the national United Jewish Appeal. The site includes links to organizational programs, as well as to a few dozen member Jewish federations and other Jewish national organizations.

United Negro College Fund
http://www.uncf.org/

The College Fund is an educational assistance organization with 40 private, historically black, member colleges and universities. The first vision that hits the screen when this page loads is a box with "Pledge to College Fund/UNCF" inside it. Obviously, a potential donor is a terrible thing to waste. With a click or two, you are transported to an on-line pledge form. There is a link to the organization's The Frederick D. Patterson Research Institute. The Institute has information and statistical data relating to African-American education.

United Way/Crusade of Mercy
http://www.unitedway.org/

The United Way system includes approximately 2,000 community-based United Way organizations, each independent, separately incorporated, and governed by local volunteers. Through a single community-wide campaign, local United Way volunteers raise funds to support local agency service providers and provide funding to 45,000 agencies and chapters. Thanks to you, this site is working. The index has a note that the site was last updated six months ago, and there is little we could find on the site that looks like it would need to be updated six months from now—the usual program information, a paragraph blurb on public policy issues, nothing particularly creative or useful, although the site is designed attractively. Clicking on the search button takes one to an index rather than a search. There is much pleasing to look at here, but little useful substance, and nothing that made us want to return. One notable exception is some useful material on outcomes measurement, which is based on a 1996 United Way publication.

World Vision USA
http://www.worldvision.org/worldvision/master.nsf/stable/home

"World Vision is one of the world's largest child sponsorship organizations. During 1996, 1,164,410 children in 47 countries were sponsored by World Vision, child sponsors from many nations...." The home page is small, linking viewers to files designated as "Learn" (About Us), "Explore" (The World), "Know" (The Facts), and "Change" (A Life). New material is posted periodically. When we reviewed this site, there was current material on the death of Mother Teresa, and newly posted articles on land mine elimination. "Know" links to the pages relating to *World Hunger* magazine, press releases, commentary, statistics about the organization's work, and information about the famine in North Korea. "Explore" links to files about the organization's programs around the world. "Change" tells viewers how they can donate and volunteer, and there is an extensive FAQ file on the site, which is a good example of how an international charity can communicate effectively with the public.

YMCA of the USA
http://www.ymca.net

Local YMCAs collectively make up the country's largest community service organization. Included on the site is information about YMCA programs, categorized by "kids," "families" and "community." Nothing fancy here.

Others Charities of Interest:

Alzheimer's Association
http://www.alz.org

This site contains the organization's mission statement, news releases, position statements, and a listing of chapters. Educational information for caregivers is provided (i.e., "10 Warning Signs"). On-line advocacy efforts include public policy FAQs, current projects, and an on-line policy newsletter. There are links to related sites, and the site is searchable by key words. With few graphics other than a logo, the site loads quickly— a plus for those with slow browsers/computers.

America's Charities
http://www.charities.org

America's Charities is a non-profit federation of about 80 national charities. In addition to links to the pages of its members, there is a link to individuals who coordinate volunteers for its membership by region. The pitch made by the organization is to purchase its services to set up payroll deduction workplace campaigns and provide the fiscal management for funneling the collections to worthy charities. And guess who's on the list of these worthy charities? Its members, of course!

Charities USA
http://www.charitiesusa.com/

Independent Charities of America, founded in 1987, "is the first and only national federated fund raising group organized by contributors. Our mission is to bring the benefits of federated group fund raising to America's finest independent nonprofit organizations, and to provide member charities and contributors alike with the finest service at the lowest cost of any charitable federation in America." The database is searchable (although a search of the word "defense" failed to turn up files relating to the Children's Defense Fund) and there is a secure, on-line form for donations.

Charity Village
www.charityvillage.com/cvhome.html

This is a bilingual site (French and English) serving Canadian charities, but it is certainly of interest to those of us down South as well. There's plenty of news about the latest developments by clicking "Charity Village NewsWeek," pages for both non-profit managers and those who donate, a career center, book reviews, and lots of useful files and links. The intent here is to imitate the one-stop shopping you find at the Internet Non-Profit Center, but for our Northern cousins. It is colorful, inviting, and frequently updated.

Make-A-Wish Foundation
http://www.wish.org/main.htm

The mission of the organization "is to ensure that wishes are granted to children in the United States with life-threatening medical conditions creating the probability the children will not survive beyond their 18th year. We accomplish this by chartering chapters and providing them with consistent policies, substantive resources, comprehensive training and wholehearted support." The site includes links to files headlined Make-A-Wish Story, Chapter Listing, What Is Make-A-Wish?, How Are Wishes Granted?, How To Donate, Myth Of Craig Shergold Wish (relating to an unauthorized Internet chain letter encouraging people to send business cards to a seriously ill boy), Potpourri Of Wishes, a Frequently-Asked Questions file, Our National Speakers Bureau, Major Make-A-Wish Sponsors, and News Center (organizational press releases).

G. Current News, Weather, and Time

News

ABC News/Realtime Audio
http://www.realaudio.com/contentp/abc.html

This site features an up-to-the-minute realtime audio news service. With appropriate software (which may not work on older computers), your Internet screen can turn into a radio transmitting news broadcasts.

Christian Science Monitor—Electronic Edition
http://www.csmonitor.com

Among other things, you can access the text of the current edition (or archived stories) of this respected national newspaper, play back radio broadcasts of particular stories you select using a form, or participate in an interactive, brain-teasing crossword puzzle. You can view the current editorial page cartoon, as well.

CNN Interactive News
http://www.cnn.com/US/index.html

Here is a popular and well-organized site. It polls readers through its "take a stand" page and confirms by allowing only one vote for a single e-mail address (however, one could vote more than once by entering an incorrect e-mail address). A "dialogue" page gives readers the chance to discuss news topics.

Crayon
http://crayon.net

"CRAYON (Create Your Own Newspaper) is a tool for managing news sources on the Internet and the World Wide Web. CRAYON uses a simple analogy that everyone can understand— a newspaper to organize periodical information." It has received most of the awards out there; and its 120,000 subscribers (no cost to subscribe!) can thank the creativity of two undergraduate students from Bucknell University, Jeff Boulter and Dave Maher (both have graduated and are now gainfully employed), for developing this site. This site lets you download parts of different news sources to create your own eclectic newspaper—say you want the front page of the *Philadelphia Inquirer*, but the editorials from the *New York Times* and the sports from the *Boston Globe*. You can add in your own sources using known URLs.

Fox News
http://www.foxnews.com/

This site is a good gateway for finding the latest general, financial, entertainment, business, science and technology, and health news, as well as sports, and weather. You can find the Associated Press, Reuters, and SportsTicker wire stories here and there are video clips that you can download to create customized newscasts. The site is colorful, searchable, animated, and uses frames to organize material. The site also offers live realtime audio broadcasts. You can access local news by clicking on a map that features links to network local affiliates.

MSNBC News
http://www.msnbc.com/

The primary drawback of this site is that it is highly graphical and can be slow to download pages, but if you are looking for pictures, video clips, and sound bites, this is a good source. It also links to other Internet sites relating to the stories presented. It features a collaboration with television broadcasts, and can be customized to respond to your information needs.

The New York Times
http://www.nytimes.com/

This site requires you to register (takes about 5-10 minutes) but is free. Once you join, you will have access to a large amount of content.

USA Today
http://www.usatoday.com/

This is a national news source with information organized topically, as well as regionally, by state. Its opinion section features a "round-up" of opinions on particular topics from newspapers around the country. The site is searchable and updated more than once each day, although stories are relatively short. But if there is only one source you can go to for current news, weather, sports, colorful pictures and graphics, lots of useful files and services, pick this one.

Weather

CNN Weather
http://www.cnn.com/WEATHER/

Here you can find five-day weather forecasts for more than 3,500 cities.

Weather Channel
http://www.weather.com/

Point your browser to this site for especially well-organized and detailed information.

Yahoo! Weather
http://weather.yahoo.com/

This URL is a good starting point for current weather information.

Time

Directorate of Time, U.S. Naval Observatory
http://www.nasw.org/users/kcarr/estclock.htm

This provides the correct time for the Eastern time zone.

World Time
http://www.stud.unit.no/USERBIN/steffent/verdensur.pl

Find the correct time here for over 100 cities around the world. The time is updated every minute, and your page reloads automatically every five minutes.

H. Publication Sites

The Bulletin (by Relief Web)
http://www.reliefWeb.int/bulletin.html

The Bulletin is available on the Web and by e-mail, and provides timely information, especially for those supporting relief efforts around the globe.

Charity Magazine
http://www.charitynet.org/infostore/charitymag/index.html

The target audience of this publication is those interested in fund-raising news in the UK.

The Electronic Newsstand
http://www.enews.com/

"The Electronic Newsstand is the Web's premiere magazine site. Founded in 1993, it was also one of the first content-based sites on the Internet. This site contains the largest and most diverse magazine-related resources anywhere on the Web...The Newsstand is home to more than 200 actual magazine sites...and is also home to a comprehensive list of links to magazine-related sites elsewhere on the Web: 2,000 in all! You can browse through these with our easy-to-use Monster Magazine List." With a colorful, animated, frame-utilizing home page, The Electronic Newsstand is the virtual home for *more* than 2,000 magazines. Most provide sample articles, and some provide their entire contents. You can usually find bargain subscription prices here and you can order them on-line using a credit card. This searchable site provides archives that can be searched as well. A search on the term "nonprofit" scored 83 hits, returned in chronological order. There are links to the home pages of many of the magazines featured. This is a good site to do research, or just browse (and there is no store clerk hovering over you annoyed that you are reading but not buying). And to think what we had to do when we were kids to view *National Geographic* without being disturbed by our parents....

Imagine's New Direction's Newsletter
http://www.Web.net/users/imagine/products/new_directions/index.html

This is a Canadian on-line newsletter about strengthening corporate community investments. There is also a related newsletter *Inter-Sector* published on-line by the same organization.

More Than Money
http://www.efn.org/~impact/mtmpage.html

More Than Money is a quarterly journal for major donors, which says that its target audience is those with inherited or earned wealth "seeking a just and sustainable world." The site has an 8-page sample copy of the publication, which provides excerpts from five issues.

NonProfit Times On-line
http://www.nptimes.com/

The on-line version of *NonProfit Times* includes the full-text of lead articles in a newspaper style format. A "teamworks" section provides a discussion forum for topics in non-profit management and fund-raising.

Philanthropy Journal On-line (see page 82)
http://www.philanthropy-journal.org/

Philanthropy Journal is a non-profit newspaper for the non-profit sector. The entire site is searchable. There is a chat discussion area with frequent guest speakers, and the transcripts of their comments are posted. There is job information, a "National Headlines" icon that links to alerts and news of interest, a free e-mail newsletter called *Philanthropy Alert* with breaking news of interest to the non-profit sector, and lots of links. There is a link to a *Meta-Index of Nonprofit Organizations*, which provides one-stop shopping for non-profit links. The foundation section, for example, has links to 110 foundations and six regional associations of grantmakers, as well as 21 mailing lists. There are additional categories relating to government sources and media.

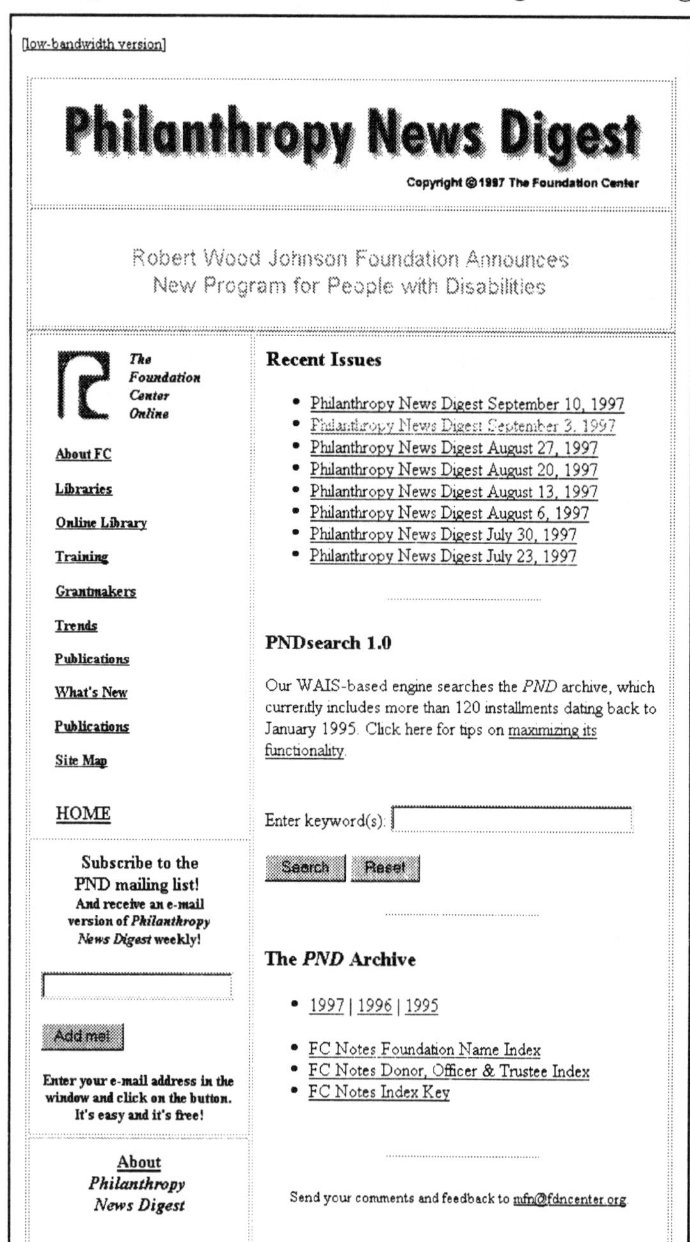

Philanthropy News Digest home page. Reprinted with permission.

Philanthropy News Digest
http://fdncenter.org/phil/philmain.html

An on-line publication of the Foundation Center, this digest provides short briefs on news in philanthropy. New issues are published weekly and are searchable by terms.

Who Cares
http://www.whocares.org

Who Cares, launched in 1993, is a national quarterly journal devoted to community services and activism. Lycos awarded it one of its top 5% Web sites. It has a searchable resource directory database, a national calendar of events, workshops and services and, of course, subscription information. Back issues are posted on-line (the Summer 1996 issue was the latest available at this site in September 1997), but even back issues of this publication have useful information.

I. Commercial Sites

Arent Fox
http://www.arentfox.com/

This award-winning site has free on-line newsletters on various topics of interest, including one on the latest developments in labor law *(Employment News)* and taxes *(Tax Bullets)*. The newsletter *TIPsheet* has the most current developments on intellectual property law. The latest issue we saw had a provocative article on Internet law.

CDB Infotek's State and County Database
http://www.cdb.com/public/

"CDB Infotek is the United States' largest source of public records on-line. We have over 1,600 databases and more than 3 billion records collected from local, county, and state governments all across the nation, as well as the federal government and various businesses." Browse through this, and you won't ever wonder again how someone got information you considered to be private. But don't worry; the material on the site says that the information about you won't be given out to subscribers to its service unless you "have a legitimate business need for the information." We feel much better. There are lots of uses for these databases for non-profit organizations, although we couldn't tell from the site how much is charged for subscriptions.

CPA's Weekly News Update (Harcourt Brace & Co.)
http://www.hbpp.com/weekup/

This page has three sets of headlines, divided by "taxation," "practice management," and "non-profit." There are instructions for saving the files as text files to your hard drive, and the articles are searchable (the term "exemption" resulted in nearly two-dozen hits). We wouldn't recommend this site as your number one source for news of interest to non-profits, but it is a worthy supplement. The Harcourt Brace Web site also boasts five financial calculation tools: Tax Interest Calculator, Loan Calculator, Retirement Spending Calculator, Retirement Savings Calculator, and the Present Value Calculator. There is also subscription information and an index of back issues of *CPA Government & Nonprofit Report*, a monthly newsletter devoted exclusively to government and non-profit accounting and auditing.

Non-Line: The Nonprofit Network
http://www.nonline.com

This site was established in 1994 by SWMG Productions, Inc., "a privately held marketing and service company specializing in services for the nonprofit community and cause-related marketing." The company also publishes an on-line magazine of interest to non-profits called *VISIONEER*. This "magazine" is organized into channels, such as poverty, education, homelessness, and 15 other categories. Each is a link to an essay about that issue. The site has a database where you can, at no cost, submit job openings in your non-profit organization, or post your résumé. There are links to (at the time of this review) 42 corporate foundations. Non-profits can post volunteer opportunities, and potential volunteers can post their availability, at no charge. This site will soon feature newsgroups and chat rooms of interest to non-profits.

Nonprofit Bulletin
http://www.milbank.com/tenews.html

The Nonprofit Bulletin, a publication of Milbank, Tweed, Hadley & McCloy, "is published periodically to alert nonprofit organizations to significant developments in the laws governing them." The site does not appear to be regularly updated, but the publication has articles of interest to the non-profit community, such as an article explaining the lobbying disclosure law and an alert about changes in IRS policy with respect to auditing small foundations. The entire site is searchable, so you can tell quickly if what you are looking for is there. Click on the button labeled "Internet resources," and you are linked to one of the better legal-related indexes of important links on the Internet.

PhilanthroTec Inc.
http://www.ptec.com/

"PhilanthroTec is a company that specializes in the design, development and distribution of Intel PC based computer software for charitable planning and planned giving." This commercial site features articles about planned giving, providing some technical information along with a focus on helping non-experts present and understand planned giving through stories and examples. It is packaged in a fun-to-read format.

Tax Analysts
http://www.tax.org/

The home page of this site fills just one screen on our monitor, a feature that is dear to our hearts. There are 15 buttons. The "Public Interest" button allows easy subscription to one of 27 discussion forums moderated by a Tax Analyst employee. There is a Daily Update that provides current information about developments in the tax field, including lots of material that is of interest to the non-profit community. "Today's Tax News" is continuously updated. The site promotes the company's commercial products (they sell databases, mostly on CD ROM).

Tax Topics Advisory (Coopers & Lybrand)
http://www.colybrand.com/tax/

This is a subscription service for the most part, but the firm's *Tax Topics Advisory* includes periodic updates on current tax issues, including many of direct interest to the non-profit community. The database of articles is searchable (a search on the term "intermediate sanctions" yielded six articles, some of which were totally devoted to this topic). The *Washington Perspective* e-letter on this site has information that you could pay hundreds of dollars for in a conventional newsletter subscription, giving clear, concise intelligence on what is happening in Washington on a broad range of issues.

J. Employment-Related Sites

America's Job Bank
http://www.ajb.dni.us/index.html

America's Job Bank is "a product of the public employment service." This site was accessed more than 167 million times in the six-month period preceding this review. It includes information for employers and job seekers, job market information, and job search tips. Employers can post job openings on-line and submit their URLs to be linked to from AJB. Job seekers can access a searchable database of jobs. We searched for the key word "volunteer" and received a listing of 21 jobs, including a manager of volunteer services paying $15.68/hr. This site links to every State Employment Service that has a Web site, 1,397 employers' Web sites, and 470 private placement agencies. Internet job search tips are also provided.

America's Job Bank home page. Reprinted with permission.

Career Path
http://www.careerpath.com/

"Today You Can Search 188,178 Help Wanted Ads From Across the Country." With a home page opening banner such as this, you get attention, and deservedly so. Career Path provides classified ads from the Sunday editions of the *Boston Globe, New York Times, Los Angeles Times, Chicago Tribune, Washington Post, Denver Post, Baltimore Sun,* and many more.

City Net
http://www.citynet.com/

This site contains local information from over 30 cities around the nation. Information includes classified ads, entertainment, malls, phone book, news, and weather.

E-SPAN
http://www.espan.com

This site offers job-search information and job listings. There is a salary calculator, which compares cost-of-living among cities. For example, we said we currently make $50,000 and are moving from Harrisburg, PA to Chicago, IL. It told us that we needed to make $67,529 to just "break even." While this page has lots of fun features, it has lots of advertising as well.

JobWeb
http://www.jobWeb.org

This site is the home page of the National Association of Colleges and Employers and includes a variety of career-related services, which are updated and expanded regularly. You'll find an employer directory of career opportunities, a searchable database with job postings (including links to federal jobs), job search information and guidance, and links to other job-search resources. It's colorful, animated, and must have been a job putting it all on-line for you.

Monster Board
http://www.monster.com

This site provides a variety of links to job-search resources and connections to job listings.

The National Assembly of National Voluntary Health and Social Welfare Organizations (National Assembly)
http://www.nassembly.org/html/search.html

This site has an on-line database of more than 2,000 paid and unpaid internships at youth development agencies such as Big Brothers/Big Sisters, Boy Scouts, Girl Scouts, YMCA, YWCA, and Volunteers of America. The database can be searched by state, city, and type of internship sought.

On-line Career Center
http://www.occ.com/

This is a job search home page sponsored by employer organizations. It includes information on companies and job listings.

Opportunity Nocs
http://www.tmcenter.org/op-noc/on-ba-jobs.html

This site lists non-profit career opportunities in the San Francisco, Sacramento, and Bay area. Paid subscribers get first crack at seeing the job listings, which are posted for the public 7-10 days after that.

The Riley Guide
http://www.dbm.com/jobguide

This excellent on-line book includes everything you need to know to conduct a job search on-line. It provides extensive guidelines for this method of job searching and must be read by anyone considering using the Internet for this purpose. It also includes links for various career areas.

USA Jobs
http://www.usajobs.opm.gov/

The United States Office of Personnel Management manages this site on Federal jobs. There is a searchable database, which allows searching by educational level, desired salary, and other factors. There is general information about applying for Federal jobs, salaries, student employment, Federal job scams, a list of jobs by college major, information on various student employment opportunities (i.e., Outstanding Scholars Program, Volunteer Service, Summer Employment, and AmeriCorps). Federal job seekers will find the on-line application form most helpful.

K. Miscellaneous Non-Profit Resource Sites

American Society of Association Executives (ASAE)
http://www.asaenet.org

ASAE, founded in 1920, is the professional association of more than 23,000 non-profit association executives and their suppliers of products and services. The home page is designed to encourage you to return again and again—it is updated each week with important, breaking news of importance to its membership. Its "CEO Center" is for members only, but click on the "Government Affairs" icon and you will find action alerts on issues of importance to non-profits. There is the usual information about publications and membership information, and a gateway to the association's members.

ARNOVA
http://www.wvu.edu/~socialwk/A/Web.html

The Association for Research on Nonprofit Organizations and Voluntary Action's Web site has links to its newsletter, as well as scores of non-profit related links. The joke and cartoon pages with non-profit-related material (click on "laughs" and "graphics" respectively at the bottom of the Web page of ARNOVA's Nonprofit and Voluntary Sector Quarterly) are worth the visit.

Aspen Institute
http://www.aspeninst.org

The Aspen Institute is "an international nonprofit educational institution dedicated to enhancing the quality of leadership through informed dialogue. It convenes men and women who represent diverse viewpoints and backgrounds from business, labor, government, the professions, the arts, and the nonprofit sector to relate timeless ideas and values to the foremost challenges facing societies, organizations, and individuals." The site includes limited information about the Institute's Program for the Advancement of Philanthropy and promotional brochures on each of its seminars (which run about $500 for each day). The site is searchable and has free, on-line access to some intriguing publications (such *as Elections in Cyberspace*).

Charity Village's Research Library
http://www.charityvillage.com/charityvillage/research/research.html

This site offers a set of materials covering the full scope of fund-raising activity for Canadian and U.S. fund-raisers. Click on "The Library" to read fund-raising book reviews and resource listings.

CNet (see next page)
http://www.cnet.com/

A free membership site (with 600,000 members), CNet is a technology resource, a place where you can find software, entertainment and news, and technology-related information.

Community Information Exchange
http://www.comminfoexch.org

The Community Information Exchange, founded in 1983, "is a national, nonprofit information service that provides community-based organizations and their partners with the information they need to successfully revitalize their communities. The Exchange provides comprehensive information about strategies and resources for affordable housing, economic and community development, customizes this information for individualized inquiries, and offers technical

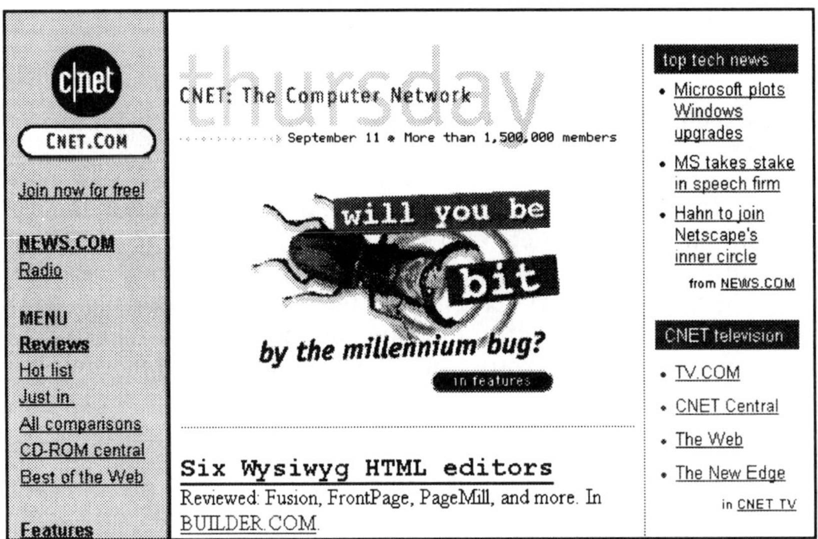

CNET home page. Reprinted with permission from CNET, Inc. Copyright 1995-7. www.cnet.com.

assistance." Click on *Computerized Information* for case studies about innovative and replicable strategies, descriptions of funding and financing sources, names of technical assistance providers, and abstracts of printed resources such as how-to-guides and sample legal documents. Bulletin boards feature the latest funding announcements, including the *Federal Register*'s, and timely news items (a subscription fee is required). There is information about the monthly newsletter *Exchange News!*, the quarterly report *Strategy Alert*, and other publications for sale. *The Washington Report* by Bud Kanitz, Executive Director of the National Neighborhood Coalition, is offered on-line for free and contains excellent material about the latest developments in Washington relating to community action agencies. There is information about internship opportunities with the organization, training and technical assistance provided by CIE, and links to other community action agency-related sites.

The Corporate Community Involvement Resource Centre
http://www.charitynet.org/caf/

This site provides a place to learn about corporate philanthropy efforts and provides corporations with a place to be recognized for their contributions to the community. For example, fund-raisers interested in the Ben and Jerry's Foundation (see page 167) can find its site here and learn what projects have been funded, its mission and guidelines, and procedures for applying. This site is a product of the UK's CHARITYnet (http://www.charitynet.org/), which serves as another resource center for non-profits and contributors. You can add your organization to its listing. Donors can learn about the tax effects of giving. Non-profit organizations can use free Internet space from CHARITYNet to build their own Web sites, which they can use for fund-raising or other purposes.

Council for the Advancement and Support of Education (CASE)
http://192.203.212.6/256/casehome.htm

CASE is a member organization for educational/institutional advancement officers. Besides information about joining, purchasing resources and publications, awards, and other programs of CASE, its site also offers four mailing lists relevant to people in this area of development and alumni work. These are for the following people and topics: (1) those working at two-year colleges, (2) senior members of the advancement profession, (3) the media and public perceptions, and (4) issues affecting independent K-12 schools. A management bulletin on issues affecting public perception about education entitled *Flashpoint* is available, as well as issue papers, links, job information, legislative alerts, and articles concerning institutional advancement.

Peter Drucker Foundation for Nonprofit Management
http://www.pfdf.org/

Founded in 1990 by Peter Drucker, *the* name in non-profit management, the site provides information about conferences, publications, awards bestowed by the Foundation, fellowships offered and, of course, information about how to purchase Drucker's best-selling non-profit management books and publications.

Fund-Raising.com
http://www.fund-raising.com/frindex

There are links at this site to organizations and companies that offer products sold as fund-raisers or used as promotional goods for fund-raising campaigns. The site also features an "idea bank" in which visitors can post their ideas for fund-raisers or provide a summary of what has worked for their organizations.

Grants Web
http://Web.fie.com/cws/sra/resource.htm

Grants Web provides an excellent and comprehensive listing of sites announcing grants available in the U.S., Canada, and around the world.

Imagine
http://www.imagine-inc.com/

This is a Canadian community site for promoting corporate giving. Members include 1,200 "Community Partners" and 436 "Caring Companies." Membership and listing of companies require only adherence to a minimum guideline of giving 1% of pretax profits to non-profit organizations and charities and a demonstration of encouraging and facilitating charitable giving and volunteering among employees. An initiative of the Canadian Centre for Philanthropy (http://www.ccp.ca/), this site is used to announce awards for creative and effective corporate/ non-profit efforts on behalf of community needs. And the world will be as one!

The National Association of Estate Planners
http://www.netplanning.com/

This site provides a listing of some 600 attorneys with experience in estate planning. In addition, the site offers a list of books, audio tapes, and videos on estate planning. From the "Keys to Wealth" page, one can learn a fair amount about estate planning and charitable gifts.

National Society of Fundraising Executives (NSFRE)
http://www.nsfre.org/

NSFRE is a national professional association for fund-raisers for charities, boasting 17,000 members and 149 chapters. Much of this site is restricted to members only. Among the useful public files on the site are a *Code of Ethical Principles of Professional Practice* (1992) and a 10-point *Donor's Bill of Rights*. Included is information about state chapters and the usual meeting times/ places. There is a link to the NSFRE Fund-raising Resource Center. This Center does provide services to non-members, but a modest fee is charged. The site provides information about the organization's three professional certifications and a bibliography on fund-raising. The "State Regulation Update" provides monthly topical information about what is happening in the states on issues affecting the regulation of fund-raising, and a "Government Relations Update" provides a monthly summary of what is brewing in Washington on major issues of interest. There is a consultant's directory and a link to pages of local chapters, which list their events and meetings.

Nonprofit "Cyber-Accountability"
http://www.bway.net/~hbograd/cyb-acc.html

This site, established by Peter Swords and Harriet Bograd, "reviews the problems and abuses and describes the system of regulation of non-profits in the United States." Also on the site is a series of links to their reports, and links to other individuals and organizations with sites relating to non-profit accountability, and information about the mailing list begun by the project.

Nonprofit Forum Interactive
http://www.nonprofit-forum.com/

This is a membership-based site requiring a $15/month fee to participate (the first month is free). While we did not join to test out this commercial "community" site, it claims that it "delivers the benefits of widely varied information resources, incorporating the experience of experts, and peer-to-peer networking among the people involved in the day-to-day operations of nonprofit organizations, all so that communities will be better served." The topics covered in its resource library include "trusteeship, leadership, management, planning, evaluation, marketing, legislative issues, and a heavy emphasis on philanthropy, fund-raising, and planned giving." You can also find information on news on non-profits, volunteerism, seminar and conference information, computer-user groups, and the application of technology for productivity. Job and career information is also available at this site. If the site lives up to its claims, it could be quite helpful for non-profit fund-raising.

Nonprofit Net
http://www.nonprofit.net

Nonprofit.net, administered by Hubris Communications, "brings together not-for-profit groups who are looking for a high quality, low cost solution to maintaining an on-line presence." The site is a gateway to the non-profits that have selected this server.

Nonprofit Prophets
http://www.kn.pacbell.com/wired/prophets/prophets.res.topics.html

Nonprofit Prophets is "an interactive project that challenges groups of students to investigate a problem that they see in the world and then create a World Wide Web Resource page on the Internet that teaches the world about the problem." The site is a directory of links organized around scores of public policy issues. At the time of the review, there were 36 topics, such as teenage pregnancy, religious discrimination, poverty, infant mortality, immigration, crime, child neglect, demographic changes, and age discrimination. There are hundreds of links on the site. While the target audience is high school students, the links are a great place to start for finding sources of material on a wide range of topics of interest to non-profits.

Nonprofit Resource Catalogue—Phillip A. Walker
http://www.clark.net/pub/pwalker/home.html

There are 2,897 links of interest to non-profits at this site, many of them newly added by Walker, who serves as the head of On-line Services for the United Way of America. This file is indexed by the following categories: Fundraising and Giving, General Nonprofit Resources, General Reference, Health and Human Services, Internet in General, News Sources, Other Nonprofit Issues, Other Personal Interests, United States Government, United Ways on the Internet, and Weather and Disasters. If you can't find what you are looking for of interest to non-profit organizations here, you probably aren't going to find it.

Joseph and Matthew Payton Philanthropic Studies Library
http://andretti.iupui.edu/philanthropy/payton.html

Affiliated with Indiana University, "the Joseph and Matthew Payton Philanthropic Studies Library staff compile and produce *Philanthropic Studies Index*, which indexes the growing body of articles written on topics and issues concerning the nonprofit sector." It serves as a repository for the historical files of some of the best known non-profit advocacy organizations. This site has information about the millions of documents that have been donated by some of these, such as Independent Sector and the Foundation Center.

Program on Non-Profit Organizations
http://www.yale.edu/isps/ponpo

"Since 1977, the Program on Non-Profit Organizations, which is based at the Institution for Social and Policy Studies, Yale University, has operated as an international center for multidisciplinary studies of philanthropy, voluntarism, and nonprofit organizations. The work of scholars affiliated with the Program has appeared in books and scholarly journals, as well as in its own working-paper series." There is almost nothing free here, and there is a price list for virtually everything. There is information about Yale's Program on Non-Profit Organizations Fellowships, such as how to apply (the deadlines had all passed at the time of the review), and ordering information for the institution's publications.

ReliefNet
http://www.reliefnet.org/

"ReliefNet™ is a non-profit organization dedicated to helping humanitarian organizations raise global awareness and encourage support for relief efforts via the Internet." The site features an innovative "virtual relief concert" in support of humanitarian relief efforts.

Relief Web
http://www.reliefWeb.int/

Relief Web is organized by the United Nations Department of Humanitarian Affairs. Emergency areas around the world are monitored by the site, allowing individuals to focus aid where it may be most needed at any particular time. The site also gives data on the amount of humanitarian assistance that has been provided each year from each nation. The U.S., for example, provided $828,259,035 in 1996, according to figures reported to DHA. The site provides data on the humanitarian assistance provided in response to complex emergencies.

Shareware.com
http://www.shareware.com/

"SHAREWARE.COM is a service from CNET: The Computer Network that features the Virtual Software Library (VSL) search engine and much more. You can search for, browse, and download the best software—including freeware, shareware, demos, fixes, patches, upgrades—from the top managed software archives and computer vendor sites on the Internet." The files are searchable by operating system (e.g., Windows® 95). There is no charge for becoming a member, and this site could be useful for the non-profit manager hoping to save a few dollars on software. Check out the "most popular" button to see which files are being downloaded the most (when we did this, a Windows® 95 zip program was in the number one spot with more than 14,000 downloads). The site's weekly newsletter, *Shareware Dispatch*, is delivered by e-mail every Wednesday evening.

The Society for Nonprofit Organizations
http://danenet.wicip.org/snpo/

The Society for Nonprofit Organizations is a Wisconsin-based membership organization of non-profits that publishes the *Nonprofit World* journal. One useful file on the site is "Did You Know," which has facts and figures about the non-profit sector. The Web page design is flashy and professional.

Support Centers of America
http://www.igc.apc.org/sca/

This site offers an e-mail newsletter, *Pulse!*, directed to non-profit management support organizations and professionals. Sent twice each month, this often contains information relevant for fund-raisers. Complementing this for fund-raisers, under the "Marketplace for Ideas" section of the Support Center's Web site, is a monthly interview with a grantmaker.

Urban Institute
http://www.urban.org/

"The Urban Institute is a nonprofit policy research organization established in Washington, DC, in 1968. The staff investigates the social and economic problems confronting the nation and government policies and public and private programs designed to alleviate them. The Institute's objectives are to sharpen thinking about society's problems and efforts to solve them, improve government decisions and their implementation, and increase citizens' awareness about important public choices." The site includes the National Center on Charitable Statistics and the Center on Non-profits and Philanthropy. It is searchable (a search on the term "non-profit" yielded scores of file matches) and has back issues of the Institute's publications, including *New Federalism: Issues and Options for States* (excellent resource material for those interested in block grants, welfare reform, Medicaid, and other federal health policy issues), *Policy and Research Report, Update, The Future of the Public Sector, Policy Bites* (the latest dated September 1995), *Opportunity in America*, and *Economic Restructuring and the Job Market*. There are files about each of the Institute's nine research centers. Doing research for a speech about a topical public policy issue? Check out the "Hot Topics" files for loads of high-quality information about current issues. There is an FAQ file, lots of information about the organization, and plenty of free, downloadable, high-quality files on public policy issues.

The Virtual Community of Associations
http://www.vcanet.org/

This site is maintained as a service of the Greater Washington Society of Association Executives (GWSAE), a 70-year-old association of association executives with 3,500 members representing 1,000 national and international associations in the Greater Washington, DC area. "The purpose of the VCA Member Directory is to provide a resource to association members and the general public for locating associations and their Web sites. The VCA Member Directory contains a master listing of all VCA member association names and Web site addresses or URLs." At this site, you can find news of interest to associations (mostly from the publication *Association News*), an interesting "National Trends" file that includes sound byte-sized summaries of current surveys and studies of interest, and an on-line e-zine called *Non-Profit Nuts and Bolts* that features sample articles from the 8-page monthly newsletter (you can order a free issue using an on-line form). Click on "Non-Profit Online Resource Room" for links and directories of related organizations, publications, and mailing lists/newsgroups of interest.

L. Search Engines

The following are some of the features of popular search engines and directories.

Alta Vista
http://altavista.digital.com/

A popular search engine (not directory), Alta Vista features the ability to search either the Web or newsgroups separately. It gives you the option to decide how much information you want about each Web site it finds for you. A search for "strategic planning" found 53,000 hits.

Alta Vista home page. Reprinted with permission.

Excite
http://www.excite.com/

Excite is both a directory and a search engine and gives options of searching the Web, the Excite directory only, Usenet newsgroups, and Usenet classified. There is also a newstracker. In addition to its directory, Excite has organized a variety of "tours" based on particular topics. If you desire, you can organize your own tour connecting a set of sites related to a particular topic, and can submit it to Excite for inclusion in its tour directory. Excite also allows you to create a personalized page similar to Yahoo!'s. Excite's "Citynet" offers you an opportunity to find information on most metropolitan areas, and its "Reviews " section evaluates various sites for the quality of information they offer. The Excite search engine is fairly large (searching for "strategic planning" gives more than 39,000 sites), and it scores sites, orders them by confidence level (showing you the top ten sites), and provides a summary. A unique feature is that Excite gives a "more like this site" option, so you can expand your search beyond your original search terms to find other sites containing similar content.

InfoSeek
http://www.infoseek.com/

In addition to English, it also includes a directory in Spanish, French, German, and Japanese. InfoSeek features the ability to search by a phrase (e.g., entering a question rather than just the words). It also gives you a value rating or "score" for each page it finds (e.g., 38%) to tell you the "confidence level" that it matches your inquiry. Factors that affect the score include the frequency that your term appears, and the proximity of it to the top of the page. The sites it finds are ordered according to these scores. InfoSeek has an enormous database (a search for "non-profit strategic planning" turned up more than 762,000 hits, and this search can be refined further by searching only within the sites identified).

Infoseek also offers a unique service in the ability to perform "specialized searches" such as:

1. searching just for pictures or graphic images.
2. limiting your search to a word or phrase in a particular Web site only.
3. searching for pages with a link to a particular Web site (e.g., so that you can find out how many people have made links to your Web page).
4. searching only the URLs on the Web or the title lines.
5. NetClock: a search engine and directory of events happening on the Internet, such as audio broadcasts and celebrity discussions.

Liszt's Directory
http://www.liszt.com/

Liszt's Directory is a leading directory and search engine of mailing lists and newsgroups.(see page 40)

Lycos
http://www.lycos.com/

When searched for "strategic planning," Lycos's search engine found 433 links. Like Yahoo, Lycos offers scores of useful services, including searching for pictures and sounds, and providing content such as news, sports, and financial information (and more than a dozen other categories, as well). This is one of the better places to begin surfing the Web.

Magellan
http://www.mckinley.com/

Magellan is run by Excite, but offers an even more expansive database. It features Web reviews, news, stock quotes, sports, weather, and other categories of information.

Net Locator
http://nln.com/

The Net Locator is a useful site if you need to use more than one search engine. Net Locator allows you to search with one engine and then instantly search with another without taking the time to go to the other's actual search site. It is a little tricky to use but, with practice, is very valuable for comprehensive searching.

TILE.NET/Lists
http://tile.net/listserv/

Tile.net is an excellent search engine and is well-organized for finding appropriate mailing lists and newsgroups.

Yahoo (see pages 92-93)
http://www.yahoo.com

M. Prospect Research and Places for Donors Sites

The Association of Prospect Researchers for Advancement
http://Weber.u.washington.edu/~dlamb/apra/APRA.html

This is a community site organizing individuals in the field of prospect research.

Hoover's On-line
http://hoovWeb.hoovers.com/

Hoover's On-line has extensive, detailed and well-organized information on more than 2,700 public and private companies. This subscription service offers much for free, including 10,000 company "capsules" (shorter information pages), which are probably sufficient for most fund-raising uses. It also offers links to Web sites for 5,000 companies and a list of the top 2,500 employers.

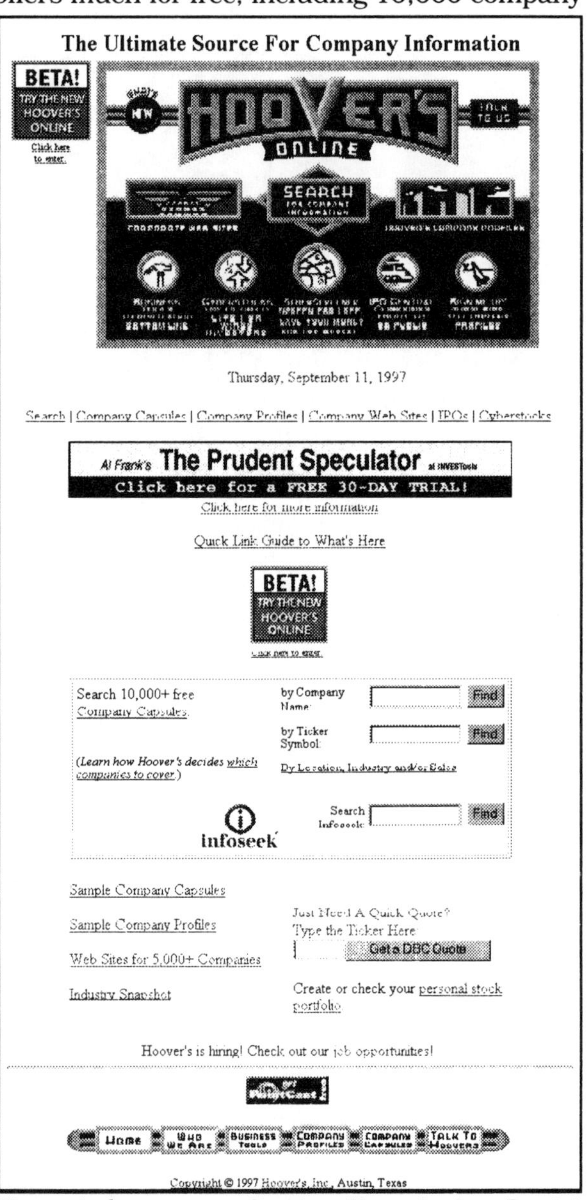

Hoover's home page. Courtesy Hoover's, Inc. Reprinted with permission.

Internet Prospector
http://plains.uwyo.edu/~prospect/

This site features a free monthly on-line newsletter directed to non-profit fund-raisers. Information on this site is gleaned by volunteers who "mine" the Internet for fund-raising nuggets and the site is organized as a collaborative effort of fund-raising colleagues. For those who may forget to check in on a regular basis, there is a subscription form for having issues sent via e-mail. Past newsletters are archived at the site. Each newsletter focuses on sites of interest to fund-raisers and prospect researchers. It is organized into categories, such as corporations, foundations/grants, people, ethics, news on-line, international, tools, and access (prospect research pages). This site is a wonderful starting point for finding many other resources related to prospect research or for brainstorming on new prospects. It is also to be applauded as one of the more friendly sites (for example, reproduction of the material with copyrights is "ENCOURAGED") and for its success as a team effort among individuals helping one another to enhance philanthropy for all.

The Informant
http://informant.dartmouth.edu/

This unique and free service is an excellent tool for doing prospect research while you sleep. Find up to three sets of Internet search terms that fit closely with your interests; then go to The Informant to enter them into your personalized informant agent page. The Informant will contact you by e-mail whenever a new site comes up fitting those terms. The Informant will also watch five of your favorite Web pages and will let you know when they are updated.

David Lamb's Prospect Research Page
http://Weber.u.washington.edu/~dlamb/research.html

This is a handy list of prospect research sites. Links here range from EDGAR (Electronic Data Analysis Gathering and Retrieval) at http://www.edgar-online.com/bin/esearch/fullsearch.shtml, a searchable form site that allows you to pull up the SEC documents filed by any company, to the Martindale & Hubble Lawyer Locator (http://www.martindale.com/maps/../locator/home.html), as well as locators of doctors, dentists, and even airplane owners.

PR Newswire
http://www.prnewswire.com/

PR Newswire presents current press releases from companies, foundations, and other organizations.

Prospex Research
http://prospex.com/Welcome.html

This site provides a three-part service. The first two parts are "FRED" and "LEADS," which both assist with EDGAR searches, giving you the capability to search EDGAR by individual names. Both of these, however, require a subscription to use. The third service lists upcoming IPO (initial public offerings) and secondary offerings.

Places for Donors

Council of Better Business Bureaus (see page 136)
http://www.bbb.org/

International Service Agencies (ISA)
http://www.charity.org/

This is an effort to increase workplace giving by providing a single site to which donors can contribute if they are interested in supporting efforts to alleviate hunger, poverty, and the effects of war, oppression, and natural disasters. Donors can give to ISA or can designate their gifts for particular organizations within ISA. ISA members are organized into categories of Children, Education, Hunger Relief, Medical Care, Refugees/Disaster Relief, and Job Creation/Economic Relief. Members do not need to have their own home pages to participate, as ISA includes a descriptive page for each member.

National Charities Information Bureau
http://www.give.org

This site is aimed toward donors who wish to ensure that they are giving to charitable organizations that fit this organization's guidelines. Interested donors can order a free *Wise Giving Guide* and by signing on will receive notification via e-mail of new information made available at the site. There is also a set of donor tips available at the site. An on-line reference guide can be used by donors to review whether any of 300 organizations evaluated comply with NCIB standards. These standards are detailed at the site and relate to the organization's governance, purpose, and its programs. They also evaluate information disclosed, methods of fund-raising, reporting, budgeting, and the use of funds, among other criteria. The quick reference guide provides an easily scanned simple alphabetical list of organizations coded as to whether they adhere to the recommended standards, or whether information has not been disclosed by the organization. Every two weeks, a new charity is featured, with the results of its report published.

GLOSSARY

404—The error message that appears when you click on a hypertext link and the URL referenced by the link does not exist.

AltaVista—A popular and free search engine on the World Wide Web.

ASCII file—A file that contains only letters, numbers, and standard punctuation symbols from the American Standard Code for Information Exchange character set, and is the standard for the exchange of information between computer programs that may otherwise be incompatible. ASCII files do not contain formatting codes (such as those indicating that text is bold or italicized).

Binary file—A file consisting of characters other than those from the ASCII character set, including all word processing, sound, video, graphics, and compressed files.

BitNet—An acronym for Because It's Time Network, BitNet, operated by the Center for Research and Education Networking, is a network linking thousands of research and educational institutions. Its best-known application is Internet mailing lists.

Baud rate—The number of bits of information that can be transmitted through a modem, usually equal to about half the BPS (bits per second) rate.

Bit—A binary (consisting of two possibilities, 0 and 1) code that is the basic unit for the transfer of data in a computer.

Bookmark—A feature of a Web browser that saves a Web site's address in a log. It permits you to return to that Web page by clicking on "bookmark" or other icon (such as "favorite places") the first time you access the page, and then return to that page by accessing the bookmark rather than having to remember and retype that page's Web address.

BBS (Bulletin Board System)—A dial-in computer host, usually community-based, that permits you to log in and view information, and download or upload files.

Browser—A computer program that permits access to the World Wide Web by reading and interpreting HTML files. A browser may be text-only (such as Lynx), or graphical (such as Netscape Navigator or Microsoft® Internet Explorer).

Byte—A basic measurement of computer storage, using a binary system. A megabyte is 1,048,576 bytes, and each byte contains a unique 8-bit string of information, which is associated with a number, letter, or symbol.

Chat—A telecommunications system that permits two or more people to use their keyboards to communicate in real time and engage in "conversations." The chatters view on their monitors what each types in.

Counter—A software program that tracks the number of accesses or hits to a web page.

Cyberspace—The virtual space in which electronic communication by computer takes place, including the physical and metaphysical residence of e-mail, Web sites, and other Internet communication modalities.

Domain name—The part of the Internet address that identifies the specific organization being communicated with and converts the numerical Internet Protocol addresses into names with letters, which can be more easily remembered.

E-mail (electronic mail)—Messages that arrive on your computer from other computers through the telephone lines via a data connection from the Internet or an Intranet or other network.

Emoticon—A drawing made by using characters from the ASCII character set, depicting emotion or body language that would otherwise not be able to be conveyed solely by conventional text-based electronic communication.

Encryption—Disguising messages for security purposes by using cryptography "keys" that permit only the sender and receiver to decode them. Those without the correct keys see only gobbledygook.

FAQ (Frequently Asked Questions)—A file of questions and answers found in UseNet News Groups, web pages, and other Internet-related documents, which is prepared to assist new participants.

File—A set of computer-generated information, such as a document, database, or Web page, that is identified by a unique name and is created, transferred, copied, or downloaded/uploaded as a distinct unit. Files are stored on hard disks or other storage media, and are organized by using directories and subdirectories.

Flame—An electronic message that contains abusive, denigrating, threatening, or inciting language, and is often directed to those deemed by the sender(s) to have violated the informal rules of Internet conduct.

Freenet—A type of Bulletin Board Service (BBS) that provides free (usually), community-based information and downloadable files, and inexpensive or free access to the Internet and e-mail.

Freeware—Software programs that are available free for public use.

FTP (File Transfer Protocol)—A standard for exchanging files over the Internet that requires log-in and use of a password (although many FTP sites permit "anonymous" or "guest" to serve as the password).

GIF (Graphic Image File)—The most popular format for graphics files on the World Wide Web.

Gopher—A text-only, menu-based system developed at the University of Minnesota that helps find files, programs, and other resources on the Internet. Gopher servers are being replaced by the World Wide Web, which is graphical and more "user-friendly."

Graphical User Interface (GUI)—Software that utilizes windows, icons, menus, buttons, and other graphics-related devices.

Hardware—The physical components of your computer and its peripheral equipment, including the disks (although the coded instructions on the disk are *software*).

Hit—A count each time someone visits a Web page. The term also refers to the number of matches a search engine accesses in response to a search term.

Home page—The World Wide Web page that is intended as the entry point to an entire Web site and usually includes introductory and identifying information, as well as links to the rest of the site's pages. It also refers to the page that appears on your browser when you first open the browser.

Host—The computer that makes its files and data available to other computers and is directly connected to the Internet. An Internet host is the computer that serves as the intermediary from the Internet to the consumer end-user.

HTML (Hyper Text Markup Language)—The programming language for World Wide Web pages, which consists of coded tag pairs using symbols from the ASCII character set, formatting documents for the World Wide Web.

Hyperlink—A part of a Web page that is coded so that when a viewer clicks on it, he/she is taken to another Web page, and can navigate back and forth between these pages. Viewers see the hyperlink as text or a graphic that is bold, underlined, or a different color, and that, depending on the browser, indicates it is a link by a change in the icon that appears when the pointing device's cursor is on it.

Internet—The system in which millions of computers worldwide are linked for the purpose of electronic mail, mailing lists, newsgroups, and the World Wide Web.

Internet Relay Chat (IRC)—An on-line version of citizens band radio that permits real time communication over the Internet.

Internet Service Provider (ISP)—A business that makes the Internet accessible to consumers via a dial-up service to a local number for a monthly fee.

IP address—The numerical address that is unique to a computer and forms the basis of its domain name, which is converted from the IP address.

ISDN (Integrated Services Digital Network)—A type of telecommunications cable that permits data transfer at several times the speed of conventional modems.

JAVA—A programming language that supports animations and other sophisticated special effects on World Wide Web pages.

JPEG—A format for World Wide Web page graphics.

Keyword—A word used by an on-line service that serves as a gateway to files, chat, newsgroups, news, and other Internet content related to that word. It also refers to a word searched by search engines to find Internet files and pages.

Link—A reference to a file or Web page placed in an HTML file that, when clicked on using an Internet browser, takes the viewer directly to that Web page or file.

Listserv®—Commercially developed mailing list software that permits the management of e-mail mailing lists.

Lurk—To observe postings in listservs, newsgroups, or chat discussions without actively participating. Lurking is recommended before active participation.

Lycos—A popular, free search engine on the Internet.

Mailing lists—A system that permits Internet users to subscribe to an e-mail discussion group that is topical, and to post a message that will be automatically sent to all other subscribers of that list. The software that manages these lists is usually either Listserv® or MajorDomo.

MajorDomo—A freeware mailing list management program manager that uses the UNIX operating system.

Megabyte—A measure of computer data storage equal to 1,048,576 bytes.

Modem—A communications hardware device that transmits computer data over telephone lines by converting the computer's digital signals to analog, and the telephone's analog signals to digital.

Netiquette—Internet etiquette, a set of unwritten (for the most part) rules that have developed in the Internet culture and serve as rules of conduct.

Newbie—An inexperienced Internet user who is not familiar with netiquette or FAQ files, and who often annoys experienced users, all of whom were once newbies.

On-line—Being connected through the telephone lines to another computer.

On-Line Service Provider—A commercial company (such as AOL, CompuServe, or Microsoft® Network) that provides an Internet connection as well as on-line content (such as forums, chat, news, and other information and files) that is accessible only to its subscribers.

Protocol—A set of technical standards that permits two different types of computer systems to interconnect, usually in a way that is transparent to the end user.

Public domain—Intellectual property (such as software, books, clip art) that is not copyrighted, and can be freely copied and distributed without paying royalties to the creator.

RAM (Random Access Memory)—The computer's primary working memory. The more you have, the more programs you can have running simultaneously.

Real Time—Communication between or among Internet users that occurs simultaneously, such as through chat, as contrasted to the exchange of e-mail.

Search engine—A computer program that searches a database (which may contain millions of World Wide Web pages) or the World Wide Web itself and that is accessed by filling out an on-line form with a word or phrase to be searched, and parameters relating to the format of the answer you desire.

Shareware—Computer programs that are made available free-of-charge on a trial basis, with an address to send a fee if the user likes it or wishes to purchase upgrades or additional software.

Signature file—A footer automatically attached to an e-mail message, providing identifying information about the sender, and, in some cases, artwork and inspirational messages or favorite quotations.

Snail mail—Communications sent via the U.S. Postal Service.

Software—The machine-language component of computer programs, which provides the instructions to the computer needed to drive applications such as word processing, database, spreadsheets, Web browsers, desktop publishing, and others.

Spam—Large numbers of inappropriate or otherwise undesirable e-mail messages, including bulk commercial messages (also called "junk e-mail"). When used as a verb, refers to the process of generating hundreds or thousands of such messages to a violator of netiquette as a form of punishment, or to sending bulk junk e-mail.

Surf—To navigate through the World Wide Web by following interesting links.

Telnet—A protocol that permits computers to access a remote computer using telephone lines, such as a Mainframe or those used on BBSs.

UNIX—A computer operating system used by many mainframe computers (because it was provided free by Bell Laboratories to hundreds of large institutions when the Internet was in its infancy), and thus continues to be in wide use, despite its reputation for not being "user friendly."

URL (uniform resource locator)—A unique address on the Internet.

Virus—A computer program, designed as a prank or sabotage, that modifies or destroys the victim's computer capabilities. A virus is uploaded to the victim's computer by deception.

World Wide Web—A feature of the Internet that uses files containing hypertext links, which permit the viewer to navigate among potentially millions of computer hosts by clicking on the part of the computer screen that shows those links.

Webmaster—The individual who designs or administers a Web site.

Web page—An individual file/document at a Web site, which has a unique address and appears when you click on the hypertext link coded with that address or when you type the address into your browser.

Web site—A collection of related and linked Web pages that is developed by one entity. Typically, a Web site has a home page that directs readers to other pages within the site using hyperlinks.

Yahoo!—A popular Internet search engine and directory.

(use additional sheets if necessary)

Non-Profit Internet Handbook
Reader Survey/Order Form

Return Survey To:
White Hat Communications
PO Box 5390
Harrisburg, PA 17110-0390

My name and address (please print legibly):

1. I would like to suggest the following corrections:

2. I would like to suggest the following topics for inclusion in a future edition:

3. I have the following comments, suggestions, or criticisms:

4. I would like to order ____ additional copies @$29.95 each plus $3.00 shipping and handling, plus $1.98 sales tax for Pennsylvania residents (total: $34.93 per book). Pennsylvania Tax-exempt organizations may reduce this amount by the $1.98 sales tax if they include a copy of their exemption certificate from the Pennsylvania Department of Revenue. Note: Quantity discounts are available.

About the Authors

Gary Grant received his B.A. in history from the University of Chicago in1987 and his J.D. from Illinois Institute of Technology, Chicago-Kent College of Law in 1994. In law school, he served on the Chicago-Kent Law Review and the Kent Justice Foundation. He worked in the legal clinic providing legal advice to indigent civil defendants and served as an Everett Fellow with Citizens for Tax Justice in Washington, DC. He has worked as a law clerk for the National Clearinghouse for Legal Services in Chicago, writing and editing articles for the *Clearinghouse Review.* Gary has also worked as a fund-raiser for the University of Chicago, and the University of Chicago School of Social Service Administration, where he currently is employed as Associate Dean for External Affairs. He is a member of the National Society of Fundraising Executives and has served on the Ethics Committee of this organization, assisting in the publication *Honorable Matters, A Guide to Ethics and the Law in Fund Raising.* In his spare time, Gary serves as a Vice President with the Hyde Park/Kenwood Community Conference, where he heads a project to build an Internet gateway to the community and to promote uses of the Internet for non-profit organizations and businesses. He teaches professional development classes on "Uses of the Internet in Social Work." Gary lives in Chicago with his wife Kerry and daughter Alyann.

Gary Grobman received his M.P.A. from Harvard University's Kennedy School of Government and his B.S. from Drexel University's College of Science. He currently is the special projects director for White Hat Communications. Prior to that, he served for 13 years as Executive Director of the Pennsylvania Jewish Coalition, the Harrisburg-based government affairs organization representing 11 Jewish federations and their agencies. He served almost five years in Washington, DC as a senior legislative assistant for two members of Congress, and was a reporter and political humor columnist for the Capitol Hill independent newspaper, *Roll Call.* In 1987, he founded the Non-Profit Advocacy Network (NPAN), which consists of more than 50 state-wide associations representing Pennsylvania charities. He is the author of *The Non-Profit Handbook, The Pennsylvania Non-Profit Handbook,* and *The Holocaust—A Guide for Pennsylvania Teachers.* He and his wife, Linda, a social worker and publisher, are the parents of Adam Gabriel Grobman.

About the Contributors

John Aravosis is the founder of Wired Strategies, a strategic Internet consulting firm based in Washington, DC. He is the former on-line lobbyist at the Children's Defense Fund, and can be reached at: john@wiredstrategies.com.

Carolyn Biondi is a graduate of the University of Chicago School of Social Service Administration, and is employed by the Sinai Family Health Centers as a grants manager. She uses the Internet every day to assist her in project planning, fund-raising, and prospect research. A newlywed, she lives in Evanston, IL.

Steve Roller is a graduate of the University of Chicago School of Social Service Administration with an A.M. in Social Administration. He is the Manager of the Grant Development Unit of the Chicago Housing Authority's Grant Administration Department, and assists in the design and management of his employer's web site.

Anna Senkevitch Anna Senkevitch is the co-developer of the Alumni Internet Training Program and editor of the manual, "The Online Social Worker," for the University of Chicago School of Social Service Administration, where she also is a doctoral student.

Robert Tell is a graduate of the University of Chicago School of Social Service Administration with an A.M. in social work. He works for the Counseling Center of Lake View in Chicago, and is the creator of Rob's Page of Social Work at http://www.enteract.com/~ratell/socwork.html.

Bibliography

Here are some suggestions for further reading. Also, check out The Unofficial Internet Booklist (http://www.savetz.com/booklist/) for an up-to-date and comprehensive list of what else is out there. We recommend that you never purchase a book about the Internet that was published more than a year ago—this field changes quickly and new developments make older books obsolete.

Broadhurst, Judith A. *The Woman's Guide to Online Services*. New York, NY: McGraw-Hill, 1995.

Clark, David. *Student Guide to the Internet (Second Edition)*. Indianapolis, IN: Que, 1996.

Crumlish, Christian. *A Guided Tour of the Internet*. Alameda, CA: Sybex, 1995.

Dern, Daniel P. *The Internet Guide for New Users*. New York, NY: McGraw-Hill, 1993.

Gibbs, Mark and Smith, Richard. *Navigating the Internet*. Carmel, Indiana: Sams Publishing, 1993.

Glister, Paul. *The New Internet Navigator*. New York: John Wiley & Sons, Inc., 1995.

Glossbrenner, Alfred and Emily. *Internet Slick Tricks*. New York, NY: Random House, 1994.

Hahn, Harley & Stout, Rick. *The Internet Complete Reference*. Berkeley, CA: Osborne McGraw-Hill, 1994.

Haskin, David. *Microsoft Internet Explorer Tour Guide*. Research Triangle Park, North Carolina: Ventana Communications Group, Inc., 1997.

Kane, Pamela. *The Hitchhiker's Guide to the Electronic Highway*. New York, NY: MIS Press, 1994.

Kehoe, Brendan P. *Zen and the Art of the Internet: A Beginners Guide* (2nd ed.). Englewood Cliffs, NJ: PTR Prentice Hall, 1992.

Kennedy, Angus J. *The Internet & World Wide Web. The Rough Guide 2.0*. London, England: Rough Guides, LtD., 1996.

Krol, Ed. *The Whole Internet User's Guide & Catalog* (2nd ed.). Sebastopol, CA: O'Reilly & Associates, 1994.

Lambert, Steve and Howe, Walt. *Internet Basics*. New York, NY: Random House, 1993.

LaQuey, Tracy with Jeanne C. Ryer; foreword by Al Gore. *The Internet Companion: A Beginner's Guide to Global Networking*. Reading, MA: Addison-Wesley. 1993.

Miller, Michael. *Easy Internet*. Indianapolis, IN: Que, 1995.

Rankin, Bob. *Dr. Bob's Painless Guide to the Internet*. San Francisco: No Starch Press, 1995.

Stout, Rick. *The World Wide Web Complete Reference.* Berkeley, CA: Osborne McGraw-Hill, 1996.

Wiggins, Richard. *The Internet for Everyone: A Guide for Users and Providers.* New York, NY: McGraw-Hill, 1994.

KEY WORD INDEX

Note: bold page numbers refer to Glossary entries.

A

B

C

D

E

F

G

H

I

J

K

L

M

N

O

P

R

S

T

U

V

W

Y

Index of Reviews

The Pennsylvania Non-Profit Handbook

1997-98 Edition

by Gary M. Grobman

Published by White Hat Communications with the cooperation of the Pennsylvania Association of Non-Profit Organizations

The Pennsylvania Association of Non-Profit Organizations' ***Pennsylvania Non-Profit Handbook*** is the most up-to-date and useful publication for those starting a non-profit or for those already operating one. Published by White Hat Communications, the 1997-98 edition features five new chapters prepared with your needs in mind.

This 234-page ***Handbook*** was originally published in 1992 with the help of more than two dozen non-profit executives and attorneys, and is now in its 4th edition. Each easy-to-read chapter includes a synopsis, useful tips, and resources to obtain more information. Pre-addressed postcards are included to obtain important government forms, instruction booklets, and informational publications.

This essential reference tool includes:

- Information about current laws, court decisions, and regulations that apply to PA non-profits
- Practical advice on running a non-profit, including chapters on communications, fundraising, lobbying, personnel, fiscal management, non-profit ethics, and 20 other chapters
- Information on applying successfully for federal and state tax-exempt status

NEW! • How to write effective grant applications
NEW! • How to hire and fire
NEW! • Internet resources for non-profits
NEW! • How to develop a strategic plan
NEW! • Recent developments affecting non-profits

We know you will find *The Pennsylvania Non-Profit Handbook* to be an essential resource for you and your organization.

"***The Pennsylvania Non-Profit Handbook*** will help you keep on track, with everything you need to know about starting up and running a non-profit all in one volume. It is an extraordinary resource for those who already manage or serve on boards of non-profits...it is a must reference guide for all non-profit executives to have at their fingertips." Joe Geiger, Executive Director, *PA Association of Non-Profit Organizations*

THE PENNSYLVANIA NON-PROFIT HANDBOOK ORDER FORM:

Name:____________ **Organization**____________

Address____________ **City**________ **State**___ **Zip**______

Please charge: ❑Mastercard ❑Visa
Expiration Date______
Card Number ____________
Cardholder's Name (Print____________
Cardholder's Signature ____________

#of Books Ordered____ @$25.95 each $______
Shipping and Handling ($3.00 per book) $______
6% PA Sales Tax* ($1.74/book if applicable) $______
PA Nonprofit Report ($105/year/subscription)$______
PA Non-Profit Handbook and PNR (subtract $10)$______
TOTAL ENCLOSED $______

❑ **Send information about PANO membership**

Pre-payment must accompany all orders.
*** Enclose PA Dept. of Revenue tax-exemption certificate if exempt.**
Please allow three weeks for delivery.

For information about rush orders or quantity discounts, call (717) 238-3787
Make check or money order payable to: White Hat Communications.
Mail to: **White Hat Communications, PO Box 5390, Harrisburg, PA 17110-0390**
telephone/fax: 717-238-3787

nih97

Table of Contents

Notes

Notes

Notes